E. Owens Blackburne

Illustrious Irishwomen

Being Memoirs of Some of the Most Noted Irishwomen From the Earliest Ages to the Present Century. Vol. 2

E. Owens Blackburne

Illustrious Irishwomen
Being Memoirs of Some of the Most Noted Irishwomen From the Earliest Ages to the Present Century. Vol. 2

ISBN/EAN: 9783744761598

Printed in Europe, USA, Canada, Australia, Japan

Cover: Foto ©ninafisch / pixelio.de

More available books at **www.hansebooks.com**

ILLUSTRIOUS IRISHWOMEN.

BEING

MEMOIRS

OF SOME OF

THE MOST NOTED IRISHWOMEN

From the Earliest Ages to the Present Century.

BY

E. OWENS BLACKBURNE,

AUTHOR OF "A WOMAN SCORNED," "THE WAY WOMEN LOVE," ETC. ETC.

IN TWO VOLUMES.

VOL. II.

LONDON:
TINSLEY BROTHERS, 8, CATHERINE STREET, STRAND.
1877.

[Right of Translation reserved by the Author.]

BOSTON COLLEGE LIBRARY
CHESTNUT HILL, MASS.

LONDON:
SAVILL, EDWARDS AND CO., PRINTERS, CHANDOS STREET,
COVENT GARDEN.

CONTENTS

OF

THE SECOND VOLUME.

LITERARY WOMEN.

	PAGE
SUSANNA CENTLIVRE	3
THE HONOURABLE MRS. MONK	16
CONSTANTIA GRIERSON	22
CHARLOTTE BROOKE	27
MRS. MARY TIGHE	52
MARY BOYLE (COUNTESS OF WARWICK)	64
HENRIETTA BOYLE (LADY O'NEIL)	70
MARIA EDGEWORTH	73
FELICIA DOROTHEA HEMANS	108
THE MISSES PORTER	143
SYDNEY, LADY MORGAN	156
MARGUERITE, COUNTESS OF BLESSINGTON	198
ELIZA RYVES	225
HELEN SELINA, COUNTESS OF DUFFERIN . .	232
LADY STIRLING-MAXWELL	239

MISCELLANEOUS.

	PAGE
THE LADY FREEMASON	275
THE BEAUTIFUL GUNNINGS	281
THE LADIES OF LLANGOLLEN	291
LADY LOUISA CONOLLY	330
SARAH CURRAN	335

PART IV.

LITERARY WOMEN.

ILLUSTRIOUS IRISHWOMEN.

SUSANNA CENTLIVRE.

BORN, A.D. 1667.   DIED, A.D. 1722.

BE it known that the Person with Pen in Hand is no other than a Woman, not a little piqued to find that neither the Nobility nor Commonality of the Year 1722, had Spirit enough to erect in *Westminster Abbey,* a monument justly due to the Manes of the never-to-be-forgotten *Mrs. Centlivre,* whose works are full of lively Incidents, Genteel Language, and Humourous Descriptions of real Life, and deserved to have been recorded by a pen equal to that* which celebrated the Life of *Pythagoras.* Some Authors have had a *Shandeian* knack of ushering in their own Praises, sounding their own Trumpet, calling Absurdity Wit, and boasting when they ought to blush; but our Poetess had Modesty,

* Madame Dacier.

the General Attendant of Merit. She was even asham'd to proclaim her own great Genius, probably because the Custom of the Times discountenanced poetical Excellence in a Female. The Gentlemen of the Quill published it not, perhaps envying her superior Talents ; and her Bookseller, complying with national Prejudices, put a fictitious name to her *Love's Contrivance* thro' Fear that the work should be condemned, if known to be Femenine. With Modest Diffidence she sent her performances, like Orphans, into the World, without so much as a Nobleman to protect them ; but they did not need to be supported by Interest, they were admired as soon as known, their real Standard Merit brought crowding Spectators to the Play-houses, and the FEMALE Author, tho' unknown, heard Applauses, such as have since been heaped upon that great Author and Actor Colley Cibber."

The foregoing is an extract from the quaint preface prefixed to the only collected edition of Mrs. Centlivre's works. One of the most remarkable women in the annals of dramatic literature, her name has been suffered to pass into comparative oblivion ; and her works—which deserve a prominent place amongst the British Classics—are not as popular as they deserve to be. The coarse novels and dramas of Mrs. Aphra Behn are well known, where the name even of Susanna Centlivre has scarcely, if ever, been heard of.

Both an actress and an authoress, she forms a fitting link between our "famous actresses" and our "literary women." Her life was full of incident, from the time when she ran away from home, at fifteen years of age, to the day of her death, thirty years afterwards.

The maiden name of Susanna Centlivre was Freeman, and her father is supposed to have been a respectable farmer living in the north of Ireland, and originally of English extraction. Her mother died when she was yet very young, and her father, marrying again, placed over her a stepmother who treated her with such harshness that at length the girl, unable to bear the tyranny any longer, determined to run away from home. She was but fifteen at this time, and the genius, which afterwards so brilliantly displayed itself, urged her to try and get to London, there to seek her fortune upon the stage. How she got from Ireland to England must ever remain a mystery; but she has herself said that upon arriving upon English soil—probably at Bristol, Liverpool, or Milford—she had so little money in her pocket that she found she must walk to London. However physical fatigue at length conquered her brave spirit, and she sat down by the wayside and cried bitterly.

Like the bailiff's daughter of Islington, who set out in search of "the squire's son," Susanna Freeman

> "Sat her down on a mossy bank,
> And a youth he came riding by."

As our heroine sat there weeping, a veritable "squire's son" came riding by. He was young and impressionable, and the sight of beauty in distress aroused all his chivalry. He stopped and inquired the cause of her tears, and the weary girl, glad to hear a friendly voice, told him her tale of woe. What conversation followed we know not, save that he told her that his name was Anthony Hammond,[*] and that if she cared to come and stay with him for awhile at the University of Cambridge—where he was then staying—that he would very willingly take her along with him.

Susanna says she demurred at first upon hearing this proposal; at all events she eventually went with Mr. Hammond. But an insuperable difficulty now presented itself. *Alma Mater*, although a lady, had a prejudice against allowing any of her sex within the sacred precincts of her college. The young people, therefore, were obliged to have recourse to a stratagem. Taking her to a village

---

[*] Subsequently a well-known literary man.

near Cambridge, Mr. Hammond had his fair companion supplied with a suit of boy's clothes, and in this attire he took her with him to live at the University, as his " Cousin Jack." At Cambridge she read and studied everything that came in her way, and there, probably, laid the foundation of those graces of style which characterised her works of later years.

For some months Susanna Freeman continued at the University, and then, fearing her sex would be discovered, Mr. Hammond persuaded her to go to London. He gave her a considerable sum of money, and a letter of recommendation to a gentlewoman of his acquaintance, promising to follow her and to marry her.

Which of them broke the contract can never be known; but in about a year after we hear of our heroine's marriage to Mr. Fox, the nephew of Sir Stephen Fox. This gentleman died about a year after the marriage, leaving his wife a young widow of between seventeen and eighteen. Her worldly affairs were not very flourishing either, for her youthful husband had married her against the consent of his family, who would not therefore do anything for the young widow. Again she married, this time an officer in the army, named Carrol; but he having been killed in a duel about a year and a half after their marriage, she had the misfortune to be again left destitute.

It was in this emergency that the idea of writing for the stage occurred to her. Her first dramatic piece was a tragedy, entitled "The Perjured Husband," which she produced in 1700. It abounds in good writing, but did not long keep the stage. Amongst her eighteen other dramatic pieces we only find one other attempt at tragedy, the natural vivacity of her temperament leading her more into the paths of comedy. It was about this time also that she went on the boards. Her success does not appear to have been very great, as she never played in any but small provincial theatres. She did not, however, long remain upon the stage, for when playing at Windsor, where the Court then was, Mr. Joseph Centlivre, Her Majesty's "yeoman of the mouth"—*i.e.*, the royal cook—fell in love with her, and married her.

Mrs. Centlivre was now in easy circumstances. Her husband took a house for her in Spring Gardens, near Charing Cross, and here she devoted herself to literature and to the society of some of the most distinguished men of learning of the day. Her own wit and attractiveness contributed in no small degree to draw around her a brilliant circle, wherein might constantly be seen Sir Richard Steele, Rowe, Budgell, Farquhar, and others equally well known, and equally famous in the social and literary worlds.

It is difficult to give anything approaching to a correct estimate of Mrs. Centlivre's merits as a dramatist. Mrs. Aphra Behn, if more coarse, is also more sparkling in her dialogue. But then Mrs. Centlivre bears away the palm in the province of plot, and the busy, unflagging way in which, through the sheer use of incident, she keeps the interest up to the mark; so that, if plot and well-defined character be the very essence of comedy, then the bays must be awarded to Mrs. Centlivre. Her best comedy is considered to be " A Bold Stroke for a Wife." Wilkes, the actor, read it, and approved of it; but such was the prejudice against a woman's writing in that age, that when he heard it emanated from the pen of Mrs. Centlivre, he said that if that got wind amongst the audience, *that not only her play would be damned, but she herself be damned for writing it.*

As a self-cultivated genius, it is astonishing to find the traces of so much learning and extensive reading of which many of her pieces bear internal evidence. She has drawn largely upon French, Dutch, and Spanish literature; and a better idea of her absolute conception of the idiosyncrasies of the various nations cannot be better shown than by quoting an extract from her own preface to her brilliant comedy of "Love's Contrivance."

"*Writing is a kind of Lottery in this fickle Age,*" she writes, "*and Dependence on the Stage as precarious as the Cast of a Die; the Chance may turn up, and a Man may write to please the Town, but 'tis uncertain, since we see our best Authors sometimes fail. The Criticks cavil most about Decorums, and cry up* ARISTOTLE'S *Rules as the most essential part of the Play. I own they are in the right of it, yet I dare venture a Wager they'll never persuade the Town to be of their Opinion, which relishes nothing so well as Humour lightly tost up with Wit, and drest with Modesty and Air. And I believe* MR. RICH *will own, he got more by the* TRIP TO THE JUBILEE, *with all its Irregularities, than by the most uniform Piece the Stage could boast of e'er since. I do not say this by way of condemning the Unity of Time, Place, and Action; quite contrary, for I think them the Greatest Beauties of a Dramatic Poem; but since the other way of writing pleases full as well, and gives the Poet a larger* SCOPE *of* FANCY, *and with less* TROUBLE, CARE, *and* PAINS *serves his and the Player's End, why should a Man torture and wrack his Brain for what will be no Advantage to him. This, I dare engage, that the Town will ne'er be entertained with Plays according to the Method of the Ancients, till they exclude this Innovation of Wit and Humour, which yet I see no likelihood of doing. The following Poem I think has nothing can disoblige the nicest ear; and tho' I did not observe the Rules of* DRAMA, *I took peculiar Care to dress my Thoughts in such a Modest Stile that it might not give Offence to any. Some Scenes, I confess, are partly taken from* MOLIERE, *and I dare be bold to say it has not suffered in the Translation. I thought 'em pretty in the French, and could not help believing they would divert in an English Dress. The French have that light airiness in their Temper, that the least Glimpse of Wit sets them a-laughing, when it would not make us so much as smile; so that when I felt the stile too poor, I endeavoured to give it a Turn; for whoever borrows from them, must take care to touch the Colours with an English Pencil, and form the piece according to our Manners."*

If Mrs. Centlivre, therefore, was under obligations to any former dramatist for hints, she had the candour to acknowledge it. Richard Brinsley Sheridan, the writer of "The School for Scandal," the best comedy in the English language, was a plagiarist, but he never acknowledged the sources whence he got the ideas which he built upon afterwards. There are critics who say, that had not the characters of *Blifill* and *Tom Jones* been conceived by Fielding, we never should have had *Joseph* and *Charles Surface;*

although his friend and partial critic, Thomas Moore, says:—

"Next to creation, the reproduction in a new and more perfect form, of materials already existing, or the full development of the thoughts that had but half blown in the hands of others, are the noblest miracles for which we look at the hands of genius. It is not my intention, therefore, to defend Mr. Sheridan from this kind of plagiarism, of which he was guilty in common with the rest of his fellow-descendants from Prometheus, who all steal the spark wherever they can find it. But the instances just alleged of his obligations to others are too questionable and trivial to be taken into any serious account."

But these critics have quite overlooked Sheridan's obligations to Mrs. Centlivre. It is acknowledged that Sheridan's farce of "The Rehearsal" was suggested and founded upon an old play of the same name by the witty Duke of Buckingham. Sheridan was a distinguished scholar, well read too in all the dramatic literature of his own and former days; so that it is only natural that a genius so observant of everything should be struck by excellences in many of the old plays, and strive to present them to the world in a more polished and finished form. Thus, "The Rivals" and Mrs. Centlivre's comedy of "A Bold

Stroke for a Wife" have many points in common. "The Platonick Lady," one of the most brilliant comedies in the English language, written by Mrs. Centlivre, has a character in it that at once suggests the country girl who marries the rich *Sir Peter Teazle*, comes up to town, and plunges into all the dissipations of fashionable life. Mrs. Centlivre's *Mrs. Dowdy* is a widow who comes up to London to learn the ways of gentlefolks. She is atrociously vulgar, and it is chiefly the remarks made about her that bear such a strong resemblance to similar remarks made by *Sir Peter* to *Lady Teazle*, and by his friends concerning her. That Sheridan was influenced by Mrs. Centlivre's writings there can be very little doubt: he who runs may read, and space alone excludes illustrative passages from the writings of each. Congreve was also laid under contribution for "The School for Scandal." *Lady Froth's* verses on her footman undoubtedly suggested the doggerel of *Sir Benjamin Backbite:*—

Sir Benj. Backbite.—But, ladies, you should be acquainted with the circumstances. You must know, that one day last week, as Lady Betty Curricle was taking the dust in Hyde Park, in a sort of duodecimo phaeton, she desired me to write some verses on her ponies, upon which I took out my pocket-book, and in one moment produced the following:—

> Sure never were seen two such beautiful ponies,
> Other horses are downs, but these macaronics;
> To give them this title I'm sure can't be wrong,
> Their legs are so slim, and their tails are so long.

Some of Mrs. Centlivre's prologues and epilogues are amongst the very best specimens of her writings. She was fortunate too in the actresses and actors chosen to deliver them. Some years later her plays became more familiarly known upon the Dublin stage. Woodward admired her writings very much, and Miss Macklin was one of their best interpreters.

The names and dates of Mrs. Centlivre's contributions to dramatic literature are as follow :—

1. Perjured Husband 1700
2. Beau's Duel 1702
3. Love's Contrivance 1703
4. Stolen Heiress 1703
5. Gamester 1705
6. Basset Table 1706
7. Love at a Venture 1706
8. Platonic Lady 1707
9. Busy Body 1709
10. Man's Bewitched 1710
11. A Bickerstaff's Burying . . No date.
12. Marplot 1711
13. Perplex'd Lovers 1712
14. Wonder a Woman Keeps a Secret 1714
15. Gotham Election 1715
16. Wife Well Managed . . . 1715
17. Cruel Gift 1717
18. A Bold Stroke for a Wife . 1718
19. Artifice 1721

Mrs. Centlivre undoubtedly takes the lead of all female writers for the stage. Mrs. Aphra Behn is the only one worthy to be put in competition with her, and she has as far failed in the true essentials of comedy as Mrs. Centlivre has grasped them. The latter excels in plot and character—the soul and body of comedy; the former in language, which may be regarded as merely the outward dress; and Mrs. Behn dazzles more through her audaciousness than from there being any real pith in her dialogues.

Mrs. Centlivre's last marriage was a very happy one. She died at her house in Spring Gardens, Charing Cross, on the first of December, 1722, aged forty-five years, and was buried in the parish church of Saint Martin's-in-the-Fields.

THE HONOURABLE MRS. MONK.

Died, a.d. 1715.

MARY, the second daughter of Robert, second Viscount Molesworth, was the wife of George Monk, Esq., of Stephen's Green, Dublin. There is no record of the year either in which this lady was born, nor of the year of her marriage; but as she left a son and two daughters, and died in 1715, we may conclude she was born about the middle of the latter half of the seventeenth century. Her thirst for knowledge early showed itself, and she is said to have pursued her studies under very disadvantageous circumstances. At that time it was not considered feminine for a woman to be possessed of much learning, and her family even tried to turn her from her favourite pursuits. But all to no purpose. Notwithstanding the opposition she met with, Mary Molesworth contrived to become a perfect mistress of the Latin, Italian, and Spanish tongues. During her lifetime her works were never published; possibly the want of sympathy which she experienced made her decide not to trouble any one with the children of her brain. The opposition which she met with is all the more remarkable as her father, Viscount Molesworth, was a man of considerable taste and learning. He had been for some years ambassador at the Court of Denmark, and, upon his return to Ireland, wrote a history of the state of politics in that country. This work was much thought of at the time, being unique of its kind, and was translated into several languages. He also wrote an able address to the House of Commons concerning the encouragement of agriculture in Ireland; and translated *Franco Gallia*, a Latin treatise, by Hottmann, giving an account of the "free state of France and other parts of Europe before the encroachments made on their liberties."

Mrs. Monk's literary fame was posthumous. She left a large collection of poems and translations in MS., and it is but just to her father to admit that in the preface to the published edition of her works he does ample, though tardy, justice to the genius of his gifted daughter. "Marinda: Poems and Translations upon several occasions," is the title of this extremely rare book, which is dedicated to Her Royal Highness Caroline, Princess of Wales, whose chief bedchamber woman was Charlotta Amelia, third daughter of Viscount Molesworth, and younger sister of the deceased poetess.

"Most of these poems," says Lord Molesworth, in his dedicatory preface to Her Royal Highness, "are the product of the leisure hours of a young gentlewoman lately dead, who, in a remote country retirement, without any assistance but that of a good library, and without omitting the daily care due to a large family, not only perfectly acquired the several languages here made use of, but the good morals and principles contained in those books, so as to put them in practice, as well during her life and languishing sickness, as at the hour of her death; in short, she died not only as a *Christian* but a *Roman* Lady, and so became at once the object of the *Grief* and *Comfort* of her relations. As much as I am obliged to be sparing in commending what belongs to me, I cannot forbear thinking some of these circumstances uncommon enough to be taken notice of: I loved her more *because she deserved it than because she was mine*, and I cannot do greater honour to her memory than by consecrating her labours, or rather her diversion, to your Royal Highness, as we found most of them in her scritoire after her death, written with her own hand; little expecting, and as little desiring the publick should have any opportunity either of applauding or condemning them."

Mrs. Monk's poems and translations have in them the spirit and ring of true poetry. They also possess no inconsiderable humour; and her epigrams, although clever, witty, and incisive, are, unfortunately, too free in expression to bear repetition in the present day. But it must be borne in mind that such was very much the fashion of the time, Wycherley's plays and the novels of Mrs. Aphra Behn, doubtless, representing whatever current literature she may have been acquainted with.

One of the best pieces in this collection is " Runaway Love," a free translation from Tasso. Venus has lost Cupid, and offers the following reward for his apprehension:—

> And he that finds the boy shall have
> The sweetest kiss I ever gave:
> But he that brings him to my arms,
> Shall master be of all my charms.

The other chief contents of the volume are—

"An Eclogue in return to a Tale sent by a Friend." This is one of the most graceful of any of Mrs. Monk's original poems. It is distinguished by delicate play of fancy, true poetic feeling, together with chaste and smoothly-flowing diction.

"The Masque of the Virtues against Love," From Guarini.

"Human Frailty."

Many pieces from Guarina and Tasso.

"Dialogue between Lucinda and Strephon, on a Butterfly that revived before the Fire, and afterwards flew into it and was burnt."

"Ode on the late Queen's Birthday."

"On sight of the present Empress of Germany."

"An Epistle to Marinda," which commences thus :—

> A just applause and an immortal name,
> Is the true object of the poet's aim;
> In quest of this they boldly quit the shore,
> And dangerous seas and unknown lands explore.
> In the whole plan their interest has no share,
> The goods of fortune are beneath their care;
> They on the smoke of publick incense live,
> Look down on wealth, and think it mean to thrive.

The epitaphs composed by Mrs. Monk are amongst the happiest efforts of her genius, and some of them, written upon liberal-minded ladies, possess wit which would not have disgraced Swift. Concerning Mrs. Monk's married life we have no details whatever, but the following lines written by her on her deathbed, in Bath, whither she had gone for her health, to her husband, tend to the conclusion that her union was a happy one :—

> Thou, who dost all my worldly thoughts employ,
> Thou pleasing source of all my earthly joy;
> Thou tend'rest husband, and best earthly friend,
> To thee this first, this last adieu, I send.
> At length the conqu'ror Death asserts his right,
> And will for ever vail me from thy sight.
> He woos me to him with a cheerful grace,
> And not one terror clouds his meagre face.
> He promises a lasting rest from pain,
> And shows that all life's fleeting joys are vain;
> The eternal scenes of Heaven he sets in view,
> And tells me that no other joys are true.
> But Love, fond love, would yet resist his power;
> Would fain awhile defer the parting hour;
> He brings thy mourning image to my eyes,
> And would obstruct my journey to the skies.
> But say, thou dearest, thou unwearied friend;
> Say, should'st thou grieve to see my sorrows end?
> Thou know'st a painful pilgrimage I've past;
> And should'st thou grieve that rest is come at last?
> Rather rejoice to see me shake off life,
> And die as I have lived—thy faithful wife.

Mrs. Monk died in 1715, and left a son, Henry-Stanley, who subsequently became Surveyor-General to the Customs, and two daughters. The elder one, Sarah, was the authoress of some poetical pieces, which, however, met with the same posthumous recognition as those of her mother, inasmuch as that they were not published during her lifetime. Her grandfather collected them, and gave them to the world under the title of "Poems by Miranda." The very best of them are far below the standard of any written by her more gifted mother.

CONSTANTIA GRIERSON.

Born, a.d. 1707.   Died, a.d. 1733.

IN a humbler rank of life than the subject of the foregoing memoir, but superior in the ranks of genius, the name of Constantia Grierson is one of the brightest and most illustrious upon the bead-roll of Irish female biography. She was born in the city of Kilkenny, in the year 1707. Her parents were respectable people, evidently with ideas somewhat in advance of their age; for seeing their little daughter early evince an aptitude for study, they furthered her desires by every means that lay in their power. Her father sought for advice in the matter, and, although his circumstances were narrow, he endeavoured to supply her with books suited, as he had been told, to the capacity of such a child. But he soon found that her abilities were not to be meted by her years; they flew beyond them. It was observed that her genius and inclination, aided by that commonplace but indispensable quality—industry—surmounted all difficulties, and, without the aid of a master, did not alone taste, but drink deep draughts of the Pierian spring.

At a very early age, Constantia Grierson was pronounced by competent judges to be a perfect mistress of the Greek and Roman tongues. This knowledge she acquired entirely through her own extraordinary perseverance, never having had any tuition up to that time in any of the branches of learning in which she excelled. History, divinity, philosophy, and mathematics were also studied by her with much success; and, in order that she might the better perfect herself in these studies, she came on a visit to Dublin, so as to obtain instruction in her favourite pursuits.

Shortly after her arrival in the Irish metropolis she made the acquaintance of George Grierson, one of the chief printers in that city. He possessed an excellent library, to which he gladly gave her free access. From admiring the genius of the earnest young student he became sensible of her charms and worth as a woman, proposed to her, and married her.

Constantia Grierson was of much service to her husband in his business. He had the monopoly of Bible-printing in Ireland, and his wife's rare classical attainments were of much value to him. She wrote "An Abridgment of the History of England," which he printed, but which did not much enhance her literary reputation. Many poems, epigrams, and occasional pieces flowed from her facile pen—written in Latin, Greek, or English; but as they did not come up to her standard of excellence, she burnt them all before her death. None of her poems have been preserved, save a few which she addressed to various friends, notably to Mrs. Barber, and which are too personal to be quoted as they could not possess any interest for the general reader; and, on the other hand, it would be unfair to give them as specimens of Mrs. Grierson's poetical abilities. Just before she was married, she addressed some lines to her intended husband. They are as follows:—

ON THE ART OF PRINTING.

Hail mystic art, which men like angels taught
To speak to eyes, and paint embody'd thought!
The deaf and dumb, blest skill, reliev'd by thee,
We make one sense perform the task of three.
We see, we hear, we touch the head and heart,
And take or give what each but yields in part;
With the hard laws of distance we dispense,
And without sound, apart commune in sense;
View, though confin'd, nay! rule this earthly ball,
And travel o'er the wide extended All!
Dead letters thus with living notions fraught
Prove to the soul the telescope of thought.
To mortal life immortal honour give;
And bid all deeds and titles last and live.
In scanty life—Eternity we taste,
View the first ages and inform the last;
Arts, history, laws—we purchase with a look,
And keep, like fate, all nature in a book.

The chief monuments of her erudition which Mrs. Grierson has left behind her are her unrivalled translations of *Tacitus* and *Terence*. Amongst classical scholars they are known and recognised as the " Dublin editions." Lord Carteret was Lord Lieutenant of Ireland at the time, and to him Mrs. Grierson dedicated *Tacitus*. The *Terence* she dedicated to his son, accompanying it by a Greek epigram. This nobleman was himself an accomplished scholar, capable of appreciating Mrs. Grierson's genius and attainments; and as a graceful way of showing his admiration and esteem for her character and abilities, he procured for her husband the patent of King's Printer in Ireland, and to distinguish and reward her uncommon merit, he had her life inserted in it.

Undoubtedly a woman of surpassing genius, yet much was due to her extraordinary perseverance and powers of application. Amidst her literary labours—which must have been very continuous, considering all she accomplished during her short life—she faithfully performed her duty as a wife and a mother. Her contemporaries say she was singularly without vanity, and most diffident concerning her own abilities. Ballard says of her:—

" As her learning and abilities raised her above her own sex, so they left her no room to envy any; on the contrary, her delight was to see others excell : she was always ready to advise and direct those who applied to her ; and was herself willing to be advised.

"So little did she value herself upon her uncommon excellencies, that it has often recalled to my mind a fine reflection of a French author—*that great genius's should be superior to their own abilities.*"

After a long and painful illness Mrs. Grierson died, in 1773, at the early age of twenty-seven years.

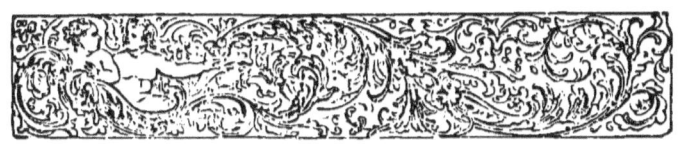

CHARLOTTE BROOKE.

DIED, A.D. 1793.

THE subjects of the preceding three memoirs —Susanna Centlivre, Hon. Mrs. Monk, and Constantia Grierson—were all women well skilled in the classical languages, and also in the more modern tongues of Europe. With the sole exception of French, we do not know if Charlotte Brooke was well acquainted with any modern language; but any deficiency in this respect was fully compensated for by the vast and accurate knowledge which she possessed of the language and literature of the ancient Irish.

Charlotte Brooke was the daughter of Henry Brooke, Esq., of Rantavan, Co. Cavan, Ireland, who married his cousin, Miss Meares—a lady for ever famous as being the only woman of whom Dean Swift was afraid. Henry Brooke was a man of much culture and learning, and a graceful and brilliant writer. His *Farmer's Letters*—after the style of the *Drapier's Letters*—are models of style; he was also the author of several plays, notably

"Gustavus Vasa," and several novels and romances. He had a numerous family, but of all his children, only two survived—a son, Arthur, who died early in the service of the East India Company, and Charlotte, the subject of this memoir.

She was literally the child of his old age, clever and intelligent beyond her years, and well fitted to be the companion of her accomplished father. He soon perceived her abilities, and spared no pains in striving to direct her literary taste. Mr. Brooke was a man of genius, and from his constant society his daughter must undoubtedly have reaped many benefits. Moreover, he was a man of high moral character—his works show this, their leading features being benevolence, patriotism almost to excess, and that ever-wakeful regard for religion and morality which delighted to employ itself in seizing or creating opportunities of advancing their cause.

Brought up in such a school, and under the tuition of such a master, Charlotte Brooke commenced her education under pleasant auspices. One of Mr. Brooke's biographers, referring to this, says :—" He had formed a plan for her education, with an unalterable determination to pursue it. In this plan he proposed to reject the severity of discipline, and to lead her mind insensibly to knowledge and exertion, by exciting her curiosity, and directing it to useful objects. By this method Miss Brooke's desire to learn became as eager as her parent's wish to teach ; and such were his talents of instruction, and her facility of retaining it, that in her fifth year she was able to read, distinctly and rapidly, any English book. He particularly attended at the same time to the cultivation of her memory, by making her learn and repeat select passages from the English poets. During this period, Miss Brooke's attention was almost equally divided between her books and a little garden, the cultivation and embellishment of which occupied all her leisure hours. Her faculties necessarily gained strength by exercise ; and the sedulity of a fond parent was without intermission exerted to add to her stock of scientific attainments. He also taught her the rudiments of drawing, in which she afterwards excelled. The quick and early improvement which she made was an ample recompense for all the pains that had been taken with her. The accomplishments generally attained with labour, expense, and waste of time, seemed with her the mere amusement of a few spare hours, and acquired with little expense or professional assistance."

Amidst such associations Charlotte Brooke passed her childhood and early girlhood. Her father had resided much in London when a young man, moving in the best literary and social circles. When he returned to Ireland, he still kept up many of the friendships he had then formed, so that some years after, when he removed with his family to Killybegs, near Naas, County Kildare, he was often visited by these friends of his younger days. This society was of great advantage to Charlotte Brooke, who was at this time a clever young girl, as much admired for the graces of her person as of her mind. Moreover, she was as modest and as unassuming as she was gifted; and, although at this time she had made many translations of poems, and had also written some herself, yet such was her diffidence and mistrust of her own powers, that she destroyed them rather than run the risk of their authorship being discovered.

During his residence at Killybegs, Mr. Brooke composed some of his finest plays. When he lived in London, he had been the intimate friend of Garrick, who at once, with his customary shrewdness, had detected the unusual talent of the brilliant young Irishman. He had offered Mr. Brooke a shilling a line for everything he should write, but this the author had refused, not wishing to sell his talent. Afterwards, when the MS. of the "Earl of Essex" was complete, Mr. Brooke offered it to Garrick; but the vain actor, who never forgave the least suspicion of a slight, refused it. The writer then sent it to Sheridan, who accepted it and brought it out at Smock Alley. It was afterwards represented at Drury Lane.*

This was the most brilliant social period of Charlotte Brooke's life. Her father went to stay in Dublin for a couple of seasons, so that she had the advantage of association with all the most distinguished persons in the brilliant Dublin society of that period. On the boards of the Dublin theatres were then to be found the best performers on the British stage. Garrick and Peg Woffington were in the Irish metropolis at the time, and Charlotte Brooke was so carried away with admiration and enthusiasm that she gave her indulgent father no peace until he introduced her to them. Night after night she spent at the theatre, so completely was she carried away by her feelings. Her rage for witnessing dramatic representations

---

* Sheridan was one day praising the language of the "Earl of Essex" in the hearing of Dr. Johnson. "Sir," said the great lexicographer, "repeat for me what you consider the finest line in the play." Sheridan promptly declaimed—

Who rule o'er freemen, should themselves be free.

"This mode of reasoning," replied the Doctor, sarcastically, "is conclusive in such a degree, that it will lose nothing of its force, even though we should apply it to a more familiar subject, as follows—

Who drives fat oxen, should himself be fat."

swept all before it; she neglected her former studious pursuits—reading, drawing, everything was laid aside; she could think of nothing but the heroes and heroines of the hour. This passion almost amounted to delirium, and was a source of much concern to her father. She wrote a tragedy, called "Belisarius," which was never acted; but whether it was during this period of theatrical infatuation or not, we have no means of ascertaining.* Remonstrance was useless, therefore her father, in despair, left Dublin, at much inconvenience to himself, and took his daughter back to the country.

Her mother had now fallen into ill-health, and Charlotte Brooke, ever an affectionate and dutiful daughter, attended her assiduously during her long and painful illness. A reaction took place in her mind, and the girl who but a few months before would have sacrificed everything to witness a representation of one of her favourite plays, now made the resolution—which she kept—never to enter a playhouse again. It is very likely that her mother's wishes had something to do with her

---

* "BELISARIUS," Trag. A scene from a MS. play under this title was printed in *The Oracle* (daily paper), Oct. 17, 1795. We know that Miss Brooke (translator of *Reliques of Irish Poetry*) wrote a tragedy under this title, the MS. of which, it is feared, is lost. Query, whether the above extract was made from Miss B.'s play ?—*Vide* "Biographia Dramatica," vol. ii. p. 56.

coming to this decision; for Mrs. Brooke was a rigid Methodist, and although she admired her husband's genius, often regretted that it led him to write for the stage, and to associate with actors and actresses.

Charlotte Brooke's life now passed very uneventfully for a good many years. Her mother's death was a serious blow to her father. They had been married for nearly fifty years, and Mr. Brooke, although he did not sympathise with his wife upon many points, chiefly relating to religion, was sincerely attached to her. In a few years his own health began to give way, and grief, years, and over-study soon reduced him to a state of complete imbecility. His daughter was unremitting in her affectionate solicitude. Mr. Brooke lived for a few years in this melancholy condition, and then died peacefully on the 10th of October, 1783.

Father, mother, and brother dead, Charlotte Brooke now found herself very much alone in the world, and with a very slender income. She was long past girlhood, and looked even older than she really was, from the anxious years of sick-nursing which she had gone through. Her spirits were quite broken, and her former literary occupations seemed to have lost all charm for her. Whilst in this state she attracted the notice of a Mr. Walker, an old friend of her father, and the author of "Historical Memoirs of the Irish Bards." This gentleman was quite aware of Miss Brooke's correct knowledge of the Irish language, and at his suggestion she undertook the translation of an Irish monody, to be inserted in the afore-mentioned work, upon which he was then engaged.

This was Miss Brooke's first published work: it stands unrivalled as a translation, from the admirable manner in which the touching pathos and simplicity of the original are preserved. Mr. Walker prefaced the poem with the following notice:—" For the benefit of the English reader, I shall here give an elegant paraphrase of this monody, by a young lady whose name I am enjoined to conceal; with the modesty ever attendant upon true merit, and with the sweet timidity natural to her sex, she shrinks from the public eye."

CAROLAN'S MONODY ON THE DEATH OF MARY MACGUIRE.

Were mine the choice of intellectual fame,
　Of spelful song, and eloquence divine,
Painting's sweet power, philosophy's pure flame,
　And Homer's lyre, and Ossian's harp were mine;
The splendid arts of Erin, Greece, and Rome,
　In *Mary* lost, would lose their wonted grace.
All would I give to snatch her from the tomb,
　Again to fold her in my fond embrace.

Desponding, sick, exhausted with my grief,
    Awhile the founts of sorrow cease to flow,
In vain—I rest not—sleep brings no relief,
    Cheerless, companionless, I wake to woe.
Nor birth, nor beauty, shall again allure,
    Nor fortune win me to another bride;
Alone I'll wander, and alone endure,
    Till death restore me to my dear one's side.

Once every thought and every scene was gay,
    Friends, mirth, and music all my hours employ'd—
Now doom'd to mourn my last sad years away,
    My life a solitude! my heart a void!
Alas, the change! the change again no more!
    For every comfort is with Mary fled;
Till ceaseless anguish shall her loss deplore,
    Till age and sorrow join me with the dead.

Adieu, each gift of nature, and of art,
    That erst adorn'd me in life's early prime!
The cloudless temper, and the social heart,
    The soul ethereal, and the flight sublime!
Thy loss, my *Mary*, chas'd them from my breast;
    Thy sweetness cheers, thy judgment aids no more;
The muse deserts a heart with grief opprest—
    And lost is every joy that charmed before.

It should be borne in mind that Miss Brooke commenced the study of the Irish language exclusively from books; but then the famous Clenard began his acquisition of the Arabic language by reading in an Arabic version of the Bible those proper names which he might suppose to be the same in the Arabic as in the Hebrew, and thus labouring to distinguish the forms and sounds of the different characters in which the names were expressed in the unknown language.

The famous Sir William Jones was much more indebted to his own ardent industry and genius, than to any aid of instructors, for the success with which he conquered all the difficulties of the most abstruse Oriental learning. Miss Brooke was no less boldly industrious, and therefore not less fortunate in her search after knowledge.

In the year 1787, yielding to the earnest solicitations of her friends, Charlotte Brooke resolved to try and conquer her constitutional timidity, and to undertake the work which has made her name famous wherever the Irish race is to be found. "The Reliques of Irish Poetry" is a sublime and lasting monument of her genius. To investigate the meagre literary remains of other times, couched in an almost obsolete language, of which few have been hardy and inquisitive enough to attempt the acquisition—to elucidate these writings and to clothe them in the vesture of modern rhyme, are achievements that might well have staggered any literary knight-errant. Yet Charlotte Brooke has accomplished all this, and her marvellously intimate acquaintance with the language of the ancient Irish may be gathered from the fact that her book was completed in one year from the time when she commenced it. She began her work by translating such Irish ballads and songs as she could collect amongst her friends, afterwards selecting the warlike and heroic odes which she considered the best specimens of ancient Irish poetry. Scarcely any true conception can be formed of the arduous nature of her task. A chief difficulty she had to contend against was the repetition of thought, plainly observable in the English versions, but not perceived in the original Irish, so great is the variety of expression peculiar to that language. The number of synonyms in which it abounds enables it, perhaps beyond any other tongue, to repeat the same thought continually without wearying the fancy or grating upon the ear. As an example of this, we may mention that there are upwards of forty names to express a ship in the Irish language, and nearly an equal number for a house.

"It is really astonishing," says Miss Brooke, in the preface to "Reliques of Irish Poetry," "of what varied and comprehensive powers this neglected language is possessed. In the pathetic it breathes the most beautiful and affecting simplicity, and in the bolder species of composition it is distinguished by a force of expression, a sublime dignity, and rapid energy, which it is scarcely possible for any translation to convey, as it sometimes fills the mind with ideas altogether new, and which, perhaps, no modern language is entirely prepared to express. One compound epithet must often be translated by two lines of English verse, and, on such occasions, much of the beauty is necessarily lost, the force and effect of the thought being weakened by too slow an introduction on the mind, just as that light which dazzles when flashing swiftly on the eye will be gazed at with indifference if let in by degrees."

Towards the conclusion of her prefatory remarks, Miss Brooke says truly :—" As yet we are too little known to our noble neighbour of Britain; were we better acquainted we should be better friends. The British muse is not yet informed that she has an elder sister in this isle; let us then introduce them to each other! Together let us walk them abroad from their bowers, sweet ambassadresses of cordial union between two countries that seem formed by nature to be joined by every bond of interest and of amity. Let them entreat of Britain to cultivate a nearer acquaintance with her neighbouring isle. Let them conciliate for us her esteem, and her affection will follow of course. Let them tell her that the portion of her blood which flows in our veins is rather ennobled than disgraced by the mingling tides that descended from our heroic ancestors!"

With the exception of "Moore's Irish Melodies," which owe their popularity chiefly to their musical accompaniments, it is much to be regretted that the poetical treasures of the Irish nation are comparatively unknown. No other people possesses in a higher degree the essentials for the production of lyrical poetry. The Celtic temperament and intellect, sensuous yet pure; graceful, impatient, and versatile, but with a want of deep mental grasp, is peculiarly suited to the flux and reflux of lyrical emotion. Moreover, the abundant use of metaphor, exquisite simplicity of expression and picturesque epithets, combine to give a poetical tone to the language. "If you plead for your life, plead in Irish," says the old adage, bearing testimony to its persuasive powers. With all these striking qualifications it would indeed be wonderful if the poetry of ancient Ireland had not attained a high degree of excellence. Poetry was the darling science of the ancient Irish, and nothing among them was left unsung. They introduced poetry into every scene, and suited it to every occasion. The bards followed their chieftains to battle, and with their heroic strains incited the kerns and galloglasses to the fight, like the European troubadours of later days, and the Scalds of Scandinavia.* For fiery declamation and head-

---

* Amongst the ancient Celtic races the office of bard was considered especially sacred, and second only in dignity to that of the king. The person of the bard was regarded with peculiar sanctity, and history furnishes but a single instance of violence towards one of their caste. At the battle of Cruachan, the songs of the bard of

long torrent of eloquence, the War Odes of the ancient Irish stand unrivalled in the literature of any nation in the world. The following extract from Miss Brooke's translation of the "WAR ODE, TO OSGUR, THE SON OF OISIN, IN THE FRONT OF THE BATTLE OF GABHRA," will illustrate this :—

> Resistless as the spirit of the night,
> In storms and terrors drest,
> Withering the force of every hostile breast,
> Rush on the ranks of fight!
> Youth of fierce deeds, and noble soul!
> Rend—scatter wide the foe!
> Swift forward rush, and lay the waving pride
> Of you high ensigns low!
> Thine be the battle—thine the sway!
> On—on to Cairbre hew thy conquering way,
> And let thy deathful arm dash safety from his side!
> As the proud wave, on whose broad back
> The storm its burden heaves,
> Drives on the scattered wreck
> Its ruin leaves;
> So let thy sweeping progress roll
> Fierce, resistless, rapid, strong,
> Pour, like the billow of the flood, o'erwhelming might along!

No language has ever been more adapted for the true and full expression of lyrical ebb and flow than has the ancient—and, indeed, it may be said, modern—Irish tongue. The poetry of many of

---

the *Ard-righ*, or Monarch of all Ireland, so enraged the King of Leinster, that he, stung by the sarcasms heaped upon him, rushed in among the enemy and slew the minstrel. The deed was held in such abhorrence that the nation unanimously gave him the name of *Cin-saleah*, or "dishonourable head." Many of his descendants yet exist, the name being modernised *Kinselagh*.

the ancient Celtic songs is almost ready-made music, without the aid of a tune. Moreover, the language is admirably constituted for the formation of word-pictures ; and in the few songs which she gives in her "Reliques of Irish Poetry," Miss Brooke has faithfully preserved this peculiarity. For instance, what can be more simple, at the same time more perfect in picturesqueness and beauty, than the following sentiment of one of these songs :—A forsaken maid compares her heart to a burning coal, bruised black ; thus retaining the heat that consumed, while it loses the light that had cheered it. The songs abound in such vivid word-pictures ; and truly of Miss Brooke it may be said that no one has done more for the poetry of her native land.

To excel in epistolary writing is no mean accomplishment, and Miss Brooke added this to her many other acquirements. She was a charming letter-writer, and her correspondence with her life-long and intimate friend, Miss T——, is as remarkable for the variety of subjects discussed as for the admirable style in which it is written. Speaking upon the subject of *self-denial*, she writes thus :—

"I agree with you perfectly as to what you say respecting the insufficiency of abstinence *for its own sake*. Nevertheless, I am assured that he who will not *of himself* take up crosses, now and then, by way of practice, will never be able to bear them when they are *laid upon* him. Observe, I include not *fasting* in abstinence. It is generally injurious to health, and when it is so, becomes sinful. But I mean *self-denial*—the *spirit of sacrifice*, which is the *spirit of love*. In general, the more we endure for a *human* friend, the more they engage our affections. And if endurance in this instance is creative of affection, affection is also creative of endurance; they mutually act upon and stimulate each other. We are even sometimes *rejoiced* in an opportunity of proving our love, by the sacrifices we are ready to make. No wonder then that we are told to 'rejoice when we are accounted worthy to suffer' *for our God!* Self-denial is also useful, and even necessary, in another point of view—to bring into subjection the 'outer man.' To make the vassal know his Lord. To keep those lubbard appetites and passions of ours in due subordination, and not suffer them, as they are perpetually inclined, to cock their arms akimbo, and flourish their fists at their masters. An enlightened heathen (Socrates) was so sensible of this that it is recorded of him that he often denied the calls of hunger and of thirst, when he found them unusually violent in their demands; and sometimes, after raising the cup to his lips, laid it down again, and took a turn in his garden, until he found that he *was* the master; and then he returned and gave his *servant* a drink."

Except in her earlier years, and during her period of theatrical infatuation, Miss Brooke had had no taste for light reading of any kind. Her mind had naturally an austerely religious bent, as may be gathered from her numerous letters, and also from the style of books she was in the habit of reading. "Law's Serious Call," the writings of Doctor Doddridge, and others of a like class, found most favour in her eyes. No doubt her early training under her mother's eye gave a bias to her religious feelings. She was truly benevolent, founded a girls' school in the country, and brought up the orphan daughter of an old friend as her own child.

In 1790, Miss Brooke met with an unexpected trial in the loss of the small patrimony which she had been left. She had scarcely sufficient to enable her to exist, and the state of her health was such as to preclude the possibility of her earning anything at literary work. In this emergency, Mr. Joseph Walker and a few other friends tried to get her appointed as housekeeper to the Royal Irish Academy, Dawson Street, Dublin, then some years in existence. The president was the Earl of Charlemont, who had been an intimate friend of the accomplished author of "Gustavus Vasa." Flattering herself with the hope of success, and elated at the prospect of obtaining at least the shelter of a roof for life, she drew up the following petition, which was presented to the Royal Irish Academy:—

"MY LORDS AND GENTLEMEN,—I should not take the liberty of this address to a society which I so highly respect, if I was not provided with an adequate claim to your attention.

"I address you as the daughter of *Gustavus Vasa*—a man who, either as a friend or a patriot, was dear to every member of your Academy.

"Since his decease I have known nothing but affliction. The death of my brother, shortly after, deprived me of my only protection, and also of a considerable share of my fortune; a principal part of what remained was involved in the failure of Captain Brooke, and *the rest* is now lost by the bankruptcy of a trader in whose hands it was placed at interest. I have lost in all to the amount of one and two hundred a year, and this without any imprudence of my own, which might have drawn down those calamities upon me.

"I find myself stripped both of friends and fortune, in a world of which I have but little knowledge—cut off from every dependence, from every protection, but that of Heaven and my country. To the most distinguished individuals of *that* country, I now address myself, as a descendant of Genius. I request to be entrusted with the care of a house destined to the purpose, and dedicated to the honour of Genius. I will undertake it, if so required, without a salary.

"Unaccustomed to solicit, I yet bend with less pain to the task, when I consider *the characters* to whom my application is addressed. To you, Gentlemen, the memory of my Father cannot plead in vain; it will, I am confident, be my advocate with *your taste*, and my own most distressing situation, with your *humanity*.

"In this protection and support for a female orphan you will also fulfil the purpose for which your elegant and respectable society was formed, by showing to the world, that to the Royal Irish Academy even the spirit of departed Genius was dear.

"I have the honour to be,
 "My Lords and Gentlemen,
  "With the utmost respect,
   "Your most obedient servant,
    "CHARLOTTE BROOKE."

From some cause, which never was explained, Miss Brooke's application was at first neglected, and then refused. Her good friend, Mr. Walker, urged her many and great claims upon the consideration of a society for the expressed fostering and encouragement of Irish literature. But his representations had no effect; and Charlotte Brooke, reduced in worldly circumstances, and in shattered health, commenced to edit an edition of her father's works. By this she gained a little money, and a year or so afterwards brought out a small book, entitled "A School for Christians," in dialogues for the use of little children. The work was not very successful; and Miss Brooke's troubles were at this time increased by hearing that an imperfect and cheap copy of her father's works was now being brought out without her knowledge or consent. She fought for her rights, and succeeded in suppressing the edition; but that was all. Shortly afterwards she brought it out in an amended form, with her own notes. In a letter written at this period, she says:—

"May, 15th, 1792.

"My dear Miss T—— will, I fear, think sadly of my silence; but in truth I am not to blame; and I can declare with the utmost sincerity, that a single day does not pass without *frequent* thoughts of, and cordial good wishes for, her welfare. I was as sure of being at Cottage a month ago as I was of my existence. Three times I was on the point of setting out, and each time detained by inevitable and disagreeable business. M'Kenzie (the College printer), who unfortunately printed my father's works, has harassed me by every species of impudence, insolence, and . . . . Until a week ago, I was not able to get the last of the books out of his hands, and I then found there was a number of the copies wanting. I refused to pay his bill till he gave them *all* up, and he threatened me with a *suit*. Any court in Christendom would have given it against him, and he was told so ; but he knew I disliked contention, and therefore bullied me to obtain what he had no right to. However, my booksellers, Archer and Jones, have taken up the matter, and say they hope to settle it. I suppose I shall lose considerably, besides the far greater vexation of having the work ill-done, which is so very dearly paid for. The paper is badly matched ; the subscribers complain, and those who do not understand the business will, to be sure, lay the blame upon *me*. But I have this consolation, that the fame of my father is justified. The work is not the less perfect in itself, for the defect of the paper ; and it will descend to posterity in a state not unworthy of its author. Any censure that may fall upon me, when compared with this consideration, is not worth a thought. I have ever lived but for my father, and I shall not *now* divide my little rivulet from the parent stream. Oh, may we never be divided! May we roll together to that sea 'from whence we never have return!' In life, my soul is his; in death I trust it shall join him! You say I know not what it is to have the heart exclusively centred in one object—you forgot my father when you said so. I am indeed incapable of any other love —my heart was *intended* for that alone; and nature has not, nor ever will have *room* for any other one. I see none on earth who resemble him, and therefore heaven alone can become his rival in my breast."

This was Miss Brooke's last literary effort. She had intended publishing a revised edition of her father's famous novel, "The Fool of Quality," but found the labour and expense would tax too heavily both her physical strength and her almost exhausted purse. For the next few years she resided principally with her friends, Mr. and Mrs. Browne, at Cottage, near Longford, and during the last winter of her life visited Dublin for the last time. She stayed alternately with Dr. Hill and with her faithful friend, Mrs. Hamilton, of Dominick Street. In the congenial and cultivated society of this lady, Miss Brooke always took an especial pleasure, and in her letters warmly eulogises Mrs. Hamilton's strong natural sense, and her unobtrusive steady friendship.

But Miss Brooke's health had been gradually declining, and her friends observed with sorrow that during this last winter she began to fail rapidly. Perhaps she felt this herself, for she abruptly shortened her Dublin visit, and returned to Cottage. Shortly after her arrival she was seized with a malignant fever, and on the 29th of March, 1793, quietly breathed her last. From the moment she was stricken down with illness she felt she had not long to live ; and during the intervals of consciousness, repeatedly expressed her resignation to the will of God, and her sole trust in the atonement and mediation of her Saviour.

Soon after Miss Brooke's death, her friend, Mr. J. C. Walker, received, anonymously, some lines upon her death, with a request that they might be published in the *Anthologia Hibernica.* Mr. Walker immediately forwarded them to the Editor of that periodical, accompanied by the following note :—

"SIR,—I was last night favoured with the enclosed lines from an unknown hand, accompanied with a modest request that I would forward them to your magazine in case they should meet my approbation. I do not lose a moment in sending them to you ; for, besides possessing many poetical beauties, they breathe a spirit of unfeigned sorrow which particularly recommends them to me, who feel such deep affliction for the ingenious and amiable subject of them.

"I am, &c. &c.,
"J. C. W.

"April 13th, 1793."

TO THE MEMORY OF MISS CHARLOTTE BROOKE.

<pre>
Let tow'ring pride erect the sculptured shrine,
And venal flattery garlands twine to deck
The vault where grandeur lies:—but come, Oh Muse!
And seek the lowly grave where CHARLOTTE rests.
Insatiate grave, and faithless! verdure gay,
In every springing flow'ret of the year
Adorn thy surface; yet thy envious depth
Veils from my aching sight the fairest flower
That grac'd our clime. Alas! for ever hid
From mortal eyes, dear maid! thy sweetness blooms
In radiant spheres beyond our feeble view.
Oh! early lost, and sudden! Mighty Powers!
Are virtue, genius, talents, only lent
A little moment just to raise our hope,
And vanish, transient, as the painted cloud
Which quick dissolves in tears? Is life no more?
And cannot worth superior ward the dart,
Or bribe a lengthened hour from ruthless death?
Ah, no! could worth prolong the fleeting date,
I had not wept o'er CHARLOTTE'S timeless urn—
Though sad my heart, no single mourner I,
For drooping friendship, in dejection fixed,
Points the mute sorrow lab'ring for a vent;
And gratitude, with lifted eye, pursues
The shade of her, whose generous bosom felt
For every human woe; nor *felt* alone,
But with delighted readiness *relieved:*
Religion too, and filial piety,
</pre>

Their vot'ry's pale remains exulting own,
Though shrouded in the dust. And lo! revealed
To fancy's wond'ring gaze, a thousand shapes,
Air-drawn, advance, bright evanescent forms,
Attuning heav'nly harps to solemn dirge;
And shadowy choirs of time-enobled bards,
Whose songs, by her from dark oblivion snatched,
And failing language charm the ear again.
While kindred genius and congenial worth
Endure, sweet maid! thou ne'er wilt be forgot:
Returning seasons still shall find thy grave
With heartfelt tears, and tributary wreaths
Due honoured; hands unseen shall dress the sod;
There pensive contemplation, too, shall steal
From scenes of thoughtless levity, to plume
Her wing for flight sublime, and learn of thee
O'er earth-born ill triumphant to arise,
To live with *virtue*, and with *hope* to die.

MRS. MARY TIGHE.
"PSYCHE."

BORN, OCTOBER 9TH, 1772. DIED, MARCH 24TH, 1810.

BORN in 1772, the daughter of the Rev. William Blachford and of Theodosia, only daughter of Lady Mary Tighe, daughter of Lord Darnley. Mary Blachford, the subject of this memoir, was scarcely in her twentieth year when she appeared in the brilliant and cultivated Dublin Society of that period. There are two original portraits of her extant; one, a miniature by Comerford, now in the possession of the Right Hon. William Tighe, of Woodstock: the other is an oil painting by Romney, the property of Lady Laura Grattan. She is depicted with rich flowing, dark-brown hair, a few tendrils of which stray upon her smooth, intellectual forehead. The eyes are of a deep blue: large and pellucid, with a wondering wistful look in them: the lower part of the face is exquisitely formed, the chiselled round chin and rather small, full, soft mouth indicating, in a remarkable degree,

sensitiveness and sensuousness—the latter an
essential of the poetic temperament—without the
slightest trace of sensuality. The general expression of the countenance is sweet, innocent, and
lofty, but tinged with a look of inexpressible
sadness.

Young, beautiful, and gifted, she was the centre
of attraction in the brilliant vice-regal Court of
Dublin before the Union. They were Dublin's
palmiest days; when the Ranelagh Gardens were
the resort of the beaux and belles, when the
Parliament was held in College Green, and the
members had their town residences in Dublin, and
when the Lord-Lieutenant danced with the mysterious shamrock-dressed lady at Saint Patrick's
Ball, who vanished as the clock struck twelve, and
kissed the knocker of Dublin Castle on her way
out.

Both as Mary Blachford and as Mary Tighe, she
must have witnessed all this : she must also have
been cognisant of that last pathetic Parliament,
held in the long low-ceiling upper room of a house
in Donnybrook, when the few members who could
not be bought, despairingly acknowledged the
death of Dublin society and of Dublin's commercial
prosperity. But although she lived through an
eventful period of her country's history, Mrs.
Tighe makes no allusion to these troublous times

in any of her writings. Of her, indeed, it may truly be said that—

> Her soul was like a star, and dwelt apart.

She lived an inner life which none might know. The following lines written by her in the year 1792, at the close of a gay Dublin season, afford a graphic picture of the tone of her mind :—

> Returned at length to solitude and peace,
>   Once more my heart resumes its lov'd pursuits,
> Once more I seek my lost poetic ease
>   And wander, searching for Castalia's fruits.
> But ah! in vain, to me the Nine refuse
>   Inspiring succour and enkindling thought,
> Too long, alas! I have renounced the Muse,
>   Her voice neglected, and her lyre forgot.
> Lost in a crowd of folly and of noise,
>   With vain delights my bosom learnt to beat,
> Resigned the pleasures I had made my choice
>   Of calm philosophy and wisdom sweet.
> For in the circles of the vain and gay,
>   No more her tranquil state my soul enjoyed,
> In busy idleness I passed the day,
>   And mirth, and dress, and song my hours employed.
> To fix the attention of admiring eyes,
>   To move with elegance and talk with ease,
> To be the object of the practised sigh,
>   To attract the notice, and the ear to please.
> The empty flattery, which my heart despised,
>   The present frenzy which the dance inspired,
> Joys, which my reason never could have prized,
>   And which, till tasted, I had ne'er desired.
> Yet these had charms which now I blush to own,
>   Powers, which I then believed not they possess'd
> The Muse to banish from her humble throne,
>   Where she so oft had fired my glowing breast.

> But the remembrance of those empty hours
>   Affords no single pleasure to my mind;
> My soul regrets her lost collective powers,
>   And sighs once more her wonted calm to find.
> For Folly's influence I yet deplore,
>   A vacant gloom she o'er my heart hath spread;
> The secret charm of solitude is o'er,
>   My thoughts are scattered, and the Muses fled.
> Such was the low ambition of my mind,
>   Such were the vain desires I formed,
> For such delights my calmer joys resigned,
>   And quenched the fires which had my bosom warmed.

She was Mary Blachford when she wrote the foregoing verses, and mingled in the society which she so despises herself for having been enthralled with, chaperoned by her aunt, Mrs. Tighe, of Rosanna, one of the most cultivated women of the day. Her father was dead; he died when she was an infant of but a few months old, and her mother, a strict unbending Puritan of ascetic habits, chose to live in retirement, and thus it was that her aunt introduced the beautiful Mary into that brilliant assemblage of which she became speedily so bright an ornament.

This Mrs. Tighe, of Rosanna, had a son named Henry, who was but one year older than her niece. The young people were much in each other's society, and Henry Tighe, who had just been returned as member for Kilkenny in the Irish Parliament, fell deeply in love with his fascinating cousin. She returned the feeling, and the youthful pair were married on October 6th, 1793, the bride being within three days of her twenty-first birthday, and the bridegroom in his twenty-third year. Henry Tighe wished to be called to the English Bar, so they went to live in London, in Manchester Square, the house they occupied belonging to his mother. But he seems to have had little taste for the drudgery of the law; and gradually allowed himself to be drawn away from more serious pursuits to take up the *rôle* of a London man of fashion. His wife's beauty and her many other superior attractions were powerful influences to gather around them a large circle of all those in the Metropolis famed for the graces of mind or person. It was a fascinating and dangerous sort of society for a young and beautiful woman to mix in, where she must have been the object of insidious flattery, and of the innumerable and intangible temptations to which a woman, excelling, as she did, in mind and in person, must have been subjected to. For a time this life seemed to charm her; but her higher nature, which no contact with the world could sully, at length asserted itself, and her feelings found vent in that magnificent outburst of poetry, which for sublimity of sentiment, graceful diction, and true poetic strength, is only second to the "Faëry Queen" of Edmund Spenser.

"Psyche," the poem here referred to, is one of

the most marvellous poems that has ever been written by any woman in any age, Elizabeth Barrett Browning alone excepted. It stands alone in the literature of Ireland—pure, polished, sublime—the outpouring of a trammelled soul yearning to be freed from its uncongenial surroundings. The publication of this poem in 1795 at once established Mrs. Tighe's reputation as a poetess (although, at first, it was only printed for private circulation), and the fanciful name of "Psyche" was bestowed upon her by her admirers. By it she is best known in literature. But there are drawbacks to every earthly triumph, and although now in the zenith of her literary fame, she was forced, through serious illness, to give up that society of which she was so distinguished an ornament, and to retire to Cheltenham in search of health. Here she became rapidly worse ; and during a dark hour, when her life hung in the balance, she gave expression to her feelings in the following sonnet :—

> O ! Thou most terrible, most dreaded Power,
>   In whatsoever form thou meetest the eye !
>   Whether thou biddest thy sudden arrow fly
> In the dread silence of the midnight hour ;
> Or whether, hovering o'er the lingering wretch,
>   Thy sad cold javelin hangs suspended long,
>   While round the couch the weeping kindred throng
> With hope and fear alternately on stretch.
> Oh say ; for me what honours are prepared ?

> Am I now doomed to meet thy fatal arm,
> Or wilt thou first from life steal every charm,
> And bear away each good my soul would guard ?
> That thus, deprived of all it loved, my heart
> From life itself contentedly may part!

However, the time was not yet ripe for Death to claim Mary Tighe as his own. She never quite recovered her health, and was continually moving about from one place to the other in a vain search for it. She was tenderly attached to her husband, and, in order to please him, associated with the companions he selected, although they must have been utterly distasteful to a woman of her pure and refined tastes. Indeed, save intellectually, there seems to have been but little sympathy between them. They returned to Ireland in 1797, and nothing can give a better idea of her intense love for the simple pleasures of a country life than the following lines to the river Vartry, written at Rosanna in the July of the same year :—

THE VARTREE.

> Sweet are thy banks, O Vartree! when at morn
> Their velvet verdure glistens with the dew ;
> When fragrant gales by softest zephyrs borne
> Unfold the flowers, and ope their petals new.
>
> How bright the lustre of thy silver tide,
> Which winds, reluctant to forsake the vale!
> How play the quivering branches on thy side,
> And lucid catch the sunbeams in the gale!

And sweet thy shade at noon's more fervid hours,
    When faint, we quit the upland gayer lawn,
To seek the freshness of thy sheltering bowers,
    Thy chestnut glooms, where day can scarcely dawn.

How soothing, in the dark sequestered grove,
    To see thy placid waters seem to sleep!
Pleased, they reflect the sober tints they love
    As, unperceived, in silent peace they creep.

The deepest foliage bending o'er thy wave,
    Tastes thy pure kisses, with embracing arms,
While each charmed Dryad stoops her limbs to lave,
    Thy smiling Naiad meets her sister charms.

Beneath the fragrant lime or spreading beech,
    The bleating flocks in panting crowds repose,
Their voice alone my dark retreat can reach,
    While peace and silence all my soul compose.

Here, Mary, rest! the dangerous path forsake
    Where folly lures thee, and where vice ensnares,
Thine innocence and peace no longer stake,
    Nor barter solid good for brilliant cares.

Shun the vain bustle of the senseless crowd,
    Where all is hollow that appears like joy;
Where, the soft claims of feeling disallowed,
    Fallacious hopes the baffled soul annoy.

Hast thou not trod each vain and giddy maze—
    By flattery led, o'er pleasure's gayest field?
Basked in the sunshine of her brightest blaze,
    And proved whate'er she can her votaries yield.

That full completion of each glowing hope,
    Which youth and novelty could scarce bestow,
From the last days of joy's exhausted cup,
    Canst thou expect thy years mature shall know?

Hast thou not tried the vanities of life,
    And all the poor mean joys of fashion known,
Blush, then, to hold with wisdom longer strife,
    Submit at length a better guide to own.

> Here woo the Muses in the scenes they love;
> Let science near thee take her patient stand;
> Each weak regret for gayer hours reprove,
> And yield thy soul to Reason's calm command.
>
> Rosanna, July, 1797.

In consequence of the unsettled state of the country, which culminated in the disastrous Irish rebellion of 1798, her husband was much away from her, his parliamentary duties occupying him when not engrossed by active service in a yeomanry corps. During this time Mrs. Tighe lived at Rosanna with her mother-in-law, who would not leave the place, although the house was once attacked by the rebels. But declining health compelled her to go elsewhere in search of strength. For the few succeeding years she resided occasionally at various English watering-places, and in 1805 returned to Ireland, never again to leave it.

After 1805 Mrs. Tighe chiefly resided in Dominick Street, Dublin, and was so far enfeebled by constant illness that she lost the use of her limbs, and was obliged always to lie on a sofa. Notwithstanding this affliction, her vigour of mind was unimpaired, and she received constant assemblies of all that was most intellectual in Dublin society. Around that lovely and patient invalid's couch might be seen gathered Charlemont, Lady St. George, Lydia White, vain Sydney Owenson,

with her carefully-arranged scarf, and Thomas
Moore, who had not at that period become
"Lord Lansdowne's piper," nor had then given
vent to those wild outbursts of hatred against the
Saxon which he sung to solace a Whig peer in
the intervals of drawing up a Coercion Bill, for
the bard's—

> Loved island of sorrow!

Letters written by her at this period, and which
are now in the possession of members of her family,
show but too plainly that her bodily pains were
not to be compared to the mental agony she underwent as the result of her ill-assorted marriage.
Her "Psyche" seemed to be rebelling against the
chains which bound her to earth, and struggled to
get free.

In 1809 she went to Woodstock, the beautiful
seat of her husband's elder brother, Mr. William
Tighe, author of "The Plants," and there she remained until her death, in 1810. She was perfectly aware that the terrible lingering disease from
which she suffered was incurable, and her last
lines—written in 1809, upon receiving a branch of
Mezerion in flower—seem prophetic of her death
before the coming springtime:—

> Odours of Spring, my sense ye charm
> With fragrance premature,
> And 'mid these days of dark alarm
> Almost to hope allure.

Methinks with purpose soft ye come
  To tell of brighter hours,
Of May's blue skies' abundant bloom,
  Her sunny gales and showers.

Alas! for me shall May in vain
  The powers of life restore,
These eyes that weep and watch in pain
  Shall see her charms no more.
No, no; this anguish cannot last—
  Beloved friends—adieu!
The bitterness of death were past
  Could I resign but you.

But oh! in every mortal pang
  That rends my soul from life,
That soul, which seems on you to hang
  Thro' each convulsive strife,
Even now, with agonising grasp
  Of terror and regret,
To all, in life, its love would clasp
  Clings close and closer yet.

Yet why—immortal, vital spark,
  Thus mortally opprest?
Look up, my soul, through prospects dark,
  And bid thy terrors rest.
Forget—forego thy earthly part,
  Thine heavenly being trust.
Ah! vain attempt! my coward heart
  Still shuddering clings to dust!

Oh! ye who soothe the pangs of death
  With love's own patient care,
Still—still retain this fleeting breath,
  Still pour the fervent prayer.
And ye—whose smile must greet my eye
  No more—nor voice my ear,
Who breathed for me the tender sigh,
  And shed the pitying tear;

> Whose kindness (tho' far, far removed)
> My grateful thoughts perceive,
> Pride of my life—esteemed—beloved—
> My last sad claim receive!
> Oh! do not quite your friend forget—
> Forget alone her faults!
> And speak of her with fond regret
> Who asks your lingering thoughts.

All her fears of death were entirely removed before she breathed her last, on March 24th, 1810. She died as she had lived, a simple, earnest Christian, an ornament of her sex, and of the social and intellectual life of the land she lived in and belonged to.

Mary Tighe is buried in the churchyard of Inistiogue. Over her remains her husband placed a handsome monumental chamber, containing a reclining statue by Flaxman; and her brother-in-law, Mr. William Tighe, inscribed upon her tomb the following lines to her memory:—

> If on this earth she passed in mortal guise
> A short and painful pilgrimage, shall we,
> Her sad survivors, grieve that love divine
> Removed her timely to perpetual bliss?
> Thou art not lost! in chastest song and pure
> With us still lives thy virtuous mind, and seems
> A beacon for the weary soul, to guide
> Her safely through affliction's winding path
> To that eternal mansion gained by thee!
>
> W. T.

MARY BOYLE.

(COUNTESS OF WARWICK.)

BORN, A.D. 1625. DIED, A.D. 1678.

MARY BOYLE, Countess of Warwick, was the thirteenth child of the first Earl of Cork. Born in 1625,* in 1641 she was married to the Earl of Warwick, whom she survived about five years. Her husband was only Mr. Rich at the time of the marriage, as the following copy of the register of marriages solemnised in the parish church of St. Nicholas, Shepperton, Middlesex, will show :—

---

* In Lord Cork's "True Remembrances," it is stated that his daughter Mary was born the 11th of November, 1624. She, however, fixes the date of her birthday on the 8th of November of the following year, as the following passage from her diary will show: "8th November, 1671.—In the morning as soon as up, I retired into the wilderness to meditate, and *it being my birthday*, it pleased God to make me call to my remembrance many of the special mercies with which my life was filled. And whilst I was doing so, I considered that God had for *forty-six* years so mercifully provided for me, that I had not ever out of necessity wanted a meal's meat, nor ever broke a bone, nor in twenty years' time been necessitated to keep my bed one day by reason of sickness; this did exceedingly draw out my heart to love God."

"Mr. Charles Rich, second son to the Right Hon. Robert Earle of Warwick, and the Lady Mary Boyle, daughter to the Right Hon. the Earle of Cork in Ireland, were married the 21st of July, 1641." Mr. Rich did not succeed to the Earldom until after the death of his eldest brother, in 1659. Two children were the issue of this marriage—a girl, named Elizabeth, who died whilst yet an infant; and a son, who died in his twenty-first year, a few months after his marriage with the daughter of Lord Devonshire. "I confess I loved him at a rate," says the Countess in her Diary, "that if my heart do not deceive me, I could, with all the willingness in the world, have died either for him or with him, if God had only seen it fit; yet I was dumb and held my peace, because God did it, and was constantly fixed in the belief that this affliction came from a merciful Father, and therefore would do me good."

The union seems to have been a singularly well-matched one; husband and wife being equally benevolent and enlightened, and zealous to promote the mental and physical welfare of those around them. A woman of rare intellectual gifts, and possessed of more than ordinary strong common sense, the Countess of Warwick's fame for charity and hospitality was such that it advanced the rent of houses in her neighbourhood. She was the common arbiter of all controversies, which she decided with so much sagacity and judgment, that she is given the credit of having averted many tedious and expensive law-suits.

The Countess of Warwick's literary remains consist of the then fashionable "Letters," and of a Diary in which she faithfully recorded almost daily, for twelve years of her life, the domestic occurrences of the period, soon after the restoration of Charles II. The letters were chiefly addressed to persons distinguished in literature; and deal justly, incisively, and comprehensively with topics of the day. Under the name of the Lady Harmonia, the Earl of Berkeley dedicated his Historical Applications to the Countess of Warwick, who, in return, wrote him "a most pious letter," of which the following safe advice forms a part:—

"I would desire you to be as chearfull as you can, and to that purpose I would recommend to you that gaiety of goodness that will make you most pleasing to your self and others. And now, my lord, as your friend, you must give me leave to give you not only good counsel, but my own experiences too (like nurses who feed their children with nothing but what they have first themselves digested into milk), and to assure you that however the devil and wicked men may persuade you that religion will make you melancholick, yet

I can assert from my own experience, that nothing can give you that comfort, serenity, and composedness of mind, as a well and orderly led life. This will free you from all those sad disquieting remorses and checks of conscience which follow an ill action, and give you that peace of God that passes all understanding, and that continual feast of a good conscience. This will calm your desires and quiet your wishes, so as you shall find the consolations of God are not small. You will find you have made a happy exchange, having gold for brass, and pearls for pebbles. For truly, my lord, I am upon trial convinced, that all the pleasures of this world are not satisfactory. We expect a great deal more from them than we find; for pleasures die in their birth; and, therefore, as Bishop Hall says, are not worthy to come into the bills of mortality. I must confess for my own part, though I had as much as most people in this kingdom to please me, and saw it in all the glories of the Court; and was both young and vain enough to endeavour having my share in all the vanities thereof; yet I never found they satisfied me; God having given me a nature uncapable of satisfaction in anything below the highest excellency."

In 1673 the Earl of Warwick died, upon St. Bartholomew's Day, to the unspeakable grief of his devoted wife. She passionately bewails his loss in her Diary; her sole comfort being in the reflection, that for the twenty years he was an invalid, she had been unremitting in her attentions to him by night and day. Her grief was so excessive that her health became seriously affected, and she says: "This greatest trial of my life did for a long time disorder my frail house of clay, and made me have thoughts that my dissolution was near; which thoughts were not at all terrible or affrighting to me, but very pleasant and delightful."

In addition to her "Letters," the Countess of Warwick wrote "Occasional Meditations upon Sundry Subjects; with pious reflections upon several Scriptures." These meditations abound in fine metaphorical language, although the subjects of some of them seem almost too trivial to be so seriously treated. They are pervaded by a spirit of fervent Christianity; and exemplify the pure and exalted mind of the writer.

The Countess of Warwick died on the 12th of April, 1678, at the age of fifty-three. Dr. Anthony Walker preached a sermon at her funeral, which speaks of her as—"truly excellent, and great in all respects; great in the honour of her birth, being born a lady and a virtuosa both; great by her marriage into a noble family; great by her tongue, for never woman used one better, speaking so gracefully, promptly, discreetly, pertinently, holily; great by her pen, as you may discover by that little taste of it the world has been happy in, the hasty fruit of one or two interrupted hours after supper; great by being the greatest mistress and promotress, not to say the foundress and inventress, of a new science—the art of obliging! in which she attained that sovereign perfection, that she reigned over all their hearts with whom she did converse; great in the unparalleled sincerity of constant, faithful, condescending friendship, and for that love of kindness which dwelt in her lips and heart."

HENRIETTA BOYLE.

(LADY O'NEIL.)

BORN, A.D. 1758. DIED, A.D. 1793.

NOTHER accomplished scion of the illustrious house of Cork and Orrery, Henrietta Boyle was the only daughter of Charles, Viscount Dungarvan, eldest son of John, Earl of Cork. Descended from a line of noble authors— her uncle Charles Boyle, Earl of Orrery, was the famous opponent of Dr. Bentley in the Boyle and Bentley controversy—who had distinguished themselves in various walks of literature, this lady was the first of her name who wooed the Muse.

At the age of nineteen Henrietta Boyle was married to John O'Neil, Esq., of Shane's Castle, in the County Antrim. The details of her life are but meagre; and she is chiefly remembered socially as being the friend of the novelist and poetess, Mrs. Charlotte Smith. This lady dedicated some of her sonnets to Lady O'Neil, and also wrote some verses upon her death. Of Lady O'Neil's poems, the following specimen will give a good idea of the finish and poetical feeling which distinguished everything that emanated from her graceful pen :—

ODE TO THE POPPY.

Not for the promise of the labour'd field,
Not for the good the yellow harvests yield,
   I bend at Ceres' shrine;
   For dull to humid eyes appear
   The golden glories of the year ;
     Alas! a melancholy worship's mine.
I hail the goddess for her scarlet flower !
   Thou brilliant weed
   That dost so far exceed
The richest gifts gay Flora can bestow,
Heedless I pass'd thee in life's morning hour—
   Thou comforter of woe—
Till sorrow taught me to confess thy power.

   In early days, when fancy cheats,
     A various wreath I wove,
   Of laughing Spring's luxuriant sweets,
     To deck ungrateful love:

The rose or thorn my numbers crown'd
As Venus smil'd, or Venus frown'd,
But love and joy, and all their train are flown.
E'en languid hope no more is mine,
And I will sing of thee alone;
Unless, perchance, the attributes of grief,
The cypress bud and willow leaf,
Their pale funereal foliage blend with thine.

   Hail! lovely blossom! thou canst ease
   The wretched victims of disease;
Canst close those weary eyes in gentle sleep,
Which never open but to weep,
     For oh! thy potent charm
     Can agonising grief disarm ;
Expel imperious Memory from her seat
And bid the throbbing heart forget to beat.

Soul-soothing plant, that can such blessings give,
  By thee the mourner bears to live!
  By thee the hopeless die!
Oh! ever friendly to despair,
  Might sorrow's pallid votary dare
Without a crime that remedy implore,
  Which bids the spirit from its bondage fly,
I'd court thy palliative aid no more.

No more I'd sue that thou shouldst spread
  Thy spell around my aching head,
  But would conjure thee to impart
  Thy balsam for a broken heart!
  And by thy soft Lethean pow'r,
    Questionable flower,
Burst these terrestrial bonds, and other regions try.

Lady O'Neil died in September, 1793; her husband survived her but a few years, dying in June, 1798, from the effects of wounds received in a sharp action with some disaffected insurgents in the County Antrim.

MARIA EDGEWORTH.

BORN, A.D. 1767. DIED, A.D. 1849.

IN the amusing chronicles of the house of Edgeworth there are many curious anecdotes recorded, which vindicate the title of Richard Lovell Edgeworth and his illustrious daughter to the combined genius and eccentricities with which they have been accredited. The lives and labours of both father and daughter are so blended and intertwined that their names and memories cannot be separated. They were connected by ties stronger than those of blood—by community of objects, habits, affections, and modes of thought. He had very plausible claims to be considered her literary parent. He divined the natural bent of her genius, and aided, without forcing, its development. He gave her the most bracing kind of education, moral and intellectual; the groundwork being scrupulous accuracy of statement, patient observation, self-knowledge, and self-respect. From her early girlhood he was her companion and friend. He read with her, wrote with her, came before an applauding public hand-in-hand with her, and, finally, he traded upon her popularity. In London literary society the two Irish lions—father and daughter—roared so loudly that Lord Byron proposed the formation of a Society for the Suppression of Edgeworth. But Richard Lovell Edgeworth was irrepressible; and, although a bore of the first magnitude, was a genial, clever, and kind-hearted Irishman. The best description of him is given by Lord Byron :—

"I have been reading the Life by himself and daughter of Mr. R. L. Edgeworth, the father of *the* Miss Edgeworth. It is altogether a great name. In 1813 I recollect to have met them in the fashionable world of London, in the assemblies of the hour, and at a breakfast of Sir Humphrey and Lady Davy's, to which I was invited for the nonce. I had been the lion of 1812; Miss Edgeworth and Madame de Staël, with the Cossack, towards the end of 1813, were the exhibitions of the succeeding year. I thought Edgeworth a fine old fellow of a clarety, elderly, red complexion, but active, brisk, and endless. He was seventy, but did not look fifty—no, nor forty-eight even. I had seen poor Fitzpatrick not very long before: a man of pleasure, wit, eloquence—all things. He tottered, but still talked like a gentleman, though feebly. Edgeworth bounced about, and talked loud and long, but he seemed neither weakly nor decrepit, and hardly old.

"He was not much admired in London, and I remember a 'ryghte merrie' and conceited jest which was rife among the gallants of the day—viz., a paper had been presented for the *recall of Mrs. Siddons to the stage*, to which all men had been called to subscribe. Whereupon Thomas Moore, of profane and poetical memory, did propose that a similar paper should be subscribed for the *recall of Mr. Edgeworth to Ireland*. The fact was everybody cared more about her. She was a nice little unassuming, 'Jeannie-Deans-looking body,' as we Scotch say; and if not handsome, certainly not ill-looking. Her conversation was as quiet as herself. One would never have guessed she could write her name; whereas her father talked, not as if he could write nothing else, but as if nothing else was worth writing."

As far back as the reign of Elizabeth we find that Edgeworthstown, in the County Longford, was in the possession of the family whence it derived its name. In 1619, Edward Edgeworth, Bishop of Down and Connor, dying without issue, left his fortune to his brother Francis. From the latter was lineally descended Richard Lovell Edgeworth, the father of the famous novelist. Mention is also made of a Lady Edgeworth, renowned for her beauty and courage. Upon her presentation at Court, she made such an impression upon the susceptible heart of Charles II., that his gallant attentions became so unmistakable as to cause her to refuse to attend the Court again. In illustration of this lady's courage, it is recorded that upon some sudden alarm at her husband's Irish castle of Lissard, she hurried to a garret for gunpowder, followed by a maidservant carrying a candle without a candlestick. When the lady had taken the quantity she wanted from the barrel, had locked the door and was half-way down the stairs again, she observed the girl had left the candle, and asked her what she had done with it. The maid replied that she had left it "stuck in the barrel of black salt." Lady Edgeworth returned by herself to the garret, put her hand carefully underneath the candle, and carried it carefully out.

"I am not a man of prejudice," Richard Lovell Edgeworth is reported to have said one day during his later years, when discoursing upon his darling themes of himself and his affairs. "I have had four wives; the second and third were sisters; and I was in love with the second during the lifetime of the first."

The first wife had been a Miss Elers, daughter of Paul Elers, Esq., of Black Bourton, in Oxford-shire, and was the mother of Maria and one son. The second and third were Honora and Elizabeth Sneyd, and the fourth, Miss Beaufort, was the sister of the late Admiral Sir Francis Beaufort. With these stepmothers and their various families, Maria Edgeworth lived on the most harmonious terms; a fact which speaks well for the tempers and dispositions of all parties.

Born in the year 1767, Maria Edgeworth was just six years old when her mother died; and in after-life remembered little more of her than having been taken to her deathbed for a last farewell. Up to this time Maria had lived at Black Bourton, but when her father married Miss Honora Sneyd, a few months after the death of his first wife, they all went to live at Edgeworthstown. The second Mrs. Edgeworth amply supplied the place of the mother the child had lost; and it was with unfeigned regret that, in consequence of her failing health, she was obliged to part with Maria, and send her to a boarding-school in Derby. She was now eight years old, a clever, mischievous little girl, who rapidly improved, and made astonishing progress in her studies. Music alone was the one branch of education which she failed to become mistress of. Her music-master gave up the attempt to teach her in despair. She also went through the usual tortures of back boards, iron collars, and dumb-bells; and used to say that the first day she entered the school-room, and heard a little girl, younger than herself, glibly repeat the nine parts of speech, she felt more admiration for her than she ever experienced afterwards for any effort of human genius.

Whilst she was at school, her father commenced, in his letters to her, that system of educating her powers of mind by analytical reflection and accurate observation, which she has so well reproduced in her "Parent's Assistant." Although during the greater part of his daughter's school-days Richard Lovell Edgeworth was chiefly employed in marrying and burying his wives, yet he did not forget Maria's mental training. He was a man of marvellous insight into character, and at a very early period of her girlhood he perceived that she had a mind of no ordinary capacity. "I beg that you will send me a tale about the length of a *Spectator*," he writes to her on one occasion, "upon the subject of Generosity; it must be taken from history or romance, and must be sent the day se'nnight after you receive this, and I beg you will take some pains about it."

The same subject was given to a young gentleman from Oxford, and when an impartial judgment was passed upon them, Maria's story was pronounced to be very much the better of the two:

—"an excellent story, and extremely well written," was the verdict, " but where is the Generosity?" This saying became a sort of proverb with her afterwards. It was her first story, and unfortunately it has not been preserved. She used to say that there was in it a sentence of inextricable confusion between a saddle, a man and his horse.

Maria Edgeworth left school when she was about sixteen, and the family now settled down permanently at Edgeworthstown, which was her home for the remainder of her life. In her memoirs of her father she gives a very detailed account of their mode of living there, their social life in general, and also introduces a graphic sketch of her father's manner of dealing with his tenantry and labourers. " His honour, God bless him! is *good pay*," was the first encomium she heard upon her return home. Richard Lovell Edgeworth was a model of what a resident landlord should be. He had no dealings with middlemen; he received his rents without the intervention of agent or subagent; he chose his tenants for their characters, the sole claims to preference being industry, honesty, and sobriety. He made no difference between Catholic and Protestant, Saxon and Celt, and his impartial administration of his magisterial duties was proverbial.

In the year 1782, at her father's suggestion,

Maria Edgeworth commenced the translation of the "Adèle et Théodore" of Madame de Genlis. The first volume was just completed when Holcroft's translation was published. She continued, under the guidance of her father, to write innumerable short tales and essays, but without any thought of their publication. They were written for private amusement—usually on a slate—she then read them aloud to her brothers and sisters, and if they approved of them she copied them. The bare sketch was always submitted to her father, who used to say, "I don't want any of your painting, none of your drapery! I can imagine all that. Let me see the bare skeleton."

"Letters for Literary Ladies" and the "Parent's Assistant" were Maria Edgeworth's first published works, but her name as an authoress first acquired notoriety by the publication of "Practical Education," in 1798. It was at once praised and abused enough to make the authors famous. The contents were of a most miscellaneous description, and included everything that could affect the mental or physical training of a rational human being. Unutterably dull, prosy, and ludicrously childish in some parts, yet the book was a step in the right direction. Hitherto, no one had taken the trouble to inaugurate any series of text-books of first principles of knowledge for the young. As this work embraced easy chapters on grammar and classical literature, geography, chronology, arithmetic, geometry, and mechanics, it is no wonder that it attracted universal attention. But one omission did not escape the watchful eyes of the reviewers : the writers taught *morality alone.* " Here, readers," said the *British Critic,* " is education *à la mode,* in the true style of modern philosophy; nearly eight hundred quarto pages on practical education, and not a word on God, religion, Christianity, or a hint that such topics are ever to be mentioned." The authors seem to have been prepared for such an outburst of opinion, for they say in their preface :—

" On religion and politics we have been silent, because we have no ambition to gain partisans or to make proselytes. The scrutinising eye of criticism, in looking over our table of contents, will also probably observe that there are no chapters on courage or chastity. To pretend to teach courage to Britons would be as ridiculous as it is unnecessary ; and except to those who are exposed to the contagion of foreign manners, we may boast of the superior delicacy of our fair countrywomen." Of this work Maria Edgeworth wrote about two-thirds, her father contributing the remainder. She particularly disliked the title of "Parent's *Assistant,*" one of her earlier publications. Originally it had been called the "Parent's Friend," but was altered by the publisher to the former. Miss Edgeworth said she disliked the name, because of its association with an old treatise on arithmetic called the "The Tutor's Assistant."

But although her well-trained, well-stored, and practical mind eminently fitted Miss Edgeworth to write upon educational subjects, yet fiction was undoubtedly her forte. The "Essay on Irish Bulls," which she wrote in partnership with her father, was published with the design of showing the English public the eloquence, wit, and talent of the lower classes of people in Ireland. There can be very little doubt but that the writing of this essay first suggested to Miss Edgeworth the first work in which she struck into her own peculiar vein. The characters in "Castle Rackrent" are but so many pegs upon which are hung the attributes analysed in the "Essay on Irish Bulls."* The first edition of "Castle Rackrent" was published anonymously in 1800, and its success was inmediate. Some person—whose name is now forgotten—not only asserted that he was the author of it, but actually took the trouble to copy

---

* A gentleman—secretary to the Irish Agricultural Society—much interested in improving the breed of Irish cattle, sent for this book, and upon discovering the real nature of its contents, threw it away in disgust.

out several pages with corrections and erasures, as if it were his original manuscript. In 1801 a second edition was published, with the author's name appended, and it was also translated into German and French. The pictures which French journalists and caricaturists used to give of the manners and customs of the English, were not more amusing than the literal manner in which they took the exceptionally ludicrous incidents of Miss Edgeworth's story as being everyday occurrences amongst the Irish. The *sweeping of the stairs with the wig* was gravely commented upon as an Irish custom. This is on a par with the French writer who seriously adduced Dean Swift's ironical proposal to relieve the Irish poor by converting their children into food for the rich English, as illustrative of the atrocities practised in that barbarous and extraordinary kingdom.

Besides preparing the second edition of "Castle Rackrent" for the press, in 1801, Miss Edgeworth appeared before the public twice in the same year. "Belinda"—one of her most popular novels—was highly successful ; so were her "Moral Tales." The latter were heralded by an elaborate preface from her father's pen, in which he explained that the tales were written by her to illustrate the opinions set forth in "Practical Education ;" he further goes on to state the moral of each—about the most effective way of repelling readers that could well be contrived by an admiring parent.

Ireland was now in a very unsettled state, from the combined effects of the recent Irish rebellion, and the agitation attendant upon the Union; so, taking advantage of the Peace of Amiens, Mr. and Mrs. Edgeworth, Maria, and her two step-sisters paid a visit to Paris in the autumn of 1802. Here they at once took their position in the best literary society, and seem to have known every one worth knowing: Madame Recamier, Comte and Comtesse de Segur, La Harpe, Suard, Boissy d'Anglas, Montmorenci, Camille Jordan, and Kosciusko. They were also acquainted with Madame de Genlis; and Miss Edgeworth, in some of her letters, gives lively sketches of the various entertainments to which they were constantly invited. At a breakfast at the Abbé Marellet's, they met Madame Sophie D'Houdetot, the original of *Julie* in Rousseau's "Nouvelle Héloïse." Miss Edgeworth thus describes her:—

"Julie is now seventy-two years of age, a thin woman in a little black bonnet; she appeared to me shockingly ugly; she squints so much that it is impossible to tell which way she is looking; but no sooner did I hear her speak than I began to like her; and no sooner was I seated beside her, than I began to find in her countenance a most benevolent and agreeable impression. She entered into conversation immediately; her manner invited and could not fail to obtain confidence. She seems as gay and open-hearted as a girl of seventeen. It has been said of her that she not only never did any harm, but never suspected any. I wish I could at seventy-two be such a woman!

"She told me that Rousseau, whilst he was writing so finely on education and leaving his own children in the Foundling Hospital, defended himself with so much eloquence that even those who blamed him in their hearts could not find tongues to answer him. Once at a dinner at Madame D'Houdetot's there was a fine pyramid of fruit. Rousseau in helping himself took the peach which formed the base of the pyramid, and the rest fell immediately. 'Rousseau,' said she, 'that is what you always do with all our systems, you pull down with a single touch, but who will build up what you pull down?' I asked if he was grateful for all the kindness shown to him. 'No—he was ungrateful: he had a thousand bad qualities, but I turned my attention from them to his genius and the good he had done mankind.'"

Many critics have found fault with the stern self-control which Miss Edgeworth always inculcates in her writings, and have said that the hard trials she imposes are superhuman. But Maria Edgeworth was too practical to do anything of the sort. She was no Madame D'Aubray with high-flown "ideas" of self-sacrifice, admirably adapted for the use of others, but shirked by herself; before setting down her ideas of self-command under temptation, she had tested them. Caroline Percy, in her novel of "Patronage," controlling her love for Count Altenberg, is Maria Edgeworth resolved upon conquering *her* own love for the Chevalier Edelcrantz.

For even practical Maria Edgeworth had a romance in her life. It did not come until she was thirty-six years of age, so she probably had her feelings under better control than if she had met her lover in earlier years. Monsieur Edelcrantz was a Swede, and the love affair, if it can be dignified by such a name, was thus announced to her relations by the lady:—"Here, my dear aunt, I was interrupted in a manner that will surprise you as much as it surprised me, by the coming in of Monsieur Edelcrantz, a Swedish gentleman, whom we have mentioned to you, of superior understanding and mild manners: he came to offer me his hand and heart!!

"My heart, you may suppose, cannot return his attachment, for I have seen but very little of him, and have not had time to have formed any judgment, except that I think nothing could tempt me to leave my own dear friends and my own country to live in Sweden,"—so, after all, Maria Edgeworth was scarcely justified in saying, "*Ich habe gelebt und geliebt.*"

Upon their return to Edgeworthstown, in 1803, "Popular Tales" appeared, with a preface by her father. Later on were published the first series of "Tales of Fashionable Life," their object being to display the errors of fashionable education, and the follies of fashionable life. They consisted of five tales of very unequal length, the first of them— that called "Ennui"—being by far the best. Of course, as might have been expected, although the authoress gives a summary of the duties of tuition, she has excluded religion from her system of education. The morality of Miss Edgeworth, as detailed in her "Tales," is a system of manners regulated by prudence and a sense of propriety, having little connexion with the heart, and rarely leading to any very difficult or important efforts of virtue. There is little in her standard of moral duty to which any one of common discretion and average goodness of disposition does not naturally conform, and scarcely anything in the motives she proposes has a nobler source than a regard for worldly and social interests.

The publication of these "Tales of Fashionable

Life" set the seal of individuality upon Maria Edgeworth's literary labours. She inaugurated what may be called the *natural* mode of novel writing, without dragging her realism through the mud of the affectation of ignoring all idealism. Maria Edgeworth scorned the traditional properties of the novelist. The traditionary villain, the traditionary seducer and his victim, and all the other cut-and-dried incidents of fiction she would have none of. She discarded them all, and with new materials resolved to make a fresh start; and, taking people as she found them, she wrote about them in like manner, thus inaugurating a new class of literature.

The chief charm of Miss Edgeworth's stories lies in their fidelity to Nature. They have an air of *probability* about them, induced by the fact that the writer presents Nature under its ordinary, not under its *extra*-ordinary—although ofttimes probable—aspects. As a writer of tales and stories Miss Edgeworth has a very marked idiosyncrasy. It is that of venturing to dispense common sense to her readers, and to bring them within the pale of real life and natural feeling. She presents us with no incredible adventures or inconceivable sentiments, no hyperbolical representations of uncommon character, or monstrous exhibitions of **exaggerated** passion. Without excluding love from her pages, she assigns it very moderate limits; at times giving the idea that if the character could have been painted without it, that it would have been more to her taste to have done so. The sentiment is toned down, and reduced to the level of the other passions. Her heroes and heroines are never miraculously good, nor detestably wicked. They are such men and women as we see and converse with every day of our lives, with the same proportionate mixture in them of what is right and what is wrong, what is great and what is little.

The second series of "Tales of Fashionable Life" was published in 1812. It comprised four tales, or, as we would now call them, "novelettes," of which the longest and the best was "The Absentee." Then followed her novel of "Patronage," which Jeffrey criticised in the *Quarterly Review* in the following terms:—

"The character we have given of Miss Edgeworth's writings in general is applicable, without any material alteration, to these volumes. We confess, however, that we think them inferior—a good deal inferior—to the best of her former productions. The length of the work makes her deficiency in the art of framing a story more conspicuous and less excusable. We are carried on easily and pleasantly for a short distance by mere sketches and dialogues, and we excuse the want of skill in a tale that is to end so soon. But when the same personages are to be kept upon the stage through four whole volumes it is but reasonable that such a demand upon our attention should be supported by a proportionate interest in the characters and situations. We expect invention, combination, unity, and the absence of these qualities is a just cause of disappointment. They come strictly within the terms of the author's implied engagement to the reader. In 'Patronage,' the persons come in and out, exhibit themselves, and describe others, in an agreeable way enough, but without our well knowing why they came or why they went, without our much caring whether or not they ever appear again. The author, too, begins to flag. She seems encumbered by the unsuccessful care of an unusual number of persons and events, and her powers of entertainment are less at her command. 'Patronage' is, in fact, another 'Tale of Fashionable Life,' almost as long as all the preceding ones put together, and yet we doubt whether more passages of distinguished merit could be selected from it than could be matched from 'The Absentee,' though it occupies three times the space. Indeed, if we might venture to offer our advice to a person of Miss Edgeworth's distinguished reputation, it would be to revert to her former method, and to break down her sketches into tales of a more manageable length. She would thus better consult the convenience of her readers, and at the same time give freer scope to her own faculties in that style in which she really excels, by not tasking them for an exertion to which they are not adapted.

"There are no Irish characters in 'Patronage' (O'Brien is scarcely an exception). Perhaps Miss Edgeworth thought the subject was exhausted. We are sorry for it. Some of her happiest efforts have been employed upon the description of them. Miss Edgeworth knows the Irish nation thoroughly, not merely in those broader and more general characteristics that distinguish it from this and from all other nations, but in those nicer shades that mark each class of society. All the materials are drawn from her own stores, and she is never obliged to supply the defect of actual observation by hearsay or conjecture. Perfect acquaintance with her subject gave freedom and originality to every stroke of her pencil, and enabled her at once to delight and instruct the public, to which, generally speaking, the peculiar manners of Ireland were less known than those of Otaheite. Her merit was not that of describing what had never been described before; it was greater; it was that of describing well what had been described ill—of substituting accurate, finished resemblances for clumsy confused daubings by the sign-post artists of modern comedy.

"But when the scene is purely English, Miss Edgeworth appears to much less advantage. Like the giant, she grows feeble when her strength is no longer recruited from her native soil. Her gaiety flags as she recedes from Nature and observation. Her comic scenes are diminished in number and even in spirit. For the first time she has had recourse to exaggeration to produce interest, and tried the effect of high colouring and artificial contrasts to supply the place of those natural tints which she used to represent with so much grace."*

"Patronage" is by no means as good a tale as "Ennui" or "The Absentee;" indeed, we question whether Miss Edgeworth has ever written anything better than the latter story. As an instance of keen powers of observation it stands unrivalled, and was written with the idea of exposing the folly and misery of renouncing the respectable position of country ladies and gentlemen to push, through intolerable expense and more intolerable scorn, into the fashionable world of

---

* *Quarterly Review*, January, 1814.

London society. The plot of the story is the worst part of it, its excellence mainly depending upon the inimitably humorous sketches with which it abounds. In " Larry Brady, the Post-Boy," we have one of the best delineations of Irish character ever conceived.

Until 1817, Miss Edgeworth did not again publish anything. But in the meantime she had not been idle, for almost simultaneously appeared " Harrington" and " Ormond," together with " Thoughts on Bores," a work in two volumes, with the inevitable preface by her father. It was the last thing ever Richard Lovell Edgeworth wrote. On the 13th of June, 1817, he died, to the inconsolable grief of his family. It is perfectly marvellous to reflect, upon looking through this egoist's memoirs, how his various wives and children believed in him. They considered him the greatest and the best of men ; and when the grave closed over him, they felt the loss which they sustained was irreparable. Miss Edgeworth's grief was so intense that it caused a disease in her eyes, which quite incapacitated her from even writing a letter for some months. However, towards the latter end of the year, she was so far recovered as to be able to prepare for the press her " Comic Dramas."

When Sheridan read Miss Edgeworth's novel of

"Belinda," he was so struck with the dramatic situations which it contained, that he advised the writer to turn her attention to writing for the stage. But even the clear-headed Sheridan made a mistake in this respect. It is one thing to be able to write *a dramatic novel;* but it is quite a different matter to keep up the interest of a drama, which depends for its excellence upon the interest being sustained by means of unflagging incident. The paths of the novelist and dramatist widely diverge, although, at first, they appear to coincide. Scarcely any author has pursued both paths with eminent success—and Maria Edgeworth is no exception to the rule.

As stage-plays, these three "Comic Dramas" are failures. They fail in the essentials of clear plot and rapid change of incident; although the dialogue and character painting can scarcely be surpassed. They did not add to her literary reputation; and were unsparingly criticised in *The Quarterly.*

From some inexplicable cause, this latter magazine—which, if it had pointed out errors in Miss Edgeworth's works, at least had done their merits ample justice—now completely changed its tone. In October, 1820, when Miss Edgeworth brought out her father's Memoirs, *The Quarterly* criticised them with extreme bitterness, and with an entire absence of the acumen and justice with which its reviews had hitherto been characterised. Every recorded circumstance in the two volumes is satirically expatiated upon and distorted in a manner which is scarcely credible. Mr. Edgeworth is charged with the violation of every sacred moral obligation, with hypocrisy, and with deliberate untruths. His four marriages—to which the reviewer has ingeniously prefixed a fifth—were made the mark for much indignation, real or simulated. "This infamous article," as Dumont called it when writing to Miss Edgeworth, excited universal attention; for there was a strong Edgeworthian clique who had pinned their faith to the loquacious Irishman. Mrs. Marcet spoke of it as a subject which made her blood boil, and "roused every feeling of contempt and abhorrence." Miss Edgeworth herself seems to have taken the whole affair more philosophically than did either her friends or her relatives. "I will never lose another night's sleep or a moment's thought on the *Quarterly Review*," she writes to her aunt; "I have never read, and I never will read it;" and she kept her word.

The same year (1820) Miss Edgeworth went to Paris with her two step-sisters. The doors of all the leading hotels and salons flew open at their approach; including those of the Faubourg St. Germain, for the name of the Abbé Edgeworth was a passport to the houses of the ancient *noblesse*. Amongst the French he had been familiarly called the Abbé de Firmont; a name he assumed from the difficulty they found in pronouncing the name of "Edgeworth."*

"Madame Maria Edgeworth, et Mesdemoiselles ses sœurs," to quote the form of visiting-card they adopted, seem to have enjoyed this visit to Paris. They knew everybody worth knowing. Leaving Paris, they proceeded to Switzerland, and stayed for a short time at Geneva, where they made the acquaintance of Madame de Staël. Miss Edgeworth records in one of her letters that she was "very happy" in the society of the latter.

After their return to England Thomas Moore met Miss Edgeworth at Bowood, and complacently enters in his diary, "She was much affected at my singing." Again, he speaks of meeting her at a breakfast at Rogers's—"Went, and found Miss Edgeworth, Luttrell, Lord Normanby, and Sharpe; Miss Edgeworth, with all her cleverness, anything but agreeable. The moment any one begins to speak, off she starts too, seldom more than a sentence behind them, and in general contrives to

---

* Byron speaks of some Russian or Polish names that would descend to posterity, if posterity could only pronounce them.

distance every speaker. Neither does what she say, though of course very sensible, make up for this over-activity of tongue."

Could anything be more characteristic of Thomas Moore's inordinate vanity ! He judged people subjectively, not objectively, forming his estimate of them from his own feelings, sympathies and antipathies, and not from their qualities, merits and demerits. We can scarcely be very far wrong in supposing that Miss Edgeworth took the wind out of his sails, by anticipating him in a favourite story, or adding a touch of Irish humour which he had let slip. Miss Edgeworth was not anxious for display of the kind Moore attributes to her. Lord Byron says her conversation was as quiet as herself. Lockhart, who was fastidious to priggishness, was delighted with her; and Sir Walter Scott says of her,—"It is scarcely possible to say more of this very remarkable person than that she not only completely answered, but exceeded, the expectations which I had formed. I am particularly pleased with her *naïveté* and good-humoured ardour of mind which she unites with such formidable powers of acute observation."

Revisiting London in 1822, Miss Edgeworth found herself again the centre of a brilliant social and literary clique. Every year she became more and more the fashion, and every year was more and more lionised. "In all societies," says Cotton, "it is advisable to associate, if possible, with the highest. In the grand theatre of life a *box-ticket* takes you through the house." Miss Edgeworth and her sisters seem to have acted upon this maxim. We find them in one day spending the morning at Newgate with Mrs. Fry, receiving Sir Humphrey Davy in the afternoon, taken by Whitbread to the ladies' gallery in the House of Commons, and finishing up with Almack's in the evening !

"Fanny and Harriet have been with me at that grand exclusive paradise of fashion, Almack's. Observe that the present Duchess of Rutland, who had been a few months away from town, and had offended the lady patronesses by not visiting them, could not at her utmost get a ticket from any one of them, and was kept out, to her amazing mortification ! This may give you some idea of the importance attached to admission to Almack's. Kind Mrs. Hope got tickets for us from Lady Gwydir and Lady Cowper (Lady Palmerston) ; the patronesses can only give tickets to those whom they personally know ; on that plea they avoided the Duchess of Rutland's application ; she had not visited them—'they really did not know her Grace,'—and Lady Cowper swallowed a camel for me, because she did not really know me. I had met her, but had never been introduced to her until I saw her at Almack's."

Here they met Lord Londonderry, who introduced Lady Londonderry, and conversed enthusiastically upon "Castle Rackrent." She speaks with a sort of maternal pride about her two pretty stepsisters, and considered that Fanny was, "if not the prettiest, certainly the most elegant-looking young woman in the room." It was during this visit to London that Miss Edgeworth became acquainted with the famous Lydia White, at whose house she met Mrs. Siddons, with whom she became very intimate. "She gave us," says Miss Edgeworth, "the history of her first acting of *Lady Macbeth*, and of her resolving, in the sleep scene, to lay down the candlestick, contrary to the precedent of Mrs. Pritchard and all the traditions, before she began to wash her hands and say, 'Out, vile spot!' Sheridan knocked violently at her door during the five minutes she had desired to have entirely to herself to compose her spirits before the play began. He burst in, and prophesied that she would ruin herself for ever if she persevered in this resolution to lay down the candlestick! She persisted, however, in her determination—succeeded, was applauded, and Sheridan begged her pardon. She described well the awe she felt, and the power of the excitement given to her by the sight of Burke, Fox, Sheridan, and Sir Joshua Reynolds in the pit."

In 1823, Miss Edgeworth visited Sir Walter Scott, at Abbotsford. "Everything about you is exactly what one ought to have wit enough to dream!" she exclaimed, when her host met her at the archway. She enjoyed this visit thoroughly, and so did Scott, who always referred it as being one of the pleasantest episodes in his life. So well he might: for, indirectly, he owed his fortune, and the feudal state which he assumed, to Maria Edgeworth. Sir Walter Scott, the *novelist*, may be regarded as the immediate offspring of the genius of the Irish authoress. Her delineations of Irish character in her "Castle Rackrent" made so deep an impression upon him that he determined to do a like service for his own country. With this object in view he commenced "Waverley," and as the work progressed he used to read the chapters to his friend James Ballantyne, "that astounding little liar,"* who never pleased the author better than when he exclaimed, "Positively this is equal to Miss Edgeworth." When the novel was published, Scott sent Miss Edgeworth a copy "from

---

* In his will he left Sir Walter Scott a legacy of 13,000*l*. His affairs having been looked into, he was proved never to have been possessed of that sum. Moreover, he died insolvent.

the author of Waverley;" he kept the secret of authorship *in the letter;* but *in truth* he revealed it to her.

"We have heard Waverley called a Scotch Castle Rackrent," says Jeffrey, "and we have ourselves alluded to a certain resemblance between these works; but we must beg leave to explain that the resemblance consists only in this, that the one is a description of the peculiarities of Scottish manners, as the other is of those of Ireland; and that we are far from placing on the same level the merits and qualities of the works. Waverley is of a much higher strain, and may be safely placed far above the amusing vulgarity of Castle Rackrent, and by the side of Ennui or the Absentee, the best undoubtedly of Miss Edgeworth's compositions."*

In 1825, when Sir Walter Scott made a tour through Ireland, he returned Miss Edgeworth's visit; staying at Edgeworthstown, where a brilliant coterie had been invited to meet him, and making daily excursions through the surrounding country. A peasant girl, who was exhibiting some of the lions of the neighbourhood, was told the strange gentleman was a poet. "*Poet!*" she exclaimed, in indignation, "the divil a bit of him! but an honourable gentleman, for he gave me half-a-

---

* *Quarterly Review*, July, 1814. Vol. xi.

crown!" Of the harmonious life of the domestic circle at Edgeworthstown he speaks in enthusiastic terms. Miss Edgeworth, together with her stepbrother and stepsister, were easily induced to join Sir Walter Scott and his friends on their tour, during which many interesting and amusing incidents occurred. When at Limerick they were very anxious to visit a well-known demesne in the neighbourhood; and, ignorant of the fact that the master of the house had died the night before, permission to enter the grounds was requested in the joint names of Miss Edgeworth and Sir Walter Scott. The reply was as follows:—

"Mrs. —— presents her kind compliments to Mr. ——, and much regrets that she cannot show the pictures to-day, as Major —— died yesterday evening by apoplexy; which Mrs. —— the more regrets, as it will prevent her having the honour to see Sir Walter Scott and Miss Edgeworth." Sir Walter Scott—who had a story to suit every occasion—said this lady reminded him of a woman in Fife, who, summing up the misfortunes of a black year in her history, said to him, "Let me see, sir—first we lost our wee callant—and then Jenny—and then the gudeman himsel died—and then the *coo* died too, poor hizzey!—but to be sure, *her* hide brought me fifteen shillings!"

In 1834, Miss Edgeworth published her last,

and—considered by some—her best novel of "Helen,"—and then, true to her didactic instincts, closed her literary career by the publication of a juvenile tale, called "Orlandino." The latter possessed the common defect of all her juvenile books, inasmuch as it demanded too much from both pupil and teacher. Scott thought so, and said to Joanna Baillie,—" I do not like her last book on education ('Harry and Lucy'), considered as a general work. She should have limited the title to 'Education in Natural Philosophy,' or some such term, for there is no great use in teaching children in general to roof houses or build bridges, which, after all, a carpenter or mason does a great deal better at two shillings and sixpence a day. Your ordinary Harry should be kept to his grammar, and your Lucy, of most common occurrence, would be kept employed on her sampler, instead of wasting wood and cutting their fingers, which I am convinced they did, though their historian says nothing of it."

As the most fertile, popular, and influential educational writer and novelist of her own age or any succeeding period, Maria Edgeworth bears away the palm. She was the first who devoted her talents to the especial department of juvenile literature; she inaugurated the novel of life as it is, not as life under exceptional circumstances; and, crowning glory of all, Maria Edgeworth drew forth Sir Walter Scott's abilities as a novelist. The general character of her productions was so ably and so exhaustively discussed in her lifetime, and the traditional estimate of them is so fixed and unanimous, that little remains to be said upon the subject. She possessed the finest powers of observation, most penetrating common sense, a high moral tone consistently maintained, fertility of invention, undeviating rectitude of purpose, varied and accurate knowledge, a clear style, exquisite humour, and some pathos. What she could not help wanting with her matter-of-fact understanding and practical turn of mind, are poetry, romance, and passion. In her opinion, the better part of life and conduct is discretion. She has no toleration for self-indulgence nor criminal weakness; neither has she sympathy with lofty, defiant, uncalculating heroism or greatness; she never snatches a vagabond grace beyond the reach of prudence, nor does she ever arrest us by scenes of melodramatic intensity. In her attempts at historic painting she signally fails. Her gaze was too superficial to admit of much depth. Miss Edgeworth is worthy of the highest admiration of the soberer kind. She does not nspire enthusiasm; and she would have been even more useful—as she would have been infintely more attractive—had she thought and written less about utility.

Miss Edgeworth's chief works are :—Castle Rackrent : Essay on Irish Bulls : Essay on Self-Justification : Forrester : The Prussian Vase : The Good Aunt : Angelina : The Good French Governess : Mademoiselle Panache : The Knapsack : Lame Jervas : The Will : The Limerick Gloves : Out of Debt, out of Danger : The Lottery : Rosanna : Murad the Unlucky : The Manufacturers : Harry and Lucy : The Contrast : The Grateful Negro : To-morrow : Ennui : The Dun : Manœuvring : Vivian : The Absentee : Madame de Fleury : Emile de Coulanges : The Modern Griselda : Belinda : Leonora : Letters : Patronage : Comic Dramas : Harrington : Thoughts on Bores : Ormond : Helen : Orlandino ; and the last volume of her father's Memoirs.

The private life of Miss Edgeworth was as decorous and as irreproachable as was that of any one of her own most unexceptionable heroines. A large family resided under the hospitable roof at Edgeworthstown, united by the closest ties of affectionate harmony. Maria Edgeworth was the good fairy of the establishment ; and Mrs. S. C. Hall, the friend of her later years, who visited her at Edgeworthstown, bears ample and loving testimony to her unselfishness and active watchfulness for the comfort and happiness of all around her.* In person Miss Edgeworth was very small, her face was pale and thin, her features irregular, and her expressive eyes of a bright blue. Her voice was low and pleasant, and her manner entirely free from affectation.

On May 7th, 1849, being then in her eighty-third year, Miss Edgeworth writes to Mrs. Richard Buller,—" I am heartily obliged and delighted by your being such a goose and Richard such a gander as to be frightened out of your wits at my going up the ladder to take off the top of the clock." Miss Edgeworth had actually performed such a feat, apparently emulous of the *traditional* fate of the old Countess of Desmond.

On the 21st of the same month she complained in the morning of not feeling as well as usual. A note was despatched to her physician, but before he could arrive Maria Edgeworth had quietly breathed her last. She died in her eighty-third year, full of years and honours. A few days afterwards the following notice of her appeared in the London *Morning Chronicle:*—

"The death of one who has done such solid service as Miss Edgeworth rendered to the cause of education and social morality cannot be recorded

---

* *Vide* Edgeworthstown, by Mrs. S. C. Hall. "Liddell's Living Age." Vol. xxii. p. 320.

without a passing word of retrospective praise. Miss Edgeworth had long since ceased to take an active part in life, or in that world of literature of which she was once so bright an ornament. But she has taken her rank, and will keep it so long as youth have to be instructed in the elements of social morality. As a woman of singular intellectual acquirements, she takes her place by the side of some of the most distinguished of her sex who have adorned the present era."

FELICIA DOROTHEA HEMANS.

Born, a.d. 1794. Died, a.d. 1835.

AMONGST her many gifted daughters there is not one which Ireland has greater reason to feel proud of than the subject of this sketch. There is no record of any other Irishwoman—save the "Speranza"* of our own day and the "Psyche" of three-quarters of a century ago—having so successfully wooed the Muse. Few writers have been so fortunate in their literary careers as was Felicia Dorothea Hemans. Adverse or unjust criticism was a thing she had but little experience of, save when—at the early age of eleven—she published her first volume of poems, for in after years the reviewers seemed to have banded together to endeavour to find expressions strong enough illustrative of their admiration of her genius. She was essentially a Christian poet, and in perusing her voluminous works the reader cannot fail to be impressed by her marvellous

---

* Jane Francesca, Lady Wilde.

perception of the true and the beautiful. These attributes, added to her extreme *womanliness*, constitute the chief charms of her poetry. Whatever subject she descanted upon, or whatever scene she described, her metaphors are always of refined and exceeding beauty. Her moral perceptions were so pure and noble that she seemed to shed a heavenly radiance upon the earthly subjects of her verse. All her poetry—from her very earliest efforts—has a tinge of sadness prevading it; as though she ever realised the fleeting nature of earthly beauty. "She saw the perfectness of the Creator's works in their most attractive forms; but she also saw that Death was in the world, and that all which was made was subject to the Destroyer."

Felicia Dorothea Browne was born in Duke Street, Liverpool, on the 25th of September, 1794. She was the second daughter of an Irishman named Browne, who carried on an extensive business as a wine merchant. Mr. Browne had married a lady named Wagner, of mixed Venetian and Italian descent, and to this mingling of nationalities Mrs. Hemans afterwards attributed much of her romantic temperament. Unfortunate pecuniary speculations—joined, it is to be feared, to improvident habits—so reduced Mr. Browne's means that he was obliged to give up his business in Liverpool and retire with his wife and five children to St. Asaph, in Wales. Here they lived in great seclusion, and Mr. Browne dying soon after, his widow and children appeared to have less reason to sorrow for his death than for the destitute condition to which they had been reduced before that event took place.

After the death of her husband, Mrs. Browne, who was a woman of high intellectual acquirements, devoted her time to the education of her children. Nothing pleased her so much as to gather her little ones around her, and to tell them some story culled from the German legends learnt in her own earlier days, or some chivalrous tale of Venetia. Her children fully appreciated her love and tenderness for them, and her anxiety concerning their mental training. All through life her gifted daughter, Felicia, was passionately attached to her, and her first poetical effort, written at the age of eight, was addressed to her mother, and runs thus :—

ON MY MOTHER'S BIRTHDAY.

Clad in all their brightest green,
This day the verdant fields are seen ;
The tuneful birds begin their lay,
To celebrate thy natal day.

The breeze is still, the sea is calm,
And the whole scene combines to charm ;
The flowers revive, this charming May,
Because it is thy natal day.

> The sky is blue, the day serene,
> And only pleasure now is seen;
> The rose, the pink, the tulip gay,
> Combine to bless thy natal day.

The young poetess henceforth constantly expressed her thoughts in verse. All her earlier poems were chiefly addressed to the members of her own family, to familiar friends, or had for their themes some of the objects of interest in the neighbourhood, but seldom dealt with abstract subjects. These poems, written at intervals between her eighth and her thirteenth years, were collected and published in 1808, under the title of "Early Blossoms." It was upon this occasion only that she tasted the bitterness of incisive and unsparing criticism. "When the severe sentence thus passed on these childish effusions had been announced," says one of her friends,* "their little author was put to bed for several days, weeping, and heart-sick of vexation and disappointment. This was the first and the last time that she tasted the bitterness of criticism."†

---

* Mrs. Lawrence, of Wavertree Hall.
† The criticism referred to ran as follows:—"We hear that these poems are the 'genuine productions of a young lady, written between the ages of eight and thirteen,' and we do not feel inclined to question the intelligence; but although the fact may insure them an indulgent reception from all who have 'children dear,' yet, when a little girl publishes a large quarto, we are disposed to examine before we admit her claims to public attention. Many of Miss Browne's compositions are extremely *jejune*. However, though

But these early poems show a prodigality and wealth of fancy and metaphor which justify the criticism being condemned as an unjust one. Her "Invocation to the Fairies" is a wonderful production to have emanated from the brain of a child; and the following "Ode to Liberty" was surely earnest of the genius which expanded so brilliantly and soared to such heights in after years:—

ODE TO LIBERTY.

Where the bold rock majestic towers on high,
 Projecting to the sky;
Where the impetuous torrent's rapid course
 Dashes with headlong force;
Where scenes less wild, less awful, meet the eye,
 And cultured vales and cottages appear;
Where softer tints the mellow landscape dye,
 More simply beautiful, more fondly dear;
  There sportive Liberty delights to rove,
   To rove unseen,
  In the dell or in the grove,
   'Midst woodlands green.

Miss Browne's poems contain some erroneous and some pitiable lines, we must praise the 'Reflections on a Ruined Castle,' and the poetic strain in which they are delivered. The lines to 'Patriotism' contain good thoughts and forcible images; and if the youthful author were to content herself for some years with reading instead of writing, we should open any future work from her pen with an expectation of pleasure, founded on our recollection of this publication; though we must, at the same time, observe that premature talents are not always to be considered as signs of future excellence. The honeysuckle attains maturity before the oak."—*Monthly Review*, 1809.

And when placid eve advancing,
  Faintly shadows all the ground;
Liberty, with Hebe dancing,
  Wanders through the meads around.
Fair wreaths of brightest flowers she loves to twine,
  Moss-rose, and bluebell wild;
The pink, the hyacinth with these combine,
  And azure violet, Nature's sweetest child!
When the moonbeam, silvery streaming,
  Pierces through the myrtle shade;
Then, her eye with pleasure beaming,
  She trips along the sylvan glade.

She loves to sing in accents soft,
  When the woodlark soars aloft;
She loves to wake the sprightly horn,
And swell the joyful note to celebrate the morn!

In the dell, or in the grove,
  Liberty delights to rove;
By the ruined moss-grown tower,
By the woodland, or the bower;
On the summit thence to view
The landscape clad in varied hue;
By the hedgerow on the lawn,
Sporting with the playful fawn;
Where the winding river flows,
And the pensile osier grows,
In the cool impervious grove,
Liberty delights to rove.

The following year Mrs. Browne removed with her family to Bronwylfa, in Flintshire, in order to afford her children additional educational advantages. Here the industrious young poetess pursued her studies indefatigably. French, German, Spanish, and Portuguese were amongst her studies. She had an extraordinary talent for acquiring languages, and there was scarcely a modern European tongue which she could not read fluently. Her numerous translations from the literature of many lands attest this, as does also the remarkable manner in which she catches the spirit of the various poets of whom she has given imitations or translations. She was also a student of German literature; but the warmth of colouring and the halo of romance surrounding the effusions of the Italian and Spanish poets were more congenial to her. Nor were other branches of her education neglected. Felicia Dorothea Browne both drew and painted well; in addition, she evinced a decided taste for music, but never devoted to it the time necessary in order to become a first-rate performer. The influence of her residence in the Principality is very distinctly evinced in Miss Browne's poems written at this period. The grand, lonely, and romantic character of the scenery with which she was surrounded made a deep impression upon her sensitive nature; and many of her best poetical pieces are upon Welsh subjects.

Whilst living at Bronwylfa, the young poetess made the acquaintance of Captain Hemans. She was then but fifteen or sixteen years of age, and in the first flush of that beauty which was destined to fade so early. "The mantling bloom of her cheeks," says Mrs. Hale, "was shaded by a profusion of natural ringlets, of a rich golden brown; and the ever-varying expression of her brilliant eyes gave a changeful play to her countenance, which would have made it impossible for any painter to do justice to it. No wonder that so fair a creature should excite the admiration of the gallant Captain." They were both very much in love with each other; but prudence forbade their immediate marriage. Captain Hemans was suddenly called to Spain with his regiment, and upon his return in 1812 they were married.

The same year, Mrs. Hemans published her poems upon the Domestic Affections. They were the last of what may be termed her juvenile productions; and there are few lines or thoughts in the whole collection which excel any to be found in her earlier volume of poems. "The Ruin and its Flowers" is by far the best. It was written on an excursion to the old fortress of Dyganwy, the remains of which are situated on a bold promontory near the entrance to the river Conway, and whose ivied walls, now fast mouldering into oblivion, once bore their part bravely in the defence of Wales. They are further endeared to the lovers of song and tradition as having echoed the complaints of the captive Elphin, and resounded to the harp of Taliesin.

Never was there a more ill-assorted marriage than that of Captain and Mrs. Hemans. He was prosaic and practical to a fault; she was equally imaginative and unpractical. She carried her romantic feelings and ideas into the commonest walks of life, where they are not always treated with consideration, and are, moreover, often looked upon as being insupportably tedious. No doubt there were faults upon both sides. She was incapable of conforming to the ordinary rules of dull domestic life; and, from what can be gathered in a fragmentary manner, he seems to have gone into the opposite extreme, and to have made no allowance for her peculiar mental construction. Captain Hemans married a young, lovely, highly-cultured, enthusiastic poetess, and he was disappointed when she did not at once settle down to the very mundane matters of suckling fools and chronicling small-beer. "Almost daily facts," says one of Mrs. Hemans's biographers, "assure us that a female assuming a decided literary character—whether the assumption spring from an early attachment and devotedness to learning, or from the hope of winning without effort the heart of some amateur of the same craft—whether it be adopted before the tender passion buds, or after it has begun to blossom—stands the least chance, in the present state of male opinions on this subject, of accomplishing her object, and becoming a wife of any importance in the world. The present and the past age have been distinguished by females no less honoured for their talents than beloved for their virtues; but most of them either died or are living in single blessedness, while the few who are remembered or known as wives were the least distinguished of the entire class as literary women."

Notwithstanding the want of sympathy between them, and the consequent absence of harmony, this unequally-yoked pair lived together for some years, and five sons were born unto them. But even the children were not peacemakers; the breach between husband and wife daily grew wider, and at length they separated with mutual consent. Captain Hemans went to reside at Rome, and his wife, to whom he made a liberal allowance, returned to her mother, with whom she lived until the death of the latter.

At the time of the separation Mrs. Hemans was but six-and-twenty, and her name was already well known and welcomed as a favourite poetess. In 1816 she had published her two first important poems—viz., "The Restoration of the Works of Art to Italy," and "Modern Greece." Few poets of that day, or, indeed, of even later times, have written about these Southern lands without the influence of Byron's works cropping up somewhere. The poems of Mrs. Hemans are striking exceptions, for she writes with a loftiness of purpose and a purity of sentiment peculiarly her own. The publication of the two afore-mentioned poems stamped Mrs. Hemans as a poetess of the first order.* Indeed, her actual career as an authoress may be said to have commenced when they appeared. Her earlier and very juvenile pro-

---

* "In our reviews of poetical productions, the better efforts of genius hold out to us a task at once more useful and delightful than those of inferior merit. In the former the beautiful predominate, and expose while they excuse the blemishes. But the public taste would receive no benefit from a detail of mediocrity, relieved only by the censure of faults uncompensated by excellences. We have great pleasure in calling the attention of our readers to the beautiful poem before us, which we believe to be the work of the same lady who last year put her name to the second edition of another poem on a kindred subject—'The Restoration of the Works of Art to Italy'—namely, Mrs. Hemans, of North Wales. That the author's fame has not altogether kept pace with her merit, we are inclined to think is a reproach to the public. Poetry is at present experiencing the fickleness of fashion, and may be said to have had its day. Very recently, the *reading* public, as the phrase is, was immersed in poetry, but seems to have had enough; and excepting always that portion of it who are found to relish genuine poetry on its own intrinsic account, and will never tire of the exquisite enjoyment which it affords, the said public seldom read poetry at all. Our readers will now cease to wonder that an author like the present, who has had no higher aim than to regale the imagination with imagery, warm the heart with sentiment and feeling, and delight the ear with music, without the foreign aid of tale or fable, has hitherto written to a select few, and passed almost unnoticed by the multitude."—*Blackwood's Magazine*, 1816.

ductions are chiefly matters of curiosity, although giving good earnest of the greater things which followed. Her intellectual career may be divided into three parts—the juvenile, the classical (commencing with the publication of "The Restoration of the Works of Art"), and the romantic, which commences with "The Forest Sanctuary," and includes "The Records of Woman," and all the later efforts of her muse.

In "Modern Greece" Mrs. Hemans displays a chaste splendour of versification and imagery which none of her later works have achieved. Moreover, no other work of hers shows more clearly the wide range of her reading. Ancient and modern history, travels, the literature of other lands, all were laid under contribution. It is doubtful whether Mrs. Hemans ever wrote anything more sublime than her "Modern Greece." After recounting in glorious verse the vain struggles of the Greeks for liberty, she says:—

> Now is that strife a tale of vanished days,
> With mightier things forgotten soon to lie;
> Yet oft hath minstrel sung, in lofty lays,
> Deeds less adventurous, energies less high.
> And the dread struggle's fearful memory still
> O'er each wild rock a wilder aspect throws;
> Sheds darker shadows o'er the frowning hill,
> More solemn quiet o'er the glen's repose;
> Lends to the rustling pines a deeper moan,
> And the hoarse river's voice a murmur not its own.

> For stillness now—the stillness of the dead—
> Hath wrapt that conflict's lone and awful scene,
> And man's forsaken homes, in ruin spread,
> Tell where the storming of the cliffs hath been.
> And there, o'er wastes magnificently rude,
> What race may rove, unconscious of the chain?
> Those realms have now no desert unsubdued,
> Where Freedom's banner may be reared again:
> Sunk are the ancient dwellings of her fame,
> The children of her sons inherit but their name.

Mrs. Hemans was an omnivorous reader. It has been said that the booksellers and librarians of every place she resided in could prove—more by the works they were not able to procure for her than by those they could furnish—the extent and variety of her studies. "She explored every possible and probable source whence she might extract fresh materials to aid and embody her bright imaginings; while her own fancy was rich and glowing, and as her piety advanced essayed more lofty flights, she drew as largely from the stores of others as they could appropriately furnish, or her time and power of thought could enable her to make their best sentiments her own. And this course she pursued at all times, in season and out of season; by night and day; on her chair, and sofa, and bed; at home and abroad; invalid, convalescent, and in perfect health; in rambles, and journeys, and visits; in company with her husband, and when her children were around her; at hours usually devoted to domestic claims, as well as in the solitude of the study and bower. Could such a mind symbolise with that of a plodding commonplace gentleman, thrown by the cessation of war into a state of official inactivity, and possessing a larger share than usually falls to the lot of one military man in a thousand of the cool, calculating 'utilitarianism' of secluded life?"

In *Blackwood's Magazine*, for April, 1818, appeared Mrs. Hemans's exquisite "Stanzas on the Death of the Princess Charlotte." It is one of the chief works of this period of her career, and is the first poem in which the womanly tenderness of the writer's heart is betrayed. Hitherto her productions had been more platonic and classical, but in these elegiac verses she is all a woman. Upon their publication the name of the author was on every lip. The poem was enthusiastically read, and studied, and wept over; it appealed to the hearts of all, as her former important poems had appealed to the intellects of her readers. Many an one besides he to whom allusion is made in the following lines echoed the sentiment of them:—

> Oh! there are griefs for Nature too intense,
> Whose first rude shock but stupefies the soul;
> Nor hath the fragile and o'erlaboured sense
> Strength e'en to *feel*, at once, their dread control.
> But when 'tis past, that still and speechless hour,
> Of the seal'd bosom and the tearless eye,

> Then the roused mind awakes, with tenfold power
> To grasp the fulness of its agony!
> Its death-like torpor vanished—and its doom,
> To cast its own dark hues o'er life and Nature's bloom.
>
> And such *his* lot, whom thou hast loved and left,
> Spirit! thus early to thy home recalled!
> So sinks the heart, of hope and thee bereft,
> A warrior's heart! which danger ne'er appalled.
> Years may pass on—and, as they roll along,
> Mellow those pangs which now his bosom rend;
> And he once more, with life's unheeding throng,
> May, though alone in soul, in seeming blend;
> Yet still, the guardian angel of his mind
> Shall thy loved image dwell, in Memory's temple shrined.

How inexpressibly touching is the allusion to the poor mad old king in the following stanza:—

> Yet there is one who loved thee—and whose soul
> With mild affections Nature formed to melt;
> His mind hath bowed beneath the stern control,
> Of many a grief—but *this* shall be unfelt!
> Years have gone by, and given his honoured head
> A diadem of snow; his eye is dim;
> Around him Heaven a solemn cloud hath spread—
> The past, the future, are a dream to him!
> Yet, in the darkness of his fate, alone
> He dwells on earth, while thou, in life's full pride, art gone!

Close upon the publication of the foregoing, followed the longest and most important of Mrs. Hemans's poems, upon Scottish themes. A member of the Highland Society, wishing to raise a suitable national monument to the memory of Wallace, offered prizes for the three best poems upon the subject. This was done with the view of giving popularity to the project. There were many competitors for the prizes, and the judges must have had a no less laborious than amusing task, to wade through the piles of manuscript which they received. One of the contributions is said to have been as long as "Paradise Lost!" But they set to work; the labour of reading the manuscripts was accomplished, and the first prize unanimously awarded to Mrs. Hemans. She had entered the lists as a competitor, at the earnest solicitation of a friend in Edinburgh, although not in the least sanguine of success. The Ettrick Shepherd was one of the unsuccessful candidates, and forgot his discomfiture in his generous laudation of his rival. "This poem," says he, speaking of his own attempt, "was hurriedly and reluctantly written, in compliance with the solicitations of a friend who would not be gainsaid, to compete for a prize offered by a gentleman for the best poem upon the subject. The prize was finally awarded to Mrs. Felicia Hemans; and, as far as the merits of mine went, very justly, hers being greatly superior both in elegance of thought and composition. Had I been constituted the judge myself, I would have given hers the preference by many degrees; and I estimated it the more highly as coming from one of the people that were the hero's foes, oppressors, and destroyers. I think my heart never warmed so much to an author for any poem that ever was written." What acceptable praise this must have been, coming from such a man as the author of "The Queen's Wake"!

There were fifty-seven competitors for the prize: that a Scottish prize, for a poem on a subject purely Scottish, should have been awarded to a candidate of another nationality, is a very clear proof of the impartiality and fair dealing of the judges.

"Mrs. Hemans so soon again!" exclaimed the *Edinburgh Review*, when the result of the competition was known, "and with a palm in her hand! We welcome her cordially, and rejoice to find the high opinion of her genius which we lately expressed so unequivocally confirmed."*

About this time Mrs. Hemans made the acquaintance of the celebrated Reginald Heber, famous throughout the world as the author of the well-known missionary hymn, "From Greenland's icy mountains." It is the least meritorious, from

---

* The same year (1819) was produced a clever and not very lenient satire. Alluding to the female writers of the age, the author first mentions Miss Baillie, and then says:—

"Next I'd place
Felicia Hemans, second in the race;
I wonder the Reviews, who make such stir
Oft about rubbish, never mention her;
They might have said, I think, from mere good-breeding,
Mistress Felicia's works are worth the reading."

a literary point of view, of any of his productions, but upon it his popular fame chiefly rests. Mr. Reginald Heber was the first literary character Mrs. Hemans ever was personally acquainted with; the secluded country life she led, occupied with her literary pursuits, her studies, and her children, debarring her from any intercourse with the great world. Heber admired her classical poems, and sought her out in the hope that she might take for her themes some of the many subjects to be found in Biblical lore. There is no doubt but that his advice exercised an influence upon her later poetry, which soon developed that sacred and seraphic character, by which, amongst female poets, she will ever be distinguished. Acting upon the advice of Mr. Heber, Mrs. Hemans offered her "Vespers of Palermo" to the stage. It was acted at Covent Garden in 1823, but proved a failure. The poet Milman interested himself in its behalf, and it was subsequently acted in Edinburgh with considerable success, the epilogue being written by Sir Walter Scott.

The enormous number of poems which flowed from the pen of the poetess is quite as remarkable as the great variety of subjects of which they treat. The brightest period of her fame is considered that when she published the "Forest Sanctuary," and, above all, her "Records of

Woman." She was now also in correspondence with some of the most noted literary women of the age : with Johanna Baillie, Anne Grant, Mary Mitford, Caroline Bowles, Mary Howitt, and Mrs. Fletcher—formerly Miss Jewsbury—the latter her devoted and admiring friend. It was certainly the most peaceful portion of her life ; but the death of her mother, in 1827, broke up the little Welsh household at St. Asaph, and Mrs. Hemans decided upon removing to Liverpool. Several reasons induced her to come to this determination: her own failing health, for which she thought her native air might prove beneficial ; her desire again to see something of society, and her wish to be in the neighbourhood of some good schools for the sake of her children. She took a small house in the suburbs, and lived there during the three most distinguished and important years of her life. The house was "the third of a row," and a friend of hers gives the following graphic account of Mrs. Hemans's visitors :—

"Scarcely had she settled herself at Wavertree than she was besieged by visitors to a number positively alarming ; a more heterogeneous company cannot be imagined. Many came merely to stare at the strange poetess, others called on regular morning visits, while a third and worst class brought in their hands small cargoes of cut-

and-dry compliment, and, as she used to declare, had primed themselves for their visit by *getting up* a certain number of her poems. Small satisfaction had they in their visits. They found a lady neither short nor tall, no longer youthful or beautiful in her appearance, yet with hair of the true auburn tinge, and as silken, profuse, and curling as it had ever been; with manners quiet and refined, a little reserved; and one, too, who lent no ear to the news of the day. The ladies, when they departed, had to tell that her room was in a sad litter with books and papers, that the strings of her harp were half of them broken, and that she wore a veil on her head like no one else."

Shortly after fixing her residence at Wavertree, Mrs. Hemans paid her first visit to Scotland. Her fame having already preceded her, she was enthusiastically received. Upon this occasion she was accompanied by two of her children, a circumstance which should be noted by those who are forward in censuring her imputed want of domestic affection. Whilst in Scotland she was lionised as much as ever was Sir Walter Scott or Miss Edgeworth in London. The former invited her to stay at Abbotsford, where she spent a few very happy days. "With him," she says in one of her letters, "I am now in constant intercourse, taking long walks over moor and woodland, and listening to song and legend of other times, till my mind forgets itself, and is carried wholly back to the days of the slogan and the fiery cross, and the wide gathering of border chivalry. I cannot say enough of his cordial kindness to me; it makes me feel when at Abbotsford as if the stately rooms of that ancestral-looking place were old familiar scenes to me." She also informs her correspondent of her having "just become acquainted with the Dominie—the veritable Dominie Sampson—being no other than a clergyman of this neighbourhood, Melrose, a tall man, with long parted hair and a wooden leg. Be it known to you all that the Dominie professeth the most profound admiration for me, after the solemn expression of which you may be well assured that all other homage must be flat and unprofitable."

Her visit to Scotland extended from June to September, and during her stay there she composed many of the "Songs of the Affections," notably, "The Spirit's Return." Mrs. Hemans always said that she preferred the latter poem to anything she had ever written. "But if there be," she writes, "as my friends say, a greater power in it than I hitherto evinced, I paid dearly for the discovery, and it almost made me tremble as I sounded the deep places of my soul."

.... I woke to love:—
O gentle Friend! to love in doubt and woe,
Shutting the heart the worshipped name above,
Is to love deeply—and *my* spirit's dower
Was a sad gift, a melancholy power
Of so adoring;—with a buried care,
And with the o'erflowing of a voiceless prayer,
And with the deepening dream, that day by day,
In the still shadow of its lonely sway,
Folded me closer;—till the world held nought,
Save the *one* Being to my centred thought.
There was no music but his voice to hear,
No joy but such as with *his* step drew near;
Light was but where he looked—life where he moved—
Silently, fervently, thus, thus I loved.
Oh! but such love is fearful!

* * * *

  He died—*he* died,
On whom my lone devotedness was cast!
I might not keep one vigil by his side,
I, whose wrung heart watched with him to the last!
I might not once his fainting head sustain,
Nor bathe his parched lips in the hour of pain,
Nor say to him "Farewell."—He passed away—
Oh! had *my* love been there, its conquering sway
Had won him back from death!—but thus removed,
Borne o'er the abyss no sounding line hath proved,
Joined with the unknown, the viewless,—he became
Unto my thoughts another, yet the same—
Changed—hallowed—glorified!—and his low grave
Seemed a bright mournful altar—mine, all mine:—
Brother and Friend soon left me *that* sole shrine,
The birthright of the Faithful!—*their* world's wave
Soon swept them from its brink.—Oh! deem thou not
That on the sad and consecrated spot
My soul grew weak!—I tell thee that a power
There kindled heart and lip;—a fiery shower
My words were made;—a might was given to prayer,
And a strong grasp to passionate despair,

And a dread triumph!—Knowest thou what I sought?
For what high boon my struggling spirit wrought?—
Communion with the dead!

During the same year Mrs. Hemans had many applications from editors and others to contribute something, were it ever so little, to various magazines and annuals. In her endeavours to keep her numerous engagements she quite overworked herself, and the winter of 1829 saw her again in delicate health, and seemingly but little benefited by her tour to Scotland. Some of the better known and more popular of her poems were composed during these few months—namely, "The Lady of Provence," "The Child's First Grief," "The Better Land," numerous shorter poems upon various subjects, and her exquisite "Ode to a Wandering Female Singer." In 1830 the "Songs of the Affections" were published; and whilst they were yet in the press the health of their author again broke down, and she was forced to try the effects of change of air and scene. Mrs. Hemans had long been an admirer of Wordsworth's poems, and now, taking advantage of her enforced holiday, she visited the veteran poet at Rydal Mount. She resided in the vicinity of Windermere for several months, having hired a tiny cottage called Dove's Nest, beautifully situated in a romantic spot near Ambleside.

Wordsworth and his family paid her much attention, and in her letters written from Dove's Nest she constantly speaks of the unremitting kindness and sympathy of the poet. To him, in 1834, Mrs. Hemans dedicated her "Scenes and Hymns of Life," in "token of deep respect for his character and fervent gratitude for moral and intellectual benefit derived from reverential communion with the spirit of his poetry." Such was the dedication which went forth to the world, prefixed to the first volume of the work. After her death, however, a letter was found bearing the inscription—"Intended Dedication of the 'Scenes and Hymns of Life,' to William Wordsworth, Esq." This letter, in which Mrs. Hemans had given free scope to her sentiments, not only of veneration for the poet, but of deep and grateful regard for the friend, was never published, but its substantial ideas are conveyed in the brief dedication before quoted. Towards the conclusion of this letter Mrs. Hemans says :—"May I be permitted on the present occasion to record my unfading recollections of enjoyment from your society—of delight in having heard from your own lips, and amidst your own lovely mountain land, many of those compositions, the remembrance of which will ever spread over its hills and waters a softer colouring of spiritual beauty. Let me also express to you, as to a dear and most honoured friend, my fervent wishes for your long enjoyment of a widely-extended influence, which cannot but be blessed—of a domestic life encircling you with yet nearer and deeper sources of happiness; and of those eternal hopes, on whose foundation you have built, as a Christian poet, the noble structure of your works."

A desire to economise, and to give her younger sons the advantages of an university education, combined with an imperative necessity for change of air, induced Mrs. Hemans to leave Wavertree in 1831, and to take up her residence in Dublin. She made a short tour through the land of her fathers during the summer, and finally fixed her residence in the Irish capital. New scenes gave her new themes for her facile pen; as numerous songs, lyrics, and other shorter pieces attest. Many of these poems are memorials of the various places she visited in Ireland. Amongst varied scenes of interest she singles out for especial mark of her regard, the tomb of Mrs. Mary Tighe, the author of " Psyche." After visiting it Mrs Hemans wrote her " Grave of a Poetess," one of the most touching poems in her " Records of Women." Later on we find another poem upon the same subject, entitled " Written after Visiting a Tomb, near Woodstock, in the County of Kilkenny":—

I stood where the lip of song lay low,
Where the dust had gathered on Beauty's brow;
Where stillness hung on the heart of Love,
And a marble weeper kept watch above.*

  * * * *

And she, that voiceless below me slept,
Flowed not her song from a heart that wept ?
O, Love and Song! though of heaven your powers,
Dark is your fate in this world of ours.

Yet, ere I turned from that silent place,
Or ceased from watching thy sunny race,
Thou, even thou, on those glancing wings
Didst waft me visions of brighter things !

Thou that dost image the freed soul's birth,
And its flight away o'er the mists of earth,
Oh ! fitly thy path is through flowers that rise
Round the dark chamber where Genius lies !

Whilst residing in Dublin one of Mrs. Hemans's chief pleasures was to attend the choral services at St. Patrick's Cathedral. She has recorded her impressions of it in a little poem, entitled "The Music of St. Patrick's." There was one anthem, frequently heard within those ancient walls, of which Mrs. Hemans used to speak with peculiar enthusiasm—that from the 3rd Psalm, "Lord, how are they increased that trouble me." The symphony to the fifth verse—"I laid me down and slept"—with its soft, dreamy vibrations, almost "steep the senses in forgetfulness," when a

---

* The marble figure in the monumental chamber, by Flaxman, above the grave of the poetess.

sudden outbreak, as it were, of life and light bursts forth with the glad announcement, "I awaked ; for the Lord sustained me." No marvel that it made a deep impression upon the sensitive mind of the poetess ; that grand old anthem once heard resounding through those dim ancient arches on a Sunday afternoon in winter, could never be effaced from the memory of any one who had listened to it.

Mrs. Hemans now wrote incessantly, notwithstanding her rapidly-failing health. Pecuniary considerations are supposed to have actuated her to do so at this period of her literary career, more than at any other time. She had a limited income, was anxious to educate her sons well, and her weak physical state required those considerations which make money a necessity. From poetry she turned her attention to prose, and in May, 1834, published a paper on " Tasso," in the *New Monthly Magazine.* Scarcely were the proofs corrected when she was seized with fever, and during her convalescence was again obliged to seek change of air and scene. She visited Wicklow a second time, residing in the neighbourhood of the lovely valley of the Dargle, which she has immortalised in verse. Whilst staying in the County Wicklow she made a pilgrimage to Rosanna, once the residence of the author of "Psyche," in memory of which gifted singer she wrote the following lines in the album there :—

> Oh! lightly tread through these deep chestnut-bowers,
>   Where a sweet spirit once in beauty moved!
> And touch with reverent hand those leaves and flowers,
>   Fair things, which well a gentle heart hath loved!
> A gentle heart, of love and grief th' abode,
>   Whence the bright stream of song in tear-drops flowed.
>
> And bid its memory sanctify the scene!
>   And let th' ideal presence of the dead
> Float round, and touch the woods with softer green,
>   And o'er the streams a charm, like moonlight, shed,
> Through the soul's depths in holy silence felt—
> A spell to raise, to chasten, and to melt!

Upon her return to Dublin Mrs. Hemans was seized with an attack of ague; and this insidious and harassing complaint continued its visitations for several weeks, reducing her poor, wasted form to the most lamentable state of debility, and at length retiring only to make way for a train of symptoms still more fatal and distressing. The following graphic account of Mrs. Hemans's situation at this time, is from the pen of her sister:—

" While the work of decay was going on thus surely and progressively upon the earthly tabernacle, the bright flame within continued to burn with a pure and holy light, and, at times, even to flash forth with more than wonted brightness. The lyric of 'Despondency and Aspiration,' which may be considered as her noblest and highest effort, and in which, from a feeling that it might be her last work, she felt anxious to concentrate all her powers, was written during the few intervals accorded her from acute suffering or powerless languor. And in the same circumstances she wrote, or rather dictated, the series of sonnets called 'Thoughts during Sickness,' which present so interesting a picture of the calm, submissive tone of her mind, whether engaged in tender remembrances of the past, or in solemn and reverential speculations on the future. The one entitled 'Sickness like Night,' discloses a view no less affecting than consolatory of the sweet and blessed peace which hovered round the couch where—

Mutely and hopelessly she lay reposing.

The last sonnet of the series, entitled 'Recovery,' was written under temporary appearances of convalescence, which proved as fugitive as they were fallacious."

The following months of November and December were spent by Mrs. Hemans at Redesdale, a country seat of Dr. Whately, then Archbishop of Dublin. Here she gave herself up to absolute quiet, and returned to Dublin much improved in health. But this slight return of strength was only fleeting, for early in the spring of 1835 her debility rapidly increased, and she felt herself that her days were numbered. One of her friends thus describes her state at this time:—" Mrs. Hemans was now too ill to leave her room, and was only laid upon a couch during the daytime, occasionally suffering severely. But all was borne with resignation and patience, and when not able to bear even the fatigue of reading, she had recourse to her mental resources, and as she lay on her sofa, she would repeat to herself whole chapters of the Bible, and page after page of Milton and Wordsworth. Her thoughts reverted frequently to the days of her childhood—to the old house by the seashore—the mountain rambles, the haunts and the books which had formed the delight of her childhood. She was wont to say to those who expressed pity for her situation, that 'she lived in a fair and happy world of her own, among gentle thoughts and pleasant images;' and in her intervals of pain she would observe that ' no poetry could express nor imagination conceive the visions of blessedness that flitted across her fancy, and made her waking hours more delightful than those even that were given to temporary repose.' At times her spirit would seem to be already half etherealised, her mind would seem to be fraught with deep and holy and incommunicable thoughts, and she would entreat to be left perfectly alone in stillness and darkness, ' to commune with her own heart, and reflect on the mercies of her Saviour.'"

Mrs. Hemans seemed to gather some vitality as the spring advanced, but towards the middle of April the former unfavourable symptoms again manifested themselves. On Sunday, the 26th of April, she dictated to her brother the "Sabbath Sonnet":—

> How many blessed groups this hour are wending,
>   Thro' England's primrose meadow-paths, their way
> Towards spire and tower, 'midst shadowy elms ascending,
>   Whence the sweet chimes proclaim the hallowed day!
> The halls, from old heroic ages grey,
>   Pour their fair children forth; and hamlets low,
> With whose thick orchard-blooms the soft winds play,
>   Send out their inmates in a happy flow,
> Like a freed vernal stream. I may not tread
> With them those pathways, to the feverish bed
> Of sickness bound; yet, O my God! I bless
> Thy mercy, that with Sabbath-peace hath filled
> My chastened heart, and all its throbbings stilled—
> To one deep calm of lowliest thankfulness.*

---

* This sonnet appeared in *Blackwood* the July following, with the subjoined remarks:—

"We cannot allow these verses to adorn, with a sad beauty, the pages of this magazine—more especially as they are the last composed by their distinguished writer, and that only a few days before her death—without at least a passing tribute of regret for an event which has cast a shadow of gloom through the sunshiny fields of contemporary literature. But two months ago the beautiful lyric entitled 'Despondency and Aspiration' appeared in these pages, and now the sweet fountain of music from which that prophetic strain gushed has ceased to flow. The highly-gifted and accomplished, the patient, the meek, and long-suffering FELICIA HEMANS is no more."

It was the last strain of the " sweet singer," whose harp was henceforth to be hung on the willows.

Exactly one month later, on the 26th of May, her sorrowing friends saw that the end was near at hand. All day she seemed to be in a stupor, and about nine o'clock in the evening the gentle spirit of Felicia Hemans passed quietly away without a struggle. She died in her house in Dawson Street, Dublin, and her remains were interred in a vault in St. Anne's Church, which is situated close to the house wherein she died. A small tablet in the wall at the right-hand side of the church tells her name, her age, and the date of her death. There are also inscribed upon it some lines from a dirge of her own.

If ever a poetess lived in her own creations it was Felicia Dorothea Hemans. The highest praise that can be accorded to her poetry, is to say that it is exceptionally feminine, and, at the same time, strong, fervid, and impassioned. Her sex could hardly wish for a better representative in the world of letters. All she has written calls for admiration, from the pure and lofty strain which pervades it, and the tone of deep religious feeling which characterises everything that has come from her pen. A noticeable feature of her poetry is her intense yearning for human affection and sympathy; and many of her sweetest poems tell of wasted feelings and disappointed hopes. Truly, of her it may be said that she " learnt in sorrow" what she " taught in song."

The poetry of Mrs. Hemans possesses three striking characteristics : ideality, picturesqueness, and a wondrous sense of harmony. In her shorter poems, she generally takes some story or incident as a skeleton, and then clothes it with her own ideal and picturesque garments. Nothing can be more polished than her versification. Every poem is like a piece of music, with its eloquent pauses, its rich combinations, and its swelling chords. Mrs. Hemans's gifted contemporary, Letitia Elizabeth Landon, concludes a short retrospect of her works with the following remarks, which also appropriately bring this brief sketch to a close :—

"Mrs. Hemans was spared some of the keenest mortifications of a literary career. She knew nothing of it as a profession which has to make its way through poverty, neglect, and obstacles ; she lived apart, in a small, affectionate circle of friends. The high-road of life, with its crowds and contention, its heat, its noise, and its dust that rests on all, was for her happily at a distance ; yet even in such green nest the bird could not fold its wings and sleep to its own music. There came the aspiring, the unrest, the aching sense of being misunderstood, the consciousness that those a thousand times inferior were yet more beloved. Genius places a woman in an unnatural position; notoriety frightens away affection; and superiority has for its attendant fear, not love. Its pleasantest emotions are too vivid to be lasting; hope may sometimes,

>Raising its bright face,
>With a free gush of sunny tears, erase
>The characters of anguish;

but, like the azure glimpses between thunder-showers, the clouds gather more darkly around for the passing sunshine. The heart sinks back on its solitary desolation. In every page of Mrs. Hemans's writings is this sentiment impressed. What is the conclusion of 'Corinne crowned at the Capitol'?

>Radiant daughter of the sun!
>Now thy living wreath is won.
>Crowned of Rome! oh, art thou not
>Happy in that glorious lot?
>Happier, happier far than thou,
>With the laurel on thy brow,
>She that makes the humblest hearth
>Lovely but to one on earth!

" What is poetry, and what is a poetical career? The first is to have an organisation of extreme sensibility, which the second exposes bareheaded to the rudest weather. The original impulse is irresistible—all professions are engrossing when once begun; and, acting with perpetual stimulus, nothing takes more complete possession of its follower than literature. But never can success repay its cost. The work appears—it lives in the light of popular applause; but truly might the writer exclaim:

> It is my youth, it is my bloom, it is my glad, free heart,
> I cast away for thee—for thee—ill-fated as thou art.

"If this be true, even of one sex, how much more true of the other! Ah! Fame to a woman is indeed but a royal mourning in purple for happiness."

THE MISSES PORTER.

JANE PORTER—Born, a.d. 1776. Died, a.d. 1850.

ANNA MARIA PORTER—Born, a.d. 1781. Died, a.d. 1832.

ALTHOUGH Jane Porter is the elder of these two gifted sisters, yet, when speaking of their literary life, Anna Maria is always considered her senior. The latter began her career as an authoress at the early age of twelve. But before alluding to their works, some notice of their perfect private life ought to possess some interest for the many who have derived pleasure or instruction—or both combined—from their writings.

Jane and Anna Maria Porter were the daughters of an Irish officer of the 6th, or Inniskilling Dragoons, who died soon after the birth of the latter. Mrs. Porter—left a young and lovely widow in very straitened circumstances—quitted the borderland of Scotland, where she was residing at the time of her husband's death, and went to live in Edinburgh. She did so with a view of affording her children the educational advantages of the Athens of the North; advantages which they appear to have availed themselves of from a very early age. With her three younger children Mrs. Porter lived in Edinburgh for some years—quietly and frugally, as her means compelled her to do—her eldest son being left at a public school in England. Whilst in Edinburgh they made the acquaintance of Sir Walter Scott, then a student at college there. Anna Maria was his chief favourite; and we are told that "he was very fond of either teasing the little female student when very gravely engaged with her book, or more often fondling her on his knees, and telling her stories of witches and warlocks, till both forgot their former playful merriment in the marvellous interest of the tale."

Here also Jane Porter listened to the stories and legends which she in after years wove into her famous historical romance of "The Scottish Chiefs." The narrator was an old woman named Luckie Forbes, whose father had fought at the battle of Culloden, and who always wore his silver brooch in her cap. "With her knitting in her hand," says Miss Porter, "she would remark on the blessed quiet of the land where we saw the cattle browsing without fear of an enemy; and then would talk to me of the 'awful times of the brave Sir William Wallace,' when he fought for

Scotland against a cruel tyrant, like unto them *Abraham* overcame, when he recovered *Lot* with all his herds and flocks, from the proud *foray* of the five robber-kings of the South; who, she added, were all rightly punished *for oppressing the stranger in a foreign land! The Lord careth for the stranger!* .... I must avow that while learning my school-lessons of general history from higher hands, to this respected old woman's endearing and often eloquent manner of relating the adventures of the Scottish Chief, I owe my early admiration for his character. Her representation of his heartrending sacrifices for the good of his country, called forth my tears and sobs; and when she told of his brave companions' sufferings and of his own eventually barbarous execution by the tyrant he had opposed, my grief was raised to its climax; and bewailing him, as I had but too recently done my own gallant father, I ceased not, during my whole future life, to remember, with something like a kindred sympathy, himself and the dauntless friends who had followed him to honour or the grave."

The two little girls were very fond of reading, and the brilliant intellect of the little Anna Maria was the admiration of their circle of acquaintances. She learnt much more quickly than did her elder sister, Jane, who was obliged laboriously to toil up the hill of knowledge. Anna Maria never had any need to sacrifice amusement for close study of any kind, the quickness of her perceptions giving her an almost intuitive knowledge of anything she wished to learn.

Mrs. Porter and her children left Edinburgh when Anna Maria was about nine, and spent a couple of years in visiting their relatives in England and Ireland. Finally they settled in London, and soon drew around them a congenial circle of friends, amongst whom were Mrs. Hannah More and Mrs. Barbauld. After residing for a year or two in London, Mrs. Porter removed to Esher, the paling of her garden dividing her little domain from the lawns and woods of Claremont Park. During the habitation of the latter place by his Royal Highness Prince Leopold, Mrs. Porter and her daughters received much attention from the Royal Family. In this unpretending cottage the happiest days of the sister novelists were passed. Jane Porter says it was "a spot which had brightened the eyes of many a tourist while loitering by its trellis porch, and looking in, admired its bowery hangings studded with singing birds; its small green stands, covered with fragrant bean-pots of every flower in the season, gathered from our own garden, or sent in greater quantities to my dear sister, she being particularly fond of

Nature's garlands, whether in their native wildness, or cultured to the perfection of the rarest exotics transplanted to our soil. But what was yet sweeter to her eye and ear were the prayer and the blessing of the hungry and the wayworn, whom we often saw and heard pouring their modest gratitude over the wicket-gate before the porch of our door. For no weary traveller or real object of charity ever stopped to lean for a moment's rest on that humble paling without attracting our mother's notice, and meeting a bounteous refreshment from her hand."

In this "little Arcadia"—as Sir Frederick Eden called it—they lived until the death of Mrs. Porter in 1831. The remains of this venerable lady were interred in the village churchyard in Esher. Her son—Sir Robert Ker Porter, famous as an historical painter—placed an altar-piece, painted by himself, over the communion-table of the village church which she had been in the habit of attending.

After the death of their mother, the Misses Porter gave up the cottage at Esher, and went to live with one of their brothers, an eminent surgeon in Bristol. Anna Maria had never been very strong, and the shock sustained by her mother's death still further enfeebled her. A few months after her arrival in Bristol she was attacked by an epidemic fever, and died on the 21st of June, 1832, aged fifty-one years. To the day of her death Miss Anna Maria Porter was remarkably elegant and graceful in figure. Her eyes were bright and expressive, and her manner attractive. In her earlier years a resemblance was traced between her features and those of Sir Joshua Reynolds; and she was wont to place a pair of large spectacles upon her nose in order to render the supposed likeness more complete. At a more advanced age, those who had known Angelica Kauffmann in her youth, observed a similarity of feature and expression between her and Miss Anna Maria Porter.

She wrote fifty-two works—a number that excites amazement, even in these days of rapid writing. Her best novel is that of "Don Sebastian," but in all her compositions she evinced the finest dramatic tact. The plots are so carefully constructed, that to remove the smallest incident would be like taking away the keystone of an arch. United to this constructive faculty were keen powers of observation and subtle analysis of character, combined with a glowing imagination. "The immortality of a work," says Mrs. Elwood, "like the happy immortality of the soul, does not lie in its superior faculties, but in the use to which they are applied—in its virtue—its power to move men's minds to good thoughts and great actions. And to accomplish such an aim was the meek but energetic object of Miss Anna Maria Porter."

Jane Porter did not commence her literary career until much later than her sister, for she was seven-and-twenty when her first novel, "Thaddeus of Warsaw," was published. It was written soon after she came to reside in London. Russia was just then endeavouring to sweep the chivalric kingdom of Poland from the map of nations, and Jane Porter's sensitive mind was deeply impressed by the stories which she heard of the sufferings of the exiled Poles. Her sympathies were further enlisted from the accounts which her brother gave her of Kosciusko. He had become acquainted with the Polish patriot when abroad, and admired and respected him. The novel attracted much attention, and as an evidence of his appreciation of the work, Kosciusko sent Miss Porter a complimentary letter, and a ring containing his portrait. The authoress was also elected a lady chanoinesse of the Teutonic order of St. Joachim, in the habit of which she appears in some of her portraits.

"The Scottish Chiefs" is the novel by which Miss Jane Porter's literary fame was firmly established. Sir Walter Scott admitted that Maria Edgeworth's pictures of Irish life had given him the idea of delineating Scottish character; but that "The Scottish Chiefs" had suggested to him the desirability of interweaving history with these traits. Joanna Baillie said of the hero of this first of the historical romances—"Wallace, in 'The Scottish Chiefs,' which, through a variety of interesting imaginary adventures conducts a character of most perfect virtue and heroism to an affecting and tragical end, is a romance deservedly popular." Not quite so flattering was the verdict of Allan Cunningham. "She has," he says, "added attributes which neither pertain to the times nor to the hero. She has drawn him with a hand much too soft and gentle." The novel passed through many editions, and Miss Porter's next work was "The Pastor's Fireside," a domestic tale in three volumes. This was followed by "Duke Christian of Luneberg," written in consequence of "His Majesty's (George IV.) gracious request that Miss Porter's next subject should be the life of his great and virtuous progenitor, Duke Christian of Luneberg." The original documents were furnished by the King, who declared the work had been completed to his fullest wishes.

Other novels followed in quick succession, one of them, "The Field of Forty Footsteps," having been dramatised. Then followed "Sir Edward

Seaward's Narrative of his Shipwreck and consequent Discovery of certain Islands in the Caribbean Sea; with a Detail of many extraordinary and highly interesting Events in his Life, from the year 1733 to 1749; as written in his own Diary. Edited by Miss Jane Porter." This clever fiction was as successful as was Sir Thomas More's "Utopia," or De Foe's "Voyage to the World of Cartesius." After elaborate researches among Admiralty records, Indian maps, &c., a critic in the *Quarterly* gravely informs his readers,— "We are compelled to state that, notwithstanding its solemn and almost sacred character, it is neither more nor less than pure unmingled fiction from first to last."* Its literary ability is commended in the same notice. Many reviewers were for a time deceived. At the merciless rummaging of Admiralty records and Indian maps, made by her critics, Miss Porter was more flattered than annoyed. When pressed as to the real origin of "Sir Edward Seaward," she would quietly say, "Sir Walter Scott had his great secret; I must be allowed to keep my little one."†

Charles Kean, in 1819, played in a tragedy by Miss Porter, called "Switzerland." It was not a success; another instance of a thoroughly dra-

---

* December, 1832.   † *Gentleman's Magazine*, August, 1850.

matic novelist being unable to write a thoroughly dramatic play.

The deaths of her mother and sister weighed heavily upon Miss Porter's mind, and her grief seriously affected her health. She had been living with her brother in Bristol, since the death of her sister, and in 1842, feeling a necessity for change of scene, accompanied her eldest brother, Sir Robert Ker Porter, on a visit to his daughter at St. Petersburg. Here a fresh trial awaited her. Just as they were on the eve of returning to England, her beloved brother was taken suddenly ill, and died in a few hours.

Miss Porter returned to England, and for the remaining years of her life resided with her younger brother, Dr. Porter, of Bristol. His house was her home, she only leaving it to pay lengthened visits to old and congenial friends. In search of health she went to Brighton for some time, and during her stay there became the object of Her Majesty's solicitude. In a preface prefixed to one of the later editions of "The Scottish Chiefs," Miss Porter thus speaks of the Royal favours which she received :—

"There is an illustrious name, the most illustrious in the country, to which I must add an honoured subject's grateful sense of its goodness—the Queen of England, who, hearing of the dangerous illness of one whom her gracious youth remembered as the authoress of 'The Scottish Chiefs,' &c.—one who had dwelt in the bosom of her family, near to the gates where Her Majesty had passed her own interesting childhood, to this now solitary and lately deeply-suffering invalid at Brighton did her young and pitying Queen no sooner hear of these circumstances, than with one of those spontaneous feelings which, like a natural fountain, spring to action in her royal heart, her command was given that the authoress of works so read and approved should, in that her, perhaps, dying hour, receive proofs of the value her gracious Sovereign set upon such talents so applied. This was a testimony to a female writer of England, which could not but be of as distinguishing an estimation in her breast as the cross or the star to the bosoms of the brave defenders of that country whose weal at home and abroad her maiden pen has ever inculcated, must rest for ever in its people's firm support of the laws, the liberties, and the throne of England."

The novels of the Misses Porter have had a wide circulation in America. In 1844 a number of the publishers, booksellers, and authors of the United States sent from New York to Miss Porter a handsome rosewood armchair, " as a memorial of high and respectful admiration for the author of some of the purest and most imaginative productions in the wide range of English literature."

A critic in *Frazer's Magazine* says: "It is to Miss Porter's fame that she began the system of historical novel-writing which attained the climax of its renown in the hands of Sir Walter Scott. And no light praise it is that she has thus pioneered the way for the greatest exhibition of the greatest genius of our time. She may parody Bishop Hall, and tell Sir Walter:

> I first adventured—follow me who list,
> And be the *second* Scottish novelist."

In addition to her works published in book form, Miss Porter was a constant contributor to the periodical literature of the day. Her last works were "The Pastor's Fireside," and some contributions to *Frazer*. The latter magazine, in 1835, published a portrait of Miss Porter, together with a brief memoir, which says: "In private, she is a quiet and good-humoured lady, rather pious, and fond of going to evening parties, where she generally contrives to be seen patronising some sucking lion or lioness. In which occupation may she long continue, devoting her mornings to the Prayer-book, and her evenings to the *conversazione*—

> And may no ill event cut shorter
> The easy course of Miss Jane Porter."

The career of Miss Jane Porter was not marked

by any very striking event ; she won her celebrity by her genius, and her unblemished character brightens the picture. She died May 24th, 1850, at the residence of her brother, Dr. Porter, of Bristol, in the seventy-fourth year of her age.

SYDNEY, LADY MORGAN.

BORN DECEMBER 25TH, ABOUT 1777. DIED APRIL 16TH, 1859.

PROTEST against dates! What has a woman got to do with dates!" exclaimed "Sydney, Lady Morgan," as she chose to call herself. She kept the secret of her birth with admirable tact; but she is supposed to have been born in the year 1777, or thereabouts. Knowing she was so sensitive upon this point, her unsparing critic and enemy, Croker, took a mean revenge against her by always speaking of her as "Miss Owenson, of the eighteenth century."

Sydney Owenson was one of the two daughters of an Irish land-steward named MacOwen, which he Anglicised to Owenson. He became stage-struck, entered the profession and went over to London, where he made his first appearance in Rowe's play of "Tamerlane." He was tolerably successful, and "Mr. Owenson, the great London actor," made a "starring" tour through the provinces. While at Shrewsbury he met a certain Miss Hill, "a simple woman of a certain age," who was completely fascinated by the handsome Irishman. She eloped with him ; they were married, and their eldest child was the subject of this memoir.

She was born on Christmas Day, on the passage between Holyhead and Dublin ; at least, that is the generally given and received account, but in Lady Morgan's own Memoirs she gives the following graphic details :—

"In the hour when I first drew breath, and felt life's first inaugural sensation-pain, the world took part in the hour and the day. It was the festival of humanity, of peace, and goodwill to man, of love and liberty and high distinction to woman, of glory to the motherhood of nations, the accomplishment of the first desire of her, who was created, not born ; the desire 'to be as gods, knowing good from evil'—the head and front of human science. I was born on *Christmas Day;* in that land where all holy days are religiously celebrated, as testimonials to faith, and are excuses for festivity—in 'Ancient Ould Dublin.'

"Bells tolled, carols were intoned, the streets resounded with joyous sounds, chimneys smoked, and friends were preparing to feast the fasters of the previous week, in that most Catholic of countries. Holly and ivy draped every wall, and many happy returns of the season were offered on all sides ; supper-tables without distinction of religion, High Church and Low Church, Catholic and Protestant, alike took the benefit of 'the good the gods provided.' Guests were assembled, and all awaited the announcing hour as it struck from the belfry of St. Patrick's Cathedral, the echoes booming down all the close old streets of Dublin, and overpowered all the minor bells of the seven churches of its most saintly neighbourhood.

"There was, however, on that joyous night one round table distinguished above most others, by the wit and humour of the *convives*. The master of the feast was as fine a type of the Irish gentleman as Ireland ever sent forth. His name was Robert Owenson; beside him sat one whose name in Ireland was long celebrated, and is not yet forgotten, as belonging to one of the greatest wits of his country and time—Edward Lysaght, long the captain of the University boys, that formidable body of learned and privileged insurbordinates, and who had lately been admitted to the Irish Bar. Others there were also, though then unknown to fame, except for their social endowments.

"The lady who had the best right to preside on the occasion of this most Christian festival, as she was herself truly the sincerest of Christians and best of women, had retired early in the evening to her chamber on the plea of 'indisposition,' but still not deeming it indicative of any immediate catastrophe. But before the great clock of St. Patrick had chimed out the second hour of the new-born anniversary, another birth had taken place, and was announced by a joyous gossip to the happy father, who instantly disappeared. The guests, far from dispersing, waited for him (though not with empty glasses), and when he returned, nearly an hour after, and announced the 'birth of a dear little Irish girl—the very thing I have always wished for!' the intelligence was responded to by a half-suppressed cheer, mellow as a Low Mass, and hearty wishes of long life to her!"*

In such wise, then, did the future poetess, novelist, dramatist, and queen of society, make her first entrance into this life. Sydney Owenson is a remarkable example of what a woman can do, unaided, who has tact and energy enough to use discreetly the brains with which she has been dowered. Who would have predicted that the small, fragile child, bred up amid actors, learning her first letters, probably, upon a playbill—conversant with properties—the pet of the green-room —whose loud merry laugh might be heard before the drop-scene was drawn up, behind the footlights—who would suppose that she would have

---

* *Vide* " Lady Morgan's Memoir," pp. 7–8.

lived to eighty-two, to figure in the most polite neighbourhood of London, among the most lettered, the most famous, and the most aristocratic society in the world?

With considerable difficulty, her mother at last succeeded in teaching Sydney to read. But before that much-to-be-desired part of her education had been accomplished, the future authoress had already had her mind well stored with hymns, poems, Irish ballads, snatches of Shakspeare, and other desultory scraps which she picked up anywhere and everywhere. Eventually, she properly learnt both reading and writing from Thomas Dermody, the Poor Scholar, who has often been called "the Irish Chatterton."

One evening, as Robert Owenson, his wife, and two little girls were sitting in their parlour adjoining the Music Hall in Fishamble Street, where Robert Owenson gave his dramatic entertainments, one of the theatre attendants announced that a boy was waiting to see the manager. Cherry, one of the actors now made his appearance, and read a satirical poem, which he said had been written by the boy who was now in the painting-room. The humour, satire, and learning which it displayed amazed and delighted the hearers, and Robert Owenson hurried off to see the author. What was his surprise at the figure that met his view! Infantine in appearance, with a meagre, half-starved, but intelligent countenance ; a coat much too large for him, and his shoulders and arms seen naked through it; without shirt, waistcoat, or stockings; with a pair of breeches made for a full-grown person, soiled and ragged, reaching to his ankles; his feet thrust into a pair of old slippers, his hair clotted with glue, and his face and almost naked body smeared and disfigured with paint of different colours—black, blue, red, green, and yellow—thus stood before them, with a pot of size in one hand and a paint-brush in the other, the translator of Horace, Virgil, and Anacreon.

Good-hearted Robert Owenson heard the boy's story, and then, touched by his poverty and his learning, not alone gave him a home in his own house, but introduced him to many influential persons. Dublin was a centre of literature and fashion at the time, and Thomas Dermody soon became a lion. But, alas! that it should be said of so many of our gifted countrymen!—Dermody fell into habits of profligacy and intemperance, and was often without the mere necessaries of life. Yet, through all, Robert Owenson's kindness was unfailing. On one occasion he wrote to his benefactor:—

" Your bounty to me has been like the ocean,

boundless and illimitable. From my appearance I am ashamed to call upon you. I shall only say I have fasted for a longer time than caused the death of Chatterton.

"THOMAS DERMODY."

To which significant epistle Owenson replied:—

"Accept the enclosed; and while so poor a man as myself can purchase a loaf, you shall never want share of it, in common with my dear girls. In answer to your former note, call at Mr. Dixon's, corner of Crow Sreet, and by my desire he will give you three pair of stockings: it will be time enough to get some of that commodity when you enter the College, if ever you should have grace enough to accomplish so desired an object. Get them of such a kind as will be useful, not fashionable. Call at Rourk's, and you will get a pair of shoes. I think you want them."

It was not until Sydney was eight years old that her sister Olivia was born. A year or two afterwards a son was born, who died in infancy. The date of Mrs. Owenson's death has never been ascertained, but it is probable it took place when Olivia was about five or six years old; for Owenson, "the exemplary widower," was long remembered in Dublin as one who would daily leave the city behind to give his little daughters the benefit of a country walk. Sydney Owenson was through life tenderly attached to her father. A more filially fond heart never existed, and to the day of her death her father's memory and portrait were venerated and treasured by her with intense enthusiasm. He was a most excellent parent, anxious in every way for the prosperity of his daughters. After the death of their mother he placed them at a good school at Clontarf, and underwent many privations in order to give his little girls the best education possible. "I remember once," said Lady Morgan, "our music mistress, Miss Buck, complained to my father of our idleness, as he sat beside us at the piano, whilst we stumbled through a duet from the overture to 'Artaxerxes.' His answer to her complaint was simple and graphic; for, drawing up the sleeve of a handsome surtout great-coat which he wore, he showed the shabby, threadbare sleeve of the black coat beneath, and said, touching the whitened seams, 'I should not be driven to the subterfuge of wearing a great-coat this hot weather to conceal the poverty of my dress beneath, if it were not that I wish to give you the advantage of such instruction as you are now neglecting.' This went home, and Miss Buck had nothing to complain of during the remainder of our tuition."

Sydney profited by the educational advantages which her father gave her; and a very few years afterwards, when he again became embarrassed in circumstances, she announced her intention of taking a situation as a governess. She entered the family of a Mrs. Featherstone, and seems to have been very happy there. At first they lived in the country, but a few months later the family removed to Dominick Street, Dublin, where Sydney commenced her search for a publisher. She had already published, by subscription, a volume of poems. Their success, however, was nothing to speak of. An evening she spent with Moore, the poet, at his brother's—the grocer of Little Longford Street, Dublin—decided her to try her fortunes seriously as an authoress. The success of the grocer's son fired her ambition, and she dreamt of name, fame, and fortune to be won by her brains and her facile pen.

So, one morning Sydney Owenson, governess, left her employer's house in Dominick Street, attired in the cook's cloak and bonnet, and set out on her travels in search of a publisher. She carried a roll of manuscript, carefully tied up with rose-coloured ribbon. It was her novel of "St. Clair." Arrived at a bookseller's shop in Henry Street, a small boy was sweeping down the steps, and in answer to her request to see "the master," inquired if she wanted the young "masther or the ould one."

The following graphic account of her interview is the last portion of her autobiography which Lady Morgan dictated :—

"Before I could make my selection, a glass door at the back of the shop opened, and a flashy young yeoman in full uniform, his musket on his shoulder, and whistling the 'Irish Volunteers,' marched straight up to me.

"The impudent boy, winking his eye, said—

"'Here's a young Miss wants to see yez, Master James.'

"Master James marched up to me, chucked me under the chin, 'and filled me from the crown to the toe-top full of direst cruelty.' I could have murdered them both.

"All that was dignified in girlhood and authorship beat at my heart, when a voice from the parlour behind the shop came to my rescue by exclaiming—

"'What are yeh doing there, Jim? Why ain't you off, sir? for the Phaynix and the lawyers' corps marched an hour ago.'

"The next moment a good-humoured-looking, middle-aged man, but in a great passion, with his face half shaved, and a razor and shaving-cloth in his hand, came forth and said—

"'Off wid yeh now, sir, like a sky-rocket.'

"Jim accordingly shouldered his musket 'like a sky-rocket,' and Scrub, leaping over the counter, seized his broom and began to sweep diligently.

"The old gentleman gave me a good-humoured glance, and saying—'Sit down, honey, and I will be with you in a jiffey,'—returned in a few minutes with the other half of his face shaved, and wiping his hands with a towel, took his place behind the counter, saying, 'Now, honey, what can I do for you?' This was altogether unlike my ideas of the Tonsons, the Dodsleys, and the great Miss Burney, that I was equally inclined to laugh and cry. So the old gentleman repeated his question, 'Well, what do you want, my dear?'

"I hesitated, and at last said—

"'I want to sell a book, please.'

"'To sell a book, dear? An ould one?—for I sell new ones myself. And what is the name of it? and what is it about?'

"I was now occupied in taking off the rose-coloured ribbon with which I had tied up my manuscript.

"'What,' he said, 'it is a manuscript—is it?'

"'The name, sir,' I said, 'is "St. Clair."'

"'Well now, my dear, I have nothing to do with Church books, neither sermons nor tracts; so you see, I take it for granted it is a Papist book, by the title.'

"'No, sir, it is one of sentiment, after the manner of "Werter."'

"He passed his hand over his face, which left the humorous smile on his face unconcealed.

"'Well, my dear, I never heard of "Werter;" and you see I am not a publisher of novels at all.'

"At this announcement—hot, hungry, flurried, and mortified—I began to tie up my MS. In spite of myself, the tears came into my eyes, and poor, good-natured Mr. Smith said—

"'Don't cry, dear—don't cry; there's money bid for you yet! But you're very young to turn author; and what's yer name, dear?'

"'Owenson, sir,' I said.

"'Owenson?' he repeated. 'Are you anything to Mr. Owenson, of the Theatre Royal?'

"'Yes, sir, I am his daughter.'

"'His daughter? You amaze me!' And running round the counter with the greatest alacrity, he said—'Come into the parlour and have some breakfast, and we will talk it over. Why, your father is the greatest friend I have in the world.'

"'Oh no, sir, impossible! I am expected to breakfast where I live—I must return.'

"'Well, then, what *can* I do for you? Will I recommend you to a publisher?'

"'Oh! sir, if you would be so good!'
"'To be sure I would.' He then took a sheet of paper, wrote a few lines, rapidly tossed a wafer about in his mouth for some minutes, sealed his letter, and directed it to Mr. Brown, bookseller and publisher, Grafton Street. 'Now here, my dear; Mr. Brown is the great publisher of novels and poems. 'Twas he brought out Counsellor Curran's poems, and Mr. O'Callaghan—beautiful poet, but rather improper. Now, dear, don't lose a minute, this is just the time for catching old Brown; and let me know your success, and what I can do for you.' And so with curtseys and blushes, and wiping away my tears, I started off for the other side of the water, and ran rather than walked to Mr. Brown's, of Grafton Street."

Mr. Brown offered to give an opinion upon the manuscript, and told the young literary aspirant to call in a few days to hear his decision. But in the meantime Mrs. Featherstone and her family left Dublin. Sydney heard nothing about her novel, and the season again returned for the family to come up to town. One day she accompanied Mrs. Featherstone to see a sick friend, and whilst she went up to the invalid's room, Sydney was left to amuse herself in the sitting-room. To pass the time, she took up a book, and found it to be her own novel of "St. Clair"!

She had not left any address with the publisher, so that he had no means of communicating with her. He presented her with four copies of the book, which was all the remuneration she received at this time. The work was re-written and improved before its publication in England. When "St. Clair" was published in Germany, a biographical notice was prefixed; this remarkable production asserted that the authoress had strangled herself with an embroidered cambric handkerchief, in a fit of despair and disappointed love!

"In spite of faults and absurdities," says William Hepworth Dixon, "'St Clair' contains the promise of better things. 'The Sorrows of Werter' was her model, but there is an idea of drawing characters and inventing situations far from hackneyed or conventional; and, in spite of the pedantry, there is an eloquence and passion which redeems its impossibility. The characters are shadows of ideas, and utterly unlike human beings, but each personage has a character and supports it; the work abounds in high-flown discourse and discussion upon the topics of love, music, poetry, and literature in general. The authoress talked out her own impressions and opinions of the books she had read, and though the display of her reading hinders the action and spoils the story, there is a freshness and enthusiasm which only needed time and practice to turn to profit. The extent of her reading is quite wonderful for so young a girl; it consists of solid works and standard authors, requiring careful and painstaking study. She had a strong passion for acquiring knowledge, stronger even than her love of displaying it. She revelled in allusions to her favourite books, in quotations and in fine-sounding words. In all her early works, her heroes and heroines indulge in wonderful digressions—historical, astronomical, and metaphysical—in the very midst of the most terrible emergencies where danger, despair, and unspeakable catastrophes are imminent and impending. No matter what laceration of their finest feelings they may be suffering, the chief characters have always their learning at their finger-ends, and never fail to make quotations from favourite authors appropriate to the occasion. It is easy to laugh at all this; but it were devoutly to be wished that the young authors of the present day would read a little before they begin to write so much."

Sydney Owenson left the Featherstones early in the summer, at the request of her father. But the quiet stay-at-home life did not suit the restless girl, ambitious always *to do something to make herself independent.* That was the secret of her success. She was, ambitious, self-reliant, and, above all, she was *industrious*. Therefore, she accepted a situation as governess in the family of a Mrs. Crawford, at Fort William, in the North of Ireland.

Her career as a governess was not an unhappy one. She possessed so many social qualities, that her presence was rather an acquisition in a dull country house. She had conciliating manners, and was not prone to take offence. As she says herself in one of her letters—" You know one of my maxims is, never to let anything in the world ruffle my temper, and by this means I continue to keep others in good humour with me." She danced well, she sang Irish songs to her harp, she was flattered and made love to, yet through it all she never lost her head.

"The Novice of St. Dominic"—her second novel—was written during these governessing-days, and the whole six volumes copied out by her lover, Francis Crossley—a most unmistakable proof of devotion! Miss Owenson determined to try her fate with a London publisher, and, at random, selected Sir Richard Phillips, merely from seeing his name in the newspapers. She wrote to him about her book, and he returned a courteous answer, saying he could not accept the work, nor even give an opinion without seeing it.

The young Irish girl had made up her mind to be an authoress, and she was determined to succeed. So upon the receipt of Sir Richard Phillips's letter, she packed up her manuscript, and set off for London. It was a long and perilous journey in those days; and she was alone, with very little money in her pocket. When the coach drove into Lad Lane, London, to the innyard of the Swan with Two Necks, the young authoress was so tired that she sat down upon her trunk in a corner of the yard, and fell fast asleep. A gentleman noticed her, and requested that she would be properly looked after. This benefactor proved to be Mr. Quentin Dick, her friend of later years.

She had an interview with Phillips, the publisher, the next day. He was charmed with her; introduced her to his wife, got her respectable lodgings, accepted her novel, and paid her at once for it. It is much to her credit that she at once sent the greater portion of the money to her father, as a help towards rescuing him from his financial embarrassments.

Out of this—the price of her first successful novel—she bought for herself an Irish harp, by Egan, and a black mode cloak. Phillips induced her to cut down the novel from six to four volumes, " and she used always to say that she believed it was regard for her feelings alone which hindered him from reducing it to three.".

"The Novice" was emphatically a success, although many of the characters were rather unnatural. The heroine is terribly well-educated, even for these days of competitive examinations. She and her accomplished lover talk Shakspeare and the musical glasses in a manner which might be edifying, were it not bewildering. Mr. Pitt thought very highly of this novel, and it was one of the last books he read.

Sydney returned from London a successful authoress, and with an order from Sir Richard Phillips for a novel upon a purely Irish subject. She went to work indefatigably; collected information from every source; even went to Connaught to look for materials, the result of her labours being "The Wild Irish Girl." When it was completed, Phillips was charmed with it, and wished to monopolise the writer upon easy terms. But she was too good a business-woman to do anything of the kind, and she wrote to Johnson, a rival publisher, about it. The correspondence upon the subject is very amusing; but the material result of it was that Phillips gave Miss Owenson three hundred pounds for the book.

No wonder the novel was a brilliant success, for the authoress painted from real life, throwing around some romantic circumstances the halo of her own vivid perceptions and imagination. At first she was about to call it "The Princess of Innismore;" and as it is based upon a curious circumstance in Miss Owenson's own life, we may be excused for giving in full the nucleus of the novel which has made the writer's name famous.

"A young man, Richard Everard,. had fallen violently in love with Miss Owenson; his father discovered it, and was displeased. This son had no money, no profession, and was a very idle young man. Miss Owenson had no money either, and it looked a very undesirable match. Mr. Everard, the father, called upon Miss Owenson, stated his objections, and begged her to use her influence to make his son Richard take to some employment, and tried to obtain her promise not to marry him. Miss Owenson had not the least inclination to marry him, but nobody likes to be peremptorily desired to refrain from a course they are 'not inclined to.' Still, Sydney Owenson spoke so wisely, and conducted herself so pleasantly, that the father actually became desirous of doing himself what he had forbidden his son to think of. Miss Owenson was no more disposed to marry the father than she had been to marry the son. He became, however, a very firm and kind friend to her father, assisting him both with counsel and money. Mr. Everard kept up a long and earnest correspondence with Miss Owenson, confiding to her, with singular frankness, all his own concerns and private affairs, and constantly entreating her to use her influence over his son to turn him from his evil courses.

"The history of this curious friendship is detailed in the story of 'The Wild Irish Girl,' where her father figures as the Prince of Innismore, Mr. Everard and his son as Lord M—— and Mortimer, though the beautiful atmosphere of romance which clothes the story in the novel was entirely absent in the matter-of-fact. The character of the Princess of Innismore was afterwards identified with Lady Morgan, and until her marriage she was always known in society by the sobriquet of Glorvina."*

"The Wild Irish Girl" was completed in 1806, and no sooner were the proofs out of her hands than Miss Owenson set to work again. The next effort of her pen was called "Patriotic Sketches," in which she dealt with the then, as now, much vexed question of Irish politics. The book was tolerably successful, and the authoress now gave herself a comparative rest. She paid visits all the while, however, gathering fresh material for

* "Memoirs," by W. H. Dixon, pp. 276-77.

other work. In 1807 she produced an operetta, called "The Whim of the Moment," in which her father played. It was his last appearance on the Dublin stage, and the following year he quitted the profession entirely. He was in very embarrassed circumstances, and the faithful Sydney did all in her power to relieve him. Her sister Olivia was very delicate, and the state of her health gave her affectionate father and sister much concern. Sydney procured a situation for her as governess to the children of General Brownrigg, then residing in Dublin. Referring to the performance of the operetta, and to the departure of Olivia, Robert Owenson writes thus to his eldest daughter:—

"I am afraid, my dear Syd, your little head will be quite turned giddy with pleasure and applause. Your dear sister, my darling Livy, will leave me on Monday, and I should be willing my life should leave me at the same time; for parting with her, and you away, is separating soul and body. Remember, however, what I say, *as if they were my last words to you*, that the very first time she finds the least thing disagreeable, that you take her away and send her back to me. She is, I am afraid, in a poor state of health. I have made her take four glasses of wine every day for ten days back, and it has done her, I think, much good. Be kind to her, and keep her two or three days with you before she goes. I got her three gowns and some other clothes, as well as I know how. Be sure you meet her at the coach-office on Tuesday evening, and have a coach ready. Bring some *male* friend with you, that she may not be imposed upon. She will leave me in *very, very* low spirits; and God only knows what I hourly feel for her, and what I am still to feel when she leaves me. She goes in the same coach you did.

"I think the terms you mention for your farce hard. If Cooke is concerned, of course he will exert himself for the benefit.

"Paying the full expenses, which I hear will be a hundred pounds, is out of all reason. I would stipulate for sixty pounds, or guineas, at most.

"Bargain I shall go up to play for you, and which I think he will not refuse, and it would be a great deal in your way. Phillips, like all the rest, is a thief. Write fully by Saturday night's mail. God bless you.

"ROBERT OWENSON."

Olivia was very beautiful, and whilst at General Brownrigg's attracted the attention of Dr. Arthur Clarke, physician to the Navy, and a man of high reputation in his profession. " Arthur Clarke was in those days one of the curiosities and celebrities of Dublin. A dwarf in height, a buck in dress, a wit, a musician, a man of science, a lover of quips and anecdotes, a maker of pleasant verses, an excellent table-talker, a lion and a lion-hunter, an adorer of learning, genius and success—such was the tiny, seductive, and most respectable gentleman who proposed to the charming governess of General Brownrigg's children." Olivia was sensible enough to accept him. He had money and position, gave her a home for her father and old Molly, and was ever a most devoted and affectionate husband. In gratitude for his skill during a severe attack of illness, the Duke of Richmond created him a knight in 1811.

But we must pass on. Sydney now had become the fashion; everywhere she was welcomed and caressed. About this time she made the acquaintance of Sir Charles Ormsby, "the ugliest fellow and the most accomplished gentleman in Dublin." That they were attached to each other there is very little doubt, but it does not appear that there had ever been any decided engagement between them. In 1808 she paid a second visit to London, where rank and literature received her with open arms. How very different from her first visit there! She quarrelled with Phillips, the publisher, about her next novel, "Ida of Athens." The exact cause of the disagreement is not known—she said he had treated her barbarously. Messrs. Longmans accepted it, and brought it out in 1809. It was the first of Miss Owenson's works that was severely criticised. The *Quarterly* honoured her with a review, more remarkable for bitterness than brilliancy. The writer never liked "Ida;" she used to call it "a bad book," and was rather ashamed of it.

The same year Miss Owenson went on a visit to Lady Abercorn, at Baron's Court, in the North of Ireland. They had read her novels, and were pleased with them; they met the authoress, and were charmed. They proposed that she should come and live with them and amuse them. At first she demurred, but, acting upon the advice of her friends, she at length acceded to the request of the Marquis and Marchioness. They were very stately and very grand, but, on the whole, extremely kind to her.* Here she met the great ones of the earth. The Abercorns took her to London with them, where she sold her book, "The Missionary," for a good sum; sat to Sir Thomas Lawrence to have her portrait painted; was presented to the Princess of Wales, and dined with her!

---

* The Marchioness of Abercorn was the original of Lady Llanberis, in "O'Donnell."

"The Missionary" was a novel upon Indian subjects, and is not worth the paper upon which it was written. She sent it to Phillips, although she had quarrelled with him; but as he would not give her her price, she disposed of it to Stockdale and Miller.

But although the family at Baron's Court treated her with every kindness and consideration, yet she had many vexations. She had to bear with all their tempers, and was expected always to be in good spirits. "She did not become discontented," says William Hepworth Dixon, "but she was disenchanted (for the time) with all that belonged to herself, and saw her own position on its true comparative scale. Sydney Owenson, from earliest childhood, had depended on herself alone for counsel and support. There is no sign that she ever felt those moments of religious aspiration, when a human being, sensible of its own weakness and ignorance, cries for help to Him who made us; there are no ejaculations of prayer, or of thanksgiving; she proudly took up her own burden, and bore it as well as she could; finding her own way and shaping her life according to her own idea of what ought to form her being's end and aim. She was a courageous, indomitable spirit; but the constant dependence on herself, the steady concentration of purpose with which she followed out her own career, without letting herself be turned aside, gave a hardness to her nature, which, though it did not destroy her kindness and honesty of heart, petrified the tender grace which makes the charm of goodness. No one can judge Sydney Owenson, because no one can know all the struggles, difficulties, temptations, flatteries, and defamation which she had to encounter, without the shelter or support of a home, or the circle of home relatives. She remained an indestructibly honest woman; but every faculty she possessed had undergone a change, which seemed to make her of a different species to other women."

Miss Owenson's literary affairs were not very flourishing at this period. "The Missionary" was not a great success, and her publishers were very dissatisfied. Casting about in her active mind for some way of retrieving her failing fortunes, she thought of writing for the stage. From her early associations, she knew all about dramatic situations; and the comparative success of her musical sketch, "The Whim of the Moment," gave her courage to try again. However, she abandoned the attempt, and went back to Baron's Court, where she became engaged to be married to Sir Charles—at that time only Dr.—Morgan.

The match was made up by the Abercorns,

whose family physician Dr. Morgan was. He was desperately in love with the lively Glorvina, and the promises of devoted affection with which his love-letters abound he amply fulfilled during the years of their happy married life. Glorvina was five or six years older than him—in later life she acknowledged to only two. She scarcely seemed to know her own mind about the matter, and appears—or pretends to appear—very much surprised at finding herself engaged. Dr. Morgan was a widower with a good income, handsome, and accomplished. "Barring his wild, unfounded love for me," says Glorvina, when writing on the subject to Mrs. Lefanu, "the creature is perfection. The most *manly*, I had almost said *daring*, tone of mind, united to more goodness of heart and disposition than I ever met with in a human being. Even with this circle, where all is acquirement and accomplishment, it is confessed that his versatility of talent is unrivalled. There is scarcely any art-science he has not cultivated with success, and the resources of his mind and memory are exhaustless. His manners are too English to be popular with the Irish, and though he is reckoned a handsome man, it is not that style of thing which, if I were to choose for beauty, I should select—it is too indicative of goodness ; a little *diablerie* would make me wild in love with him."

Such was the man who eventually became the husband of "The Wild Irish Girl."

The Duke of Richmond, then Lord Lieutenant of Ireland, knighted Dr. Morgan, out of compliment to the Abercorns. He had done nothing to deserve the distinction upon public grounds, and cared very little about the title. But Miss Owenson *did*. She scarcely thought it worth her while to take upon her the cares of matrimony as a mere "Mrs."; so Dr. Morgan submitted to have the Viceregal sword laid across his shoulder.

She delayed and temporised about the marriage so long, that Sir Charles and the Abercorns were very nearly being angry with her. At length they resolved to take her by surprise. So one cold morning in January, as she was sitting by the library fire in her morning wrapper, Lady Abercorn opened the door and said—

"Glorvina, come upstairs directly, and be married; there must be no more trifling."

Glorvina was led by the arm up to Lady Abercorn's dressing-room, where she found chaplain and bridegroom awaiting her. There was no chance of escape, and the "Wild Irish Girl" was married before she had time to think about it.

Lady Morgan did not come to her husband

> A penniless lass, wi' a lang pedigree;

she brought him about five thousand pounds, the

fruit of her savings. This money was settled upon herself, and it was also stipulated in the marriage settlements that she should have the exclusive control over any of her future earnings. For more than a year after their marriage Sir Charles and Lady Morgan resided with the Abercorns; but the independent little lady longed for a home of her own, so she and her husband set up housekeeping in Kildare Street, Dublin. The house was not very large, but it was eminently respectable-looking, and stood facing the old Kildare Street Clubhouse, which was burnt down about fifteen years ago.* Lady Morgan at once took her place in Dublin society, and became the fashion. But before coming to live in Dublin, she experienced the great grief of her later years in the death of her father. He died at the residence of his daughter, Lady Clarke, in Great George Street.

"O'Donnell" made its appearance about two years after Lady Morgan's marriage. It is the best novel she ever wrote, and deals boldly and incisively with many of the Irish questions of the day. The authoress received five hundred and fifty pounds for the copyright. The *Quarterly*

---

* In Lady Morgan's time the house was numbered 35; it has been changed to 39, and is now occupied by Mr. Charles Thorp, solicitor.

launched forth against it a bitter tide of invective and sarcasm, which had the effect of bringing the work all the more prominently before the public. It decided her position as a writer of fiction, and is considered her masterpiece.

She and her husband went to France in 1815, in order to enable her to collect material for a work on that country. Colburn offered her a good price for it. She thoroughly enjoyed the society of the French capital, and her sketches of life, politics, and manners are inimitable, notwithstanding the grave charges of impiety and immorality brought against her by the reviewers. "France" was Lady Morgan's best work, and was so great a pecuniary success that Colburn suggested she should write a similar work on Italy. In the meantime, she had brought out her novel of "Florence Macarthy," in which she revenged herself upon Croker, the *Quarterly* reviewer, by giving a ludicrous sketch of him. It is full of pictures of Dublin society, and if not so romantic, is certainly far more amusing than "O'Donnell."

Colburn offered two thousand pounds for "Italy;" and the lively little lady and her husband set off in search of material. Their progress on the Continent was one series of successes. Judging from her own letters, it might appear that the picture was overdrawn; but Thomas Moore, who was in Rome at the same time, corroborates all she says. When the work appeared, it created an enormous sensation—greater even than the excitement produced by the publication of "France;" for Italian society was even less known than Parisian,· and the habits of the people and the condition of the country were quite unknown to the majority of readers.

Of course, the *Quarterly* abused the book, which it characterised as "a series of offences against good morals, good politics, good sense, and good taste." Further on, the same review says: "We are convinced that this woman is utterly incorrigible; secondly, we hope that her indelicacy, ignorance, vanity, and malignity, are inimitable, and that, therefore, her example is little dangerous."*

Never was there a woman so well abused as Lady Morgan. But she steadily pursued her indomitable course. Byron called her "Italy" "a fearless and excellent work." Lady Morgan usually told the truth about things she saw, and the truth is not always pleasant.

"Salvator Rosa" next appeared, in two volumes, and Colburn gave Lady Morgan five hundred pounds and a velvet dress for the copyright.

---

* *Quarterly Review*, July, 1818.

She was continually fighting with her publisher, and, marvellous to record, generally got the best of it! Colburn made well by her writings, however, and removed his publishing house from his circulating library. He set up at No. 8, New Burlington Street, W., next door to Lady Cork, who, he feared, would be rather angry at his presumption, coming next door to her, shop and all.

Lady Morgan held her mimic court in the Kildare Street house, season after season. All the wit, rank, beauty, and intellect of the Irish metropolis were to be found congregated in her two small drawing-rooms on her assembly nights. She was the centre round which the Liberal party rallied; although, indeed, all creeds and all parties were welcome. She never seemed to care particularly for O'Connell. "That

> First flower of the earth,
> First gem of the sea,

O'Connell," she says, "wants back the days of Brian Borru, himself to be king, with a crown of emerald shamrocks, a train of yellow velvet, and a mantle of Irish tabinet; a sceptre in one hand, and a cross in the other, and the people crying, 'Long live King O'Connell!' This is the object of his views and his ambition. Should he ever be

King of Ireland, he should take Charley Phillips for his prime minister, Tom Moore for chief bard, J. O'Meara for attorney-general, and Counsellor Bethel for his chief justice. O'Connell is not a man of genius; he has a sort of conventional talent applicable to his purpose as it exists in Ireland—a *nisi prius* talent which has won much popularity."*

Lady Morgan and her husband were always popular with the Castle set, and no private dinner-party at the Viceregal Lodge was considered complete without the "Wild Irish Girl." Not a "girl" in any sense of the word at this time, but bravely keeping up the semblance of youth. She was "odd," and she amused people as much by her appearance and the *audacity* of her dress as she fascinated by her ready flow of wit. Fancy a little, slightly deformed woman of between fifty and sixty in a girlish white muslin dress, and a green sash! Yet such was the costume she not infrequently wore. In that most impartial sketch, "The Friends and Foes of Lady Morgan," the chronicler says :—

"Lady Morgan was a frequent guest at the Viceregal drawing-rooms of the Marquis and Marchioness Wellesley. 'Here it was,' wrote one who

---

* "Memoirs," vol. ii. p. 225.

participated in the Castle festivities—'here it was that I saw Lady Morgan for the first time; and as I had long pictured her to my imagination as a sylph-like person, nothing could equal my astonishment when the celebrated authoress, in *propria persona*, stood before me. She certainly formed a strange figure in the midst of that dazzling scene of beauty and splendour. Every female present wore feathers and trains, but Lady Morgan scorned both appendages. Hardly more than four feet high, with a slightly curved spine, uneven shoulders and eyes, Lady Morgan glided about in a close-cropped wig, bound by a fillet or solid band of gold, her face all animation, and with a witty word for everybody. I afterwards saw her in the dress-circle at the theatre. She was cheered enthusiastically. Her dress was different from the former occasion, but not less original. A red Celtic cloak, formed exactly on the plan of Grana Wail's, fastened by a rich gold fibula, or Irish Tara brooch, imparted to her little ladyship a gorgeous and withal a picturesque appearance, which antecedent associations considerably strengthened.'"

Lady Morgan's novel of "The O'Briens and the O'Flahertys" came out in 1827. The subject of it was more canvassed than that of any of her previous works. Catholic Emancipation had not yet been carried, and the country was in a state of ferment. The story dealt with Irish society before and after the Union, and may be referred to as a standard work illustrative of the state of political feeling of the times it purports to represent. Her old enemy, the *Quarterly*, characterised it as "a strange farrago of nonsense, licentiousness, and Jacobinism;" and the *Literary Gazette*, edited by William Jerdan, also attacked it with unexampled rancour. To the accident of the latter attack may be attributed the founding of the *Athenæum*. There was a split in the camp, and the rebels who could not agree to annihilate Lady Morgan set up the new censor, with James Silk Buckingham as the editor. He was followed by Wentworth Dilke, the true friend of the much satirised little authoress. Colburn gave her one thousand three hundred pounds down for the copyright, one hundred pounds on the second edition, and another hundred on the third edition; all things considered, she made a good bargain—and so did her publisher.

"The Book of the Boudoir" succeeded, and was more unfavourably received than any of her previous works. This was probably owing to the personal nature of the contents. It was merely a reprint of her commonplace book, and possesses all her faults of style, in addition to many graces. A second work on "France" followed, and was the cause of a quarrel between Lady Morgan and Colburn. The authoress knew her own value. She wanted to raise her terms, and when her old publisher refused, she left him. Colburn was in a rage, and vowed to be revenged; and the newspapers of the next day announced LADY MORGAN AT HALF PRICE! The advertisement further stated that, in consequence of the great losses Mr. Colburn had sustained by all Lady Morgan's works, he had *declined* the present book on "France," and that copies of all her books might be had at half price. This was more than damaging; it was insulting. The new publishers were in despair, and the matter was brought into Court, where Colburn admitted he had done his best to injure Lady Morgan, but was sorry for it.

Sir Charles was her fellow-labourer at this time in writing for the *New Monthly* and the *Athenæum*. They had their hands full, yet contrived to see as much society as ever. Every foreigner of note, who came to Dublin, went to Lady Morgan's receptions, where she flirted her green fan and fancied herself "The Wild Irish Girl" of thirty years before. She divided the palm for popularity with O'Connell, and was thus immortalised in a local ballad:—

> Och, Dublin city, there is no doubtin',
> Bates every city upon th' say;
> 'Tis there you'd hear O'Connell spoutin',
> And Lady Morgan makin' tay.
> For 'tis th' capital o' th' finest Nation,
> Wid charmin' pisantry on a fruitful sod,
> Fightin' like divils for conciliation,
> An' hatin' each other for th' love o' God.

And what a curiosity was not that drawing-room in Kildare Street! Everything in it had a history which the indefatigable little hostess was not slow to make a fruitful subject of conversation. She was a wonderful woman in the way in which she kept every one in good humour. Her own family adored her; her friends were ever ready to forgive her inconsistencies, and society was ever ready to applaud whatever she said or did.

After Catholic Emancipation was carried, Dublin society was shorn of much of its glory. A new, wealthy, and vulgar element sprang up, and Lady Morgan was too old—although no one dare whisper such a thing!—to try and accommodate herself to a new state of things. So she followed the old society to London. This was in 1838, and the same year her pecuniary circumstances were augmented by a pension of 300*l.* a year, in recognition of her services to Irish literature.

Lady Morgan's mode of life in London was little different to that in Dublin. She went a great deal into society, and received a great deal of society at her house at Albert Gate. All who were distinguished in the world of fashion or of letters visited her, and she was the queen of a little circle. To struggling talent she always stretched forth a helping hand; and her love for her native land was, to the end, one of her distinguishing characteristics. To her credit be it spoken, Lady Morgan was one of the first who strongly advised that every girl, no matter what her rank in life, should be taught some trade or profession, to enable her to earn a livelihood in case of necessity.

In 1840, Lady Morgan gave to the world the first two volumes of what she considered the most important work of her life—viz., "Woman and her Master." She never finished it. The work was to be of a most comprehensive character, but her eyesight failed, and she was compelled to give up the project. It deals with the condition of women in all times; the leading motive is, that in all ages, women, in spite of the systematic depression and subordination in which they have been kept, and in spite of all difficulties, have not only *never* been subordinated, but have, on the contrary, been always the depositories of the vital and leading IDEA of the time; that the spiritual life in women has always been more pure and vigorous than in men; that women have a more subtle and delicate instinct for whatsoever is "pure, lovely, and of good report;" and that, alike among the most degraded savage tribes (those in Australia and New Guinea) as among the Hebrew of old, women were held the oracles, and proved themselves to be of "finer clay" than their so-called "master"—man. Contrary to what might have been expected from the title, there is nothing strong-minded about this book, and the tone of it has nothing in common with the "Woman's Rights" question. Next appeared "The Book Without a Name," the joint production of Sir Charles and Lady Morgan, which was merely a collection of their magazine sketches and articles.

Lady Morgan was perfectly happy in her married life, and the death of her husband in 1843 was a severe trial to her. He was a man singularly beloved, both in public and in private, and, after his death, it was a long time before Lady Morgan was ever able to refer to her loss.

"Oh, my husband! I cannot endure this. I was quite unprepared for this. So ends my life!"

The foregoing is the first entry in her diary after her widowhood. That she sincerely mourned for her faithful friend and husband there can be no doubt, but the natural elasticity of her temperament asserted itself, and after a time she figured in the gay world the same as of yore. However, time soon showed her the fleeting nature of all things earthly, and in 1847 the death of her beloved sister Olivia completely prostrated her. "I cannot weep," she says, "and have none to weep with, for I am alone. All my old friends and new acquaintances have been to my door to offer me their sympathy, but I am beyond the reach, *the reach of solace now*. I almost think this last blow has struck home. So I reel on! The world is my gin or opium; I take it for a few hours per diem—excitement, intoxication, absence! I return to my desolate home, and awaken to all the horrors of sobriety."

We find her still holding her receptions, paying visits and receiving them. Her old, antagonistic Celtic spirit flashed forth in her memorable controversy with Cardinal Wiseman concerning that venerable relic of ancient upholstery so carefully preserved in the Vatican—the Chair of St. Peter. In her work on "Italy" Lady Morgan had said, "that the sacrilegious curiosity of the French broke through all obstacles to their seeing the Chair of St. Peter. They actually removed its superb casket, and discovered the relic. Upon its mouldering and dusty surface were traced carvings, which bore the appearance of letters. The Chair was quickly brought into a better light, the dust and cobwebs removed, and the inscription (for inscription it was) faithfully copied. The writing is in Arabic characters, and is the well-known confession of the Mahometan faith : ' *There is but one God, and Mahomet is his Prophet.*' It is supposed that this Chair had been, among the spoils of the Crusaders, offered to the Church, at a time when a taste for antiquarian lore and the deciphering of inscriptions was not yet in fashion. This story has since been hushed up, the Chair replaced, and none but the unhallowed remember the fact, and none but the audacious repeat it. Yet such there are even in Rome." The controversy excited some discussion, and was one of Lady Morgan's latest literary distractions.

The gradual dropping off of her old friends, one by one, warned Lady Morgan that "The Wild Irish Girl" must before very long pay the debt of Nature. Her eyesight had long since been very precarious, and her health not by any means good. But still she held on. Her spirits and energy were undiminished. She dictated in the morning, and then dressed for the day, received her visitors, and generally had a reception in the evening.

On the 17th of March, 1859—St. Patrick's Day —Lady Morgan gave a musical party. It was one of the gayest she had ever given, and no guest there could have fancied the end was so near. Upon that day she caught a cold from which she never rallied, and died, quietly and calmly, on the 16th of April, 1859. She was in the eighty-third year of her age.

Probably no woman has ever achieved greater social and literary triumphs than has Sydney, Lady Morgan. She was vain and egoistical; but she would have been more than mortal woman had she been otherwise. Flattered, caressed, and looked up to, she was always persuaded she was an oracle, and she enjoyed the position. But with all her vanity, she had an enormous fund of common sense; she never went in debt, and she was persevering and industrious. She used to say herself, that she valued herself much more on her industry than on her genius, because the one "she owed to her organisation, but the other was a virtue of her own rearing."

MARGUERITE, COUNTESS OF BLESSINGTON.

BORN SEPTEMBER 1ST, 1790. DIED JUNE 4TH, 1849.

ONE of the most brilliant women of this century, Marguerite, Countess of Blessington, was the third child and second daughter of an Irish squireen, named Edmund Power, of Knockbritt, near Clonmel, in the County Tipperary. A good-looking Irishman, with a certain amount of dash and swagger about him, Power lived as best he could upon his very small estate, the income from which never exceeded a few hundreds a year. Familiarly known throughout the county as " Beau Power" or " Shiver the Frills," he kept up an appearance of hospitality, which his actual circumstances did not, by any means, warrant. The natural result was continual debt and embarrassment. He was a thoroughly unprincipled man—" a rough, rude specimen of the Irish middle class of sixty years ago; handsome and rollicking, illiterate and pretentious,

fond of rioting and revellings, of field-sports and
garrison society, dissipated abroad and brutal at
home. In '98 he was a magistrate, hunting
rebels, though a Roman Catholic himself; the
end of which hunting was, that he shot one under
suspicious circumstances of undue haste, was tried
for murder, but acquitted. The mother, of the
name of Sheehy, was a plain, uncultivated woman,
without pretension of any sort ; a negation of all
gifts, of whom nothing particular is recorded, but
that she died in Clarendon Street, Dublin, some
twenty years ago."*

Such were the parents of the beautiful Marguerite Power. She had two sisters, who became
respectively Viscountess Canterbury and Countess
de St. Marsault. From the village of Knockbritt
to the summits of the best society in the world
was a long way ; yet the three daughters of the
Irish squireen reached the goal, and each one
adorned her respective position in her own peculiar way.

As a child, Marguerite Power was weakly and
ailing, and gave no promise of the rare and witching beauty for which she was celebrated in after
life. The sensitive, delicate child was regarded

---

* *Vide* Lady Wilde's article, "The Countess of Blessington," in
the *Dublin University Magazine* for March, 1855.

as little likely to grow up to womanhood. The atmosphere of her home was uncongenial to her: her father was a tyrant, and her mother a most commonplace person; so that she was comparatively lonely, and the imaginative little girl lived in a world of her own.

When she was about ten years of age, her father removed with his family, and went to live at Clonmel. It was a garrison town, and the society-loving Irishman soon made many acquaintances amongst the officers quartered there. His three pretty growing-up daughters were no inconsiderable attractions. Marguerite was but fifteen when she became the object of the attentions of a Captain Murray and a Captain Farmer; the latter proposed to her father for her, was accepted by him, and in 1805 they were married.

Marguerite Power disliked the man whom her father, with threats and oaths, desired her to receive as her future husband. He was subject to fits of ungovernable passion, at which times he lost all control over himself. Report said he was insane, and that Power was aware of this when he made his daughter marry him. Certainly his conduct was such as to give colour to the rumour; for he treated his child-wife with unparalleled cruelty and violence. After enduring this treatment for about three months, she left him and returned to her father's house. Here she was so coldly received that she left it again, and went to live with an aunt. She led a wandering desultory life for some years, being occasionally heard of in Dublin, in Hampshire, and lastly, in Manchester Square, London, where she had set up housekeeping in conjunction with her brother Robert.

Permanently separated from her husband, Mrs. Farmer, notwithstanding the troubles she had undergone, had blossomed into a beautiful young woman. Her house in Manchester Square was the resort of the most distinguished men of the day, conspicuous amongst them being Charles John Gardiner, Earl of Blessington. In 1817, Mrs. Farmer was freed from the legal ties which bound her. Her husband was killed in a drunken fit, and the following year she married the Earl of Blessington. His lordship had been previously married, and, at the time of his union with Mrs. Farmer, had one daughter living—Lady Harriet Anne Frances Gardiner, who married first, in 1827, the Count D'Orsay, and secondly, in 1853, the Hon. Charles Spencer Cowper.

Lady Blessington and her husband passed the first years of their married life in London, and their house was the resort of the most distinguished statesmen, poets, and wits of the day. Canning and Castlereagh, Lords Palmerston and

Russell, Erskine, Kemble, and Mathews, Lawrence and Wilkie, all frequented the drawing-rooms of the beautiful Lady Blessington, for at this period she was in the brightest summer of her matchless beauty. "Those who watched and were fascinated by her graces, tried in vain to analyse them, and say in what her witchery consisted. Her dazzlingly clear complexion, dark hair, and rich dark eyebrows and lashes, delicate features, ever radiant with the light of her mirthful nature, small mouth and thin pink lips curling with playful irony, small white hands, tiny feet, and incomparable shape, were the theme of universal admiration, not less than her frank, generous, and cordial manner—Irish in its heartiness, French in its piquancy, and English in its delicacy and refinement; and her rich soft voice, which, alike in laughter and in speech, enlivened its hearers with a sense of new-found happiness. But what most elicited enthusiastic praise was the perfect harmony of her entire appearance in rest and in action. The emotion of the moment was as manifest in her step, her form, her slightest alteration of attitude, as in her countenance. She was young and triumphant, gentle, and of a constitution naturally mirthful; these were her halcyon days: every moment brought with it a fresh joy, and the delight she experienced, manifested in the strangely subtle language of her beauty, was itself the quality with which, beyond all her other charms, she swayed the affections and imaginations of her astonished and almost incredulous admirers." Her ready sympathy won the confidence of all, and this, perhaps, was one cause of the fascination which she exerted over others.

For three years Lord and Lady Blessington lived in London after their marriage; and then set out for a tour on the Continent. Lady Blessington did not wish to leave the brilliant society which they had gathered around them in London, but she yielded in deference to her husband's wishes. During the latter year of their residence in St. James's Square, the Duc de Grammont and his brother-in-law, the young Count D'Orsay, were amongst their most frequent visitors. The latter accompanied Lord and Lady Blessington on their tour to Italy; Miss Mary Ann Power—her ladyship's sister—and the now veteran comedian, Charles Mathews, being also of the party. The latter was a *protégé* of Lord Blessington's, and was an agreeable addition to the suite.

"Charles Mathews," says Dr. Madden, "could hardly then have been twenty years of age. He had been intended for the profession of an architect, and was articled to a person of eminence in London in that profession. Lord Blessington had kindly offered his father to take charge of the young man, and to afford him every facility of pursuing his professional studies in Italy. That offer was accepted, and for upwards of two years young Mathews remained with the Blessingtons on the Continent, and was no slight acquisition to their party. A merrier man, within the limits of becoming mirth, it would be difficult to find. He was an admirable mimic, had a marvellous facility in catching peculiarities of manners, picking up the different dialects of the several parts of Italy he passed through. But with all his comic talents, love of fun and frolic, ludicrous fancies, and overflowing gaiety of heart, he never ceased to be a gentleman, and to act and feel like a man wellbred, well-disposed, and well-principled."

They became acquainted with Byron during their sojourn in Italy, and Lady Blessington has left it upon record that neither in conversation nor in appearance did he answer the expectations she had formed of him. "Were I asked to point out the prominent defect of Byron's manner, I should pronounce it to be a flippancy incompatible with the notion we attach to the author of 'Childe Harold' and 'Manfred,' and a want of self-possession and dignity that ought to characterise a man of birth and genius. Notwithstanding this defect, his manners are very fascinating, more so, perhaps, than if they were dignified; but he is too gay, too flippant for a poet."*

Count D'Orsay travelled with the Blessingtons everywhere, and this "glass of fashion and mould of form" was an universal favourite wherever he went. Extraordinarily gifted, both in mind and in person, he consented to wreck his powers and wealth on the paltry ambition of fashionable notoriety—to give laws to tailors, and furnish designs for new carriages to Long Acre.

In the year 1823, whilst Lord and Lady Blessington were yet at Genoa, news reached them of the death of Lord Mountjoy, his lordship's son and heir by his first marriage. The boy was in his tenth year, and was the only legitimate son of the Earl; who, upon this child's death, made a strange disposal of his property. The chief provisions of Lord Blessington's revised will were, after providing for his wife, that Count Alfred D'Orsay was to hold in trust a large portion of his property, which was to become his upon his marriage with either of the daughters of his lordship. He had only one legitimate daughter, but his natural daughter, Emily Rosalie Hamilton, was treated with equal consideration. It was optional which of the young ladies the Count married. He chose

---

* *Vide* "Idler in Italy," p. 392.

Lady Harriet Frances Gardiner, without having ever seen her, her legitimacy probably turning the balance in her favour with the proud D'Orsays.

They were married on the 1st of December, 1827, Lady Harriet being then fifteen years and four months old. The wedding took place at Rome, and the marriage was an unhappy one. "Taken from school without any knowledge of the world, acquaintance with society, or its usages and forms, wholly inexperienced, transferred to the care of strangers, and naturally indisposed to any exertion that might lead to efforts to conciliate them; she was brought from her own country to a distant land, to wed a man she had never seen, up to the period of her arrival in Italy, where, within a few weeks of her first meeting with that foreign gentleman who had been on terms of intimacy with her father, she was destined to become his bride.

"Lady Harriet was exceedingly girlish-looking, pale, and rather inanimate in expression, silent and reserved. There was no appearance of familiarity with any one around her, no air or look of womanhood, no semblance of satisfaction in her new position, were to be observed in her demeanour or deportment. She seldom or never spoke; she was little noticed; she was looked on as a mere school-girl. I think her feelings were crushed, repressed, and her emotions driven inwards, by the sense of slight and indifference, and by the strangeness and coldness of everything around her; and she became indifferent and strange and cold, and apparently devoid of all vivacity and interest in society, or in the company of any person in it. People were mistaken in her; and she, perhaps, was also mistaken in others. Her father's act had led to all these misconceptions and misconstructions, ending in suspicions, animosities, aversions, and total estrangements."*

Count D'Orsay received about 40,000*l.* fortune with his wife, from whom he parted almost at the church door. They never cared for each other, and soon separated, although living under the same roof and in the same house with the Blessingtons. The marriage was a grave mistake, and nothing to any purpose can be urged in extenuation of it.

The Italian life of Lord and Lady Blessington and their party must, on the whole, have been a pleasant one. Their wealth, station, and intellectual acquirements, made them welcome everywhere; and it is significant that, notwithstanding the unhappy rumours of later years, the friends which Lady Blessington then made continued faithful to her through life.

* "Memoirs of Lady Blessington," vol. i. p. 126.

In 1828 they returned to Paris, on their way home to England. For a year they stayed in the gay French capital, residing at first in the Hôtel de Terasse. After a time they rented the Hôtel Ney, the most magnificent mansion in Paris. Not content with its splendour, Lord Blessington redecorated it in a lavish style, more befitting the income of a prince than that of an Irish landlord. It is impossible to avoid remarking that in doing so his lordship was laying the foundation of the Encumbered Estates Court Jurisdiction in Ireland. Everything was on a scale of sumptuous magnificence; but the crowning effort of the upholsterer's taste was reserved for her ladyship's bedroom and dressing-room. "The whole fitting-up," says Lady Blessington, in one of her letters, "is in exquisite taste; and, as usual, when my most gallant of all gallant husbands that it ever fell to the happy lot of woman to possess, interferes, no expense has been spared. The bed, which is silvered instead of gilt, rests on the backs of two large silver swans, so exquisitely sculptured, that every feather is in alto-relievo, and looks as fleecy as those of the living bird. The recess in which it is placed is lined with white fluted silk, bordered with blue embossed lace; and from the columns that support the frieze of the recess, pale blue silk curtains, lined with white, are hung, which, when drawn, conceal the recess altogether.

"A silvered sofa has been made to fit the side of the room opposite the fireplace, near to which stands a most inviting *bergère*. An *escritoire* occupies one panel, a bookstand the other, and a rich coffer for jewels forms a pendant to a similar one for lace or India shawls. A carpet of uncut pile, of a pale blue, a silver lamp, and a Psyche glass, the ornaments silvered, to correspond with the decorations of the chamber, complete the furniture. The hangings of the dressing-room are of blue silk, covered with lace, and trimmed with rich frills of the same material, as are also the dressing-stands and *chaire longue*; and the carpet and lamp are similar to those of the bed. A toilette-table stands before the window, and small *jardinières* are placed in front of each panel of looking-glass, but so low as not to impede a full view of the person dressing in this beautiful little sanctuary. The *salle du bain* is draped with white muslin, trimmed with lace; and the sofa and the *bergère* are covered with the same. The bath is of marble, inserted in the floor, with which its surface is level. On the ceiling over it is a painting of Flora, scattering flowers with one hand, while from the other is suspended an alabaster lamp, in the form of a lotus."

Their sojourn in Paris was a brilliant one, but it was suddenly brought to a close in May, 1829, by the unexpected death, from apoplexy, of Lord Blessington. He had only returned from London a few days previously, whither he had gone on business connected with the Emancipation Bill. By his death Lady Blessington was reduced to an income of 2000*l.*, in place of 30,000*l.* So the Hôtel Ney was given up, and in 1830 Lady Blessington, accompanied by the Count and Countess D'Orsay, returned to London. Not very long after their return, the Count and Countess were formally separated; and for the sum of 100,000*l.* he consented to give up his claim upon the Blessington estates. The terms were agreed to, and the money paid by instalments. The Countess retired to Paris, and the Count took up his residence with Lady Blessington at Gore House. When she had first come to London, she had rented a house in Seamore Place, and the Count had lived in Curzon Street, almost next door to her.

No sooner had Lady Blessington removed to Gore House, than the world began to talk about her. She was too beautiful, too clever, too fascinating, and too independent to escape from the tongue of calumny. The world gave her Count D'Orsay for a lover, although she was twelve years older than him, the consequence being that the beautiful hostess was the only lady to be seen amongst the brilliant society which frequented Gore House.

Every man of note was to be seen in Lady Blessington's *salons* during the season. She had now seriously turned her thoughts to literature as a means of augmenting her income, and in *The New Monthly* appeared her "Conversations with Lord Byron," which was subsequently published in one volume. It at once established her literary reputation, and novels, tales, verses, reviews, and all kinds of miscellaneous literary matter flowed from her ready pen. They were all of an ephemeral nature, and nothing that Lady Blessington has written has survived the time when she, herself, was the fashion. We find her verses and sketches embalmed in "Annuals," "Keepsakes," "Forget-me-nots," and "Books of Beauty;" for it was during her time that the epidemic of illustrated Annuals broke out in England, and raged with equal flimsiness and platitude for about twenty years.

A titled editress was necessary for the success of these literary speculations, and her ladyship entered the ranks. It was one of her ways of gaining popularity, for it brought her into contact with many eminent literary men. At the same time it involved her in much expense, for she was under the necessity of entertaining the people she asked for contributions. Moreover, it called for much mechanical drudgery—in a word, it made her life miserable.

"The whole system of the Annuals," says Lady Wilde, "was, in fact, a speculation based on personal vanity. Court beauties had their pictures engraved with (as Dickens describes) the traditional background of flower-pots; and then verses were ordered by the editor to suit these portraits. When the mothers of the nobility were exhausted, the annualists turned to the children of the nobility, whose portraits came out with impossible eyes and hair, white frocks, the flower-pot, and a dog. For them verses were in like manner ordered; and, of course, the sale was unprecedented. Thus we find Lady Blessington petitioning a contributor, and really a man of genius, though he had caught the epidemic—Dr. William Beattie—for 'three or four stanzas for the work named "Buds and Blossoms," to contain the portraits of all the children of the nobility—the children for the illustration are the three sons of the Duke of Buccleugh, and an allusion to the family would add interest to the subject.'

"To the same poet—too yielding, perhaps, not to be made the prey of these infantile bores—she writes again with lamentable pertinacity—

"'Will you write me a page of verse for the

portrait of Miss Forrester; the young lady is seated with a little dog on her lap, which she looks at rather pensively; she is fair, with light hair, and is in mourning.'"

At this period Lady Blessington made about 2000*l.* a year by the Annuals. She did not pay contributors, except when a great name was necessary for a bait. Thomas Moore was offered 600*l.* for one hundred and twenty lines for "The Keepsake," but he declined. After a time the public began to tire of this species of literature, and a corresponding falling off in Lady Blessington's income was the result. Moreover, her novels did not sell so well as formerly. Her best works of fiction were "The Confessions of an Elderly Lady" and "The Confessions of an Elderly Gentleman;" they appeared respectively in 1837 and 1838. The *quarrelsome Quarterly*—as it might with justice be called during these few years— ignored them altogether, but the *Edinburgh Review* says :—

"Modern society, which is not very rich in materials for the stage, produces the exact varieties of life most favourable to the genius of the novelist. The comic dramatist requires strong contrasts and marked effects; and the wider the distinctions between ranks and classes, the deeper the divisions that circumstances draw between man and man, the better for the purposes of the stage. The novelist, on the contrary, more subtle, analytic, and refining than the dramatist, inclining rather to delicate fidelity, to minute details, than to bold exaggeration of vehement contrasts, finds scope for his art precisely where society appears most level and uniform; and in proportion to the apparent similarity of the general flock is the skill and beauty with which individualities are discovered and enforced.

"The novels of Lady Blessington are strongly characterised by the social phenomena of the times —they are peculiarly the *Romans de Société*—the characters that move and breathe throughout them are the actual persons of the great world, and the reflections with which they abound belong to the philosophy of one who has well examined the existing manners. In her writing there has been a marked and progressive improvement, as if by the self-study that belongs to application, powers previously unknown to herself had been gradually developed.

"The 'Confessions of an Elderly Lady' and 'Confessions of an Elderly Gentleman' are more popular in their nature than the 'Victims of Society,' and more sparkling in their execution. They contain much shrewd but quiet satire, and much subtlety of observation; while here and there, in the midst of their most lively irony, there are charming touches of reflective morality and unconscious pathos."

But, despite all this praise, Lady Blessington's fame as a writer of fiction was on the wane, and pressing pecuniary matters urged her to cast about in her fertile mind for some other way of supplementing her rapidly decreasing income. Her last novel was called "Country Quarters," and, despairing of finding a publisher, she ran it through a newspaper. The *Daily News* offered her 400*l.* a year for contributing *Exclusive Intelligence, or Gossiping News from High Quarters.* She rated her services at double the sum, and threw up the engagement in six months, for which term the proprietors of the paper paid her 250*l.*

The triteness of the saying that "troubles never come singly" is a good test of its truth; and Lady Blessington bitterly proved the applicability of the proverb. Not only was her income reduced in consequence of the failure of her literary speculations, but her jointure began to be paid very irregularly. It is but another instance of how the extremes of society are connected! Because the fields are lying black around an Irish cabin, the great London world of life and light is thrown into terror and dismay.

"The potato blight fell on Gore House, Irish

rents were not paid, and as soon as the suspicion of inability to meet demands got abroad, demands poured in. There were no means of meeting them. Lady Blessington's expenditure had long been more than double her receipts. Confusion and dismay came gathering darkly over the magnificence."

There is very little doubt but that Count D'Orsay's extravagance was a fruitful source of the monetary embarrassments at Gore House. He had the tastes of a Sybarite; it was a sort of religion with him to have the best of everything in life; and he used to say that when so far reduced that he could not have the best brougham, he would have the best umbrella. Tradesmen gave him unlimited credit, for the mere sake of having the honour of announcing that he employed them. But when a bill for 400*l.* was presented for Count D'Orsay's boots, and the money not being forthcoming, the fact was whispered abroad, and the house was besieged by bailiffs.

Finally, to meet the most urgent ordinary demands, Lady Blessington was obliged to pawn her diamonds. With radiant smiles on her beautiful face, the hostess received her guests night after night, but with terror in her heart lest the next person to walk into the room might be a bailiff. This state of things continued for two years. The Count never went out except on Sundays, and the hall door was never opened without precautions. At length, however, a bailiff effected an entrance in disguise. His valet told the Count, who replied with his customary nonchalance, "Bah! bah!" But Lady Blessington saw that the last stake had been played for and lost, and, going to his studio, implored of him to fly. So, with only a valet and a portmanteau, the brilliant D'Orsay escaped by a back door, and fled to France, leaving behind him debts to the amount of a hundred thousand pounds.

Lady Blessington did not stay long after him in London. Seeing there was no possibility of retrieving her fallen fortunes, she gave up Gore House and its artistic treasures to her creditors, and, accompanied by her two nieces, followed Count D'Orsay to Paris.

Everything was sold by auction. The sale realised over 13,000*l*., out of which a balance of eleven pounds was paid to Lady Blessington after the creditors' demands had been satisfied. Gore House and its contents were on view for some days previous to the sale, and above twenty thousand persons came to gaze upon the wreck. Many of them had been welcomed and feasted in those halls; yet, of all who came to see the show, Thackeray, the caustic satirist, the bitter denouncer of women, was the only one who showed any visible emotion. It was a realistic "Vanity Fair" to the great novelist, and one thinks the better of him for those tears.

Never was there a more complete wreck. Dr. Madden thus describes the sale:—

"There was a large assemblage of people of rank. Every room was thronged; the well-known library saloon in which the *convérsaziones* took place was crowded, but not with guests. The armchair, in which the lady of the mansion was wont to sit, was occupied by a stout, coarse gentleman of the Jewish persuasion, busily engaged in examining a marble hand extended on a book, the fingers of which were modelled from a cast of those of the absent mistress of the establishment. People, as they passed through the room, poked the furniture, pulled about the precious objects of art and ornaments of various kinds that lay on the table, and some made jests and ribald jokes on the scene they witnessed. In another apartment, where the pictures were being sold, portraits by Lawrence, sketches by Landseer and Maclise, innumerable likenesses of Lady Blessington by various artists; several of the Count D'Orsay, representing him driving, riding out on horseback, sporting and at work in his studio; his own collection of portraits of all the frequenters of Gore House, in quick succession, were brought to the hammer. It was the most signal ruin of an establishment of a person. of high rank I had ever witnessed."

Before it had come into the possession of Lady Blessington, Gore House had belonged to William Wilberforce, of anti-slavery memory, who records that in it he "repeated the 119th Psalm in great comfort." *Apropos* of these two occupants, James Smith, one of the authors of "Rejected Addresses," wrote—

> The chains from which he freed the Blacks,
> She rivets on the Whites!

Eventually it passed into the hands of the famous Soyer. "The culinary replaced the literary;" and so, for ever after, Gore House will be associated with social freedom, mental light, and corporeal regeneration.

Lady Blessington was now sixty years of age, —youth, beauty, wealth, and her brilliant, though equivocal, position gone. She came to Paris in April, 1849, and after a little time her old energy appeared to return. She seems to have hoped a good deal from the friendship of Louis Napoleon, who, when a nameless nobody in London, had been a constant visitor at Gore House. But the President, as he was then, did not give his former friend and benefactress a very warm reception. The future Emperor once invited her to dinner, and she went with her nieces and Count D'Orsay, but there his attention began and ended.

"Ah! Ah! Lady Blessington!" said the Prince President shortly after, when his open carriage was locked in a street stoppage with that of her ladyship, "are you going to stop long in Paris?"

With inimitable satire, accompanied by an arch look, she replied,—"I don't know—*are you?*"

Many heard the polished sarcasm, and ere night it was repeated in every salon in the City of Pleasure.

Lady Blessington's jointure now began to be paid more regularly, and she took a house in Paris, which she furnished with something of her former magnificence. She determined again to devote herself to literary labour, and had already planned several works; but insidious disease had been gradually gaining power. On the 3rd of June she removed into her new house, apparently in better health and spirits than she had been for some time. She became ill during the night with an attack of spasms of the heart. Her devoted nieces used every means in their power to relieve her. The first violence of the agony passed away, and turning to her niece she asked, "*Quelle heure est-il?*" They were the last words she ever spoke; and so quietly did she pass away, that those around her did not know the moment when for her Time was no more.

Count D'Orsay's grief at her death was excessive. "Much as she was to us," writes her niece, "we cannot but feel that to him she was all—the centre of his existence, round which his recollections, thoughts, hopes, and plans turned." He designed her monument at St. Germain. It is a pyramid of granite, standing on a square platform, on a level with the surrounding ground, but divided from it by a deep fosse, whose sloping sides are covered with green turf and Irish ivy, transplanted from the garden of the house where she was born. Within are two stone sarcophagi. One contains the coffin of Marguerite, Countess of Blessington: the other that of Count D'Orsay, who survived his beloved companion but three years.

Two epitaphs were written upon her—one by Barry Cornwall, the other, in Latin, by Walter Savage Landor. Both bear ample testimony to her gentleness, genius, and generosity. The latter was proverbial; and for years she supported a number of needy Irish relatives, besides being ready at all times with both money and sympathy whenever she heard a tale of distress.

Lady Blessington was born for society, and her writings were for the society of the day. Graceful and sparkling, they enjoyed a butterfly popularity so long as their writer was the fashion. Far more interesting than her novels are her "Conversations with Lord Byron" and her "Idler in Italy;" for she had wonderful powers of observation, and the inestimable faculty of saying a great deal in a few words. Her correspondence was enormous, Walter Savage Landor being one of her constant correspondents—indeed, it includes every name of note of the day. Her own letters are charming—perhaps a little too complimentary sometimes, but invariably genial and kind. She always had a pleasant word to say, and she said it well and gracefully. What she lacked was a power of deep mental grasp; there was nothing intense, nothing deeply in earnest about her. She lived on passionately from day to day, charmed with all that was pleasant, and charming every one.

Mr. S. C. Hall, in his pleasant "Book of Memories," gives the following account of her:—

"It was in the year 1832 I first knew Lady Blessington. I was then editor of the *New Monthly Magazine*, and I had called upon her (in Seamore Place) in consequence of her having expressed a wish to write for that journal. She had then done but little with her pen, and that little not calculated to make a sensation. The subjects she suggested were not tempting; but she fell into discourse of Lord Byron, telling me some striking anecdotes concerning him. It was obvious to say what I did say—'If you desire to write for the *New Monthly*, why not put on paper what you have been saying in words?' Out of that thought grew the 'Conversations with Lord Byron, by Lady Blessington,' which obtained large popularity, and led to her becoming an author by profession.

"She may be considered and described as then in 'her prime,' although past forty. It is only English, and, perhaps more so, Irishwomen, at that period of life who are even more lovely in age than in youth. She was inclined to *embonpoint*, her hair abundant, and of a lightish brown, but she always wore caps fastened under the chin; her complexion fair and healthily tinged, deriving no aid from art. She was too stout to be graceful, but she had a natural grace that regulated all her movements. There was nothing artificial in aught she said or did; nothing hurried or self-distrustful about her; she seemed perfectly conscious of power, but without the slightest assumption or pretence. It was easy to believe in her fascinating influence over all with whom she came in contact; but it was as little difficult to feel assured that such influence would be exercised with generosity, consideration, and sympathy. No one more carefully studied how to grow old gracefully than did Lady Blessington; no one knew better that the charms of youth are not the attractions of age. She was ever admirably dressed, but affected none of the adornments that become deformities when out of harmony with Time."

ELIZA RYVES.

Died 1797.

BEYOND the mere fact that she was an Irishwoman who had come to London hoping to earn a living by writing, we know nothing more of the private life of Eliza Ryves. D'Israeli says she was descended from an Irish family of distinction, and as there was, about the beginning of the eighteenth century, a Jerome Ryves, D.D., Dean of St. Patrick's Cathedral, Dublin, it is not improbable but that she was a member of this family.

In her earlier days she had possessed considerable property, but was deprived of it through the chicanery of the law. Being thus left destitute, she looked to her pen as a source of existence.

Her first literary effort was a comic opera, called "The Prude," which she wrote in 1777. Failing in her endeavours to have it acted, she published it amongst a collection of her poems. The dialogue of this piece is chaste, animated, and original; and it is very likely that the high tone which pervades it was the cause of its failure in an age when a certain amount of coarseness was necessary to make a comic piece take the taste of the audience. The Prude of the piece is a pretended one, being none other than an intriguing old woman, aunt to the heroine of the drama. She is represented as concerting with a friar, Dominick Doubleface, to force her niece into a nunnery, and to trick her brother out of his property. These schemes are frustrated by means of a nobleman in disguise, a lover of the lady, who in the end is united to her. The period of the action of this performance is in the reign of Queen Mary. The incidents are rapid, and the treatment original.

Notwithstanding this failure, Miss Ryves again essayed dramatic literature. She tried comedy this time, and produced "The Debt of Honour," which was never printed. She sent it to a manager—probably Harris of Covent Garden—who, after keeping it for some years, returned it. He did his best, however, to make reparation for the delay, for, hearing the authoress was in pecuniary distress, he forwarded to her, along with her manuscript, a bank-note for one hundred pounds.

Finding dramatic writing did not pay her, Miss Ryves turned her attention to what was then called "elegant literature." She wrote verses for the few periodicals of the day. They were written in the Chloe and Strephon style then fashionable; but when the authoress found she was only repaid by a return copy of verses in the next number, she abandoned this unfruitful field. Her verses are much above the average of the Della Cruscan school, and, like everything else she has written, seem more like the productions of a man than those of a woman. Out of many we select the following:—

ODE TO SENSIBILITY.

The sordid wretch who ne'er has known,
To feel for miseries not his own;
Whose lazy pulse serenely beats,
While injured worth her wrongs repeats;
Dead to each sense of joy or pain,
A useless link in Nature's chain,
May boast the calm which I disdain.

Give me a generous soul that glows
With others' transports, others' woes,
Whose noble nature scorns to bend,
Though Fate her iron scourge extend;
But bravely bears the galling yoke,
And smiles superior to the stroke,
With spirit free and mind unbroke.

Yet, by compassion touched, not fear,
Sheds the soft sympathising tear,
In tribute to Affliction's claim
Or envied Merit's wounded fame.
Let Stoics scoff, I'd rather be
Thus curst with Sensibility,
Than share their boasted Apathy.

Miss Ryves's perseverance was enormous. When the drama and poetry failed to procure her even the commonest necessaries of life, she was advised to try translations from modern authors. Although an excellent classical scholar, she was quite unacquainted with any modern continental language. To remedy this defect she took an obscure lodging at Islington, and lived there in complete solitude until she had produced an excellent version of Rousseau's "Social Compact," Raynal's "Letter to the National Assembly," and finally translated De la Croix's "Review of the Constitutions of the Principal States of Europe." To these translations she appended erudite and valuable notes. From a pecuniary point of view these efforts were not successful, and she returned to London broken in health and bitterly disappointed.

"Yet," says D'Israeli the elder, "even at a moment so unfavourable, her ardent spirit engaged in a translation of Froissart. At the British Museum I have seen her conning over the magnificent and voluminous MS. of the old chronicler, and by its side Lord Berners' version, printed in the reign of Henry VIII. It was evident that his lordship was employed as a spy upon Froissart, to inform her of what was going forward in the French camp; and she soon perceived, for her taste was delicate, that it required an ancient lord and knight, with all his antiquity of phrase, to break a lance with the still more ancient chivalric

Frenchman. The familiar elegance of modern style failed to preserve the picturesque touches and the naïve graces of the chronicler, who wrote as the mailed knight combated—roughly or gracefully, as suited the tilt or the field. She vailed to Lord Berners; while she felt it was here necessary to understand old French, and then to write in old English."

Again were her labours almost profitless. She now turned her thoughts to novel writing, and "The Hermit of Snowdon" was published in about 1794. It possessed much merit; it is full of indescribable pathos, and in it the authoress is supposed to have reproduced her own unfortunate and unsuccessful literary career. In common with everything written by Miss Ryves, it bears the impress of having emanated from the mind of a refined and educated gentlewoman.

She was a woman of vast reading and extraordinary attainments. When Dodsley, the founder of the *Annual Register*, gave up the management of it, Miss Ryves was engaged to conduct the historical and political department. This she did creditably for some years, and was very badly paid for her work. Some conception of the dignity and magnitude of the situation may be formed, when we record that Edmund Burke did not disdain to fill the same post.

So little profitable were all these varied labours, that Miss Ryves could not, at length, make her "daily bread." Her contemporaries say of her, that she was modest and unassuming; and a writer in the *Gentleman's Magazine* for July, 1797, bears the following testimony to her amiable character :—

"A woman more benevolent than this God never created. When her affairs were in a most '*poetical posture*' (as indeed they often were, for she managed them but inconsiderately), and she lodged in an obscure part of the City, she would spend her last shillings, herself unprovided with a dinner, in the purchase of a joint of meat for a starving family that occupied the room above her."

Eliza Ryves was a woman of learning and genius, and an unsuccessful authoress. Her literary work compares favourably with the masculine writing of the day; yet, because she was a sensitive, unpractical woman, her labours were either stolen or paid for with such a pittance, that it did not suffice to keep body and soul together. She died of absolute want, in a miserable lodging in Store Street, London, on April 29th, 1797.

Such was Eliza Ryves. Not beautiful nor interesting in her person, but with an almost masculine grasp of mind, yet susceptible of all the delicacy of feminine softness, and a virtuous woman amidst all her despair. Genius allied with success has hitherto been our theme. Because of her misfortunes it did not seem just that the name of Eliza Ryves should be omitted from this roll of talented Irishwomen; therefore, we have endeavoured to glean these brief details of her career, which serves further to endorse the assertion that the world will not believe in genius unless it be allied with success.

HELEN SELINA, COUNTESS OF GIFFORD.

BORN 1807. DIED 1867.

BETTER known by her name of Lady Dufferin, the Countess of Gifford was the eldest daughter of Thomas Sheridan, and grand-daughter of the famous Richard Brinsley Sheridan. This family has been almost unique in the brilliancy and attractiveness of its members, from the witty dramatist down to his three grand-daughters: "The beautiful sisters," Lady Dufferin, the Hon. Mrs. Norton, and the Duchess of Somerset.

Helen Selina Sheridan—who afterwards became successively Lady Dufferin and Countess of Gifford—was born in 1807. Whilst she and her sisters were yet children, their father died at the Cape of Good Hope, whither he had gone in the hope of renovating his failing health; and henceforth their mother devoted herself to their education. They lived at Hampton Court, and here the genius of the two gifted elder sisters first found vent in poetry. They produced, jointly, the "Dandie's Rout," in which the foppery of the day was quizzed by both pen and pencil.

In 1825, Helen Selina Sheridan married Captain the Honourable Price Blackwood, who subsequently became Lord Dufferin and Clandeboye; and by whom she had a son, the present Lord Dufferin. Her husband died in 1841, not very long after he had succeeded to the title; and in October, 1862, Lady Dufferin married, secondly, the late Earl of Gifford, eldest son of the Marquis of Tweeddale, who died in the December of the same year.

As Lady Dufferin she played no unimportant part in the brilliant society her distinguished position entitled her to, and of which her wit and genius made her so great an ornament. Less strikingly beautiful than her more popularly known sister, Mrs. Norton, the Countess of Gifford was remarkable for sweetness of voice, and a rare fascination of manner. This sweetness is observable in her songs and ballads, which are amongst the best in the English language. Wherever that language is spoken, the beautiful and pathetic ballad of "The Irish Emigrant" is known; and had this gifted daughter, of a gifted race, never written another line, these beautiful verses would have been enough to endear her name for ever to the hearts of her country people. As they cannot be too widely known we subjoin them in their entirety :—

THE LAMENT OF THE IRISH EMIGRANT.

I'm sittin' on the stile, Mary,
   Where we sat side by side,
On a bright May mornin', long ago,
   When first you were my bride;
The corn was springin' fresh and green,
   And the lark sang loud and high—
And the red was on your lip, Mary,
   And the love-light in your eye.

The *place* is little changed, Mary,
   The day is bright as then,
The lark's loud song is in my ear,
   And the corn is green again;
But I miss the soft clasp of your hand,
   And your breath, warm on my cheek,
And I still keep list'nin' for the words
   You never more will speak.

'Tis but a step down yonder lane,
   And the little church stands near—
The church where we were wed, Mary,
   I see the spire from here.
But the graveyard lies between, Mary,
   And my step might break your rest—
For I've laid you, darling! down to sleep,
   With your baby on your breast.

I'm very lonely now, Mary,
   For the poor make no new friends;
But, oh! they love the better still,
   The few our Father sends!
And you were all *I* had, Mary,
   My blessin' and my pride!
There's nothin' left to care for now,
   Since my poor Mary died.

Yours was the good, brave heart, Mary,
  That still kept hoping on,
When the trust in God had left my soul,
  And my arm's young strength was gone;
There was comfort even on *your* lip,
  And the kind look on your brow—
I bless you, Mary, for that same,
  Though you cannot hear me now.

I thank you for the patient smile
  When your heart was fit to break,
When the hunger pain was gnawin' there
  And you hid it for *my* sake;
I bless you for the pleasant word,
  When your heart was sad and sore—
Oh! I'm thankful you are gone, Mary,
  Where grief can't reach you more!

I'm biddin' you a long farewell,
  My Mary—kind and true!
But I'll not forget *you*, darling,
  In the land I'm goin' to:
They say there's bread and work for all,
  And the sun shines always there—
But I'll not forget old Ireland,
  Were it fifty times as fair!

And often in those grand old woods
  I'll sit and shut my eyes,
And my heart will travel back again
  To the place where Mary lies;
And I'll think I see the little stile
  Where we sat side by side,
And the springin' corn, and the bright May morn,
  When first you were my bride.

The Countess of Gifford was thoroughly Irish in her style of ballad writing. She has happily blended the humorous with the pathetic, and not one of her ballads more happily combines these attributes than does the following :—

TERENCE'S FAREWELL.

So, my Kathleen, you're goin' to lave me, all alone by meself in this place,
But I'm sure that you'll never desave me, oh no! if there's truth in that face!
Tho' England's a beautiful counthry, full of illigant boys, oh! what then?
You wouldn't forget your poor Terence, you'll come back to poor Ireland agen?

Och! them English, desavers by nature! tho' maybe you'd think them sincere,
They'll say you're a sweet, charmin' creature, but don't you believe them, me dear!
No! Kathleen agra! don't be mindin' the flattherin' speeches they make,
Just tell them a poor boy in Ireland, is brakin' his heart for yer sake.

It's a folly to keep you from goin'—tho' faith it's a mighty hard case,
For Kathleen, you know, there's no knowin' when next I may see your sweet face!—
And when ye come back to me, Kathleen, none the betther will I be off then,
You'll be spakin' sich beautiful English! sure I wont know me Kathleen agen.

Eh! now! where's the need of this hurry! don't flusther me so in this way!
I've forgot 'tween the grief and the flurry, every word I was manin' to say:
Now, just wait a minute, I bid ye, can I talk if yeh bother me so!
Och! Kathleen, my blessin' go wid yeh, every inch of the way that ye go!

But there is certainly more pathos, as there is a more decidedly Hibernian ring, in—

THE BAY OF DUBLIN.

Oh! Bay of Dublin! my heart you're troublin',
Your beauty haunts me like a fever dream,
Like frozen fountains that the sun sets bubblin',
My heart's blood warms when I but hear your name,
And never till this life-pulse ceases,
My earliest, latest thought you'll cease to be,
There's no one here knows how fair that place is,
And no one cares how dear it is to me.

Sweet Wicklow mountains! the sunlight sleepin'
On your sweet banks is a picture rare;
You crowd around me, like young girls peepin',
And puzzlin' me to say which is most fair,
As tho' you'd see your own sweet faces
Reflected in that smooth and silver sea;
Oh! my blessin' on those lovely places—
Tho' no one cares how dear they are to me!

How often when at work I'm sittin',
And musing sadly on the days of yore,
I think I see my Katie knittin',
And the childher playin' round the cabin door.
I think I see the neighbours' faces,
All gathered round, their long-lost friend to see;
Oh! tho' no one here knows how fair that place is,
Heav'n knows how dear my poor home was to me!

The two latter ballads are not as well known as they deserve to be. "Katie's Letter," another of the Countess of Gifford's songs, divides the palm for popularity with "The Irish Emigrant." Mrs. Thomas Sheridan, her mother, wrote a novel upon a Scottish subject, called "Carwell;" and in it we find a ballad written by the Countess of

Gifford. It is in Scottish dialect, and is an excellent imitation of one of the old Border ballads.

It is by her songs and few poetical pieces that this one of the beautiful Sheridan sisters is chiefly known, although she has not unsuccessfully turned her attention to other departments of literature. Her "Lispings from Low Latitudes, being an Account of the Travels of the Hon. Selina Gushington," is full of inimitable humour. She was also a frequent contributor to the various "Annuals" which were popular in her earlier literary days.

Save the few ballads we have mentioned, the Countess of Gifford's literary productions have all been of an ephemeral character; but these ballads, and especially "The Irish Emigrant," will ever hold a high position amongst the songs of our land.

During the latter years of her life, the Countess of Gifford suffered much, bearing her great physical pain with her customary sweetness and patience. She died June 13th, 1867, universally beloved and regretted.

LADY STIRLING-MAXWELL.
(HONOURABLE Mrs. NORTON.)

BORN 1808. DIED 1877.

HE brilliancy and attractiveness of the Sheridans has already been commented upon; but of the whole literary portion of the race—commencing with and excepting the witty Richard Brinsley—not one has been so distinguished as Caroline Elizabeth Sarah, the second daughter of Thomas Sheridan, and the granddaughter of the great dramatist.

She was brought up, like her sisters, Lady Dufferin and the Duchess of Somerset,* in comparative retirement at Hampton Court. Their mother, who was the daughter of Colonel and Lady Elizabeth Callander,† was a wise and good woman, and carefully educated her three beautiful daughters. The eldest made a happy marriage; the youngest, one equally happy and brilliant;

---

* At the Eglinton Tournament the Duchess of Somerset was universally elected Queen of Beauty.

† "The last week's obituary records the death of Mrs. Thomas Sheridan, the mother of a family remarkable for beauty and talent,

and the second sister, and the subject of this memoir, became the wife of a man who ill-treated her and held her fair fame up to public scorn.

When Caroline Elizabeth Sarah Sheridan was about sixteen, she attracted the attention of the Hon. George Chapple Norton, brother of Lord Grantley. He proposed to her mother for her, who refused the offer on the plea of her daughter's

and not less in her own person distinguished by both. She died at the house of Lady Dufferin, 39, Grosvenor Place, and was the daughter of Colonel Callandar, of Craigforth and Ardkinlas, and Lady Elizabeth Callandar. Mrs. Sheridan was the author of 'Carwell,' a very striking story, illustrating the inequalities of punishment in the laws against forgery. We remember not only the graceful style of many scenes in that book, but the truth and passion which affected us in others. In a later novel ('Aims and Ends') the same feminine and truthful spirit showed itself in lighter scenes of social life, observing keenly and satirising kindly. Mrs. Sheridan wrote always with ease, unaffectedness, and goodbreeding, her books everywhere giving evidence of the place she might have taken in society if she had not rather desired to refrain from mingling with it, and keep herself comparatively unknown. After her husband's early death she had devoted herself in retirement to the education of her orphan children; when she reappeared in society it seemed to be solely for the sake of her daughters, on whose marriages she again withdrew from it; and to none of her writings did she ever attach her name. Into the private sphere where her virtues freely displayed themselves, and her patient yet energetic life was spent, it is not permitted us to enter; but we could not pass without this brief record what we know to have been a life as much marked by earnestness, energy, and self-sacrifice, as by those qualities of wit and genius which are for ever associated with the name of Sheridan. Three daughters survive her, and one son—Lady Dufferin, the Hon. Mrs. Norton, Lady Seymour, and Mr. Brinsley Sheridan, the Member for Shaftesbury."
—*The Critic*, July 1st, 1851.

youth. Three years later he again proposed, and in her nineteenth year Miss Caroline Sheridan became the Hon. Mrs. Norton, the name by which she is best known in literature. In the meantime, however, she had become acquainted with and deeply attached to a gentleman, whose early death alone hindered their union.

Her marriage was not a happy one; and she and her husband were permanently separated in 1840. The world is quite aware of the slanders to which this unhappy woman was exposed, and also knows that she was triumphantly acquitted of the base charges preferred against her. Her unsullied reputation was established; and her memory deserves to be held in veneration and admiration for the courageous manner in which she overcame the malignity of unmerited persecution, pursued and persevered in for interested and sordid motives.

Never was there a woman whose actions were more wantonly and cruelly misrepresented than those of Lady Stirling-Maxwell when Mrs. Norton. She was married to a man whose barbarity and vindictiveness of disposition bordered on insanity; who used physical violence to her; whom she supported by her literary labours; and who squandered her earnings upon his own pleasures. He took her children from her and gave them into the custody of a woman with whom he was intimate. Finally he dragged her great name through the mire, and, in a public common police-court, charged her with the grossest crimes.

"Mr. Norton," says a recent writer in the *Athenæum,* " was a younger son, with a small fortune, a barrister without capacity or business, and a sensualist who was not particular how his enjoyments were paid for. He coaxed his wife into asking the Home Secretary to make him a police magistrate ; and he bullied her into earning more than his salary by her pen. Writing against time in periodicals of all kinds, from week to week, and month to month, without leisure for study or revision, it could not be expected that her compositions should display the highest degree of excellence. But from 1830 to 1836 her name was up, and half the publishers of London were competing for fragments, sketches, tales, verses, or anything else she chose to give them. In one year she reminded her ungrateful husband that she had made 1400*l.* in this way ; and as she was then in the zenith of female loveliness, she was universally sought after in society, and became the centre of a circle to which every one of wit or celebrity longed to be admitted. The once gay and still fascinating Melbourne came with the rest, and, having been her father's contemporary and friend, soon grew familiar. Mr. Norton tried hard to turn his acquaintance to account, alternately begging for a more lucrative office or a loan of money. The Minister was disgusted, and, with Leycester Stanhope and Edward Ellice, tried to make him treat his wife more worthily."

The world knows what was the result of all this. Mr. Norton finally sought 10,000*l.* damages from Lord Melbourne, as compensation for alleged familiarity with his wife. The trial was the great event of 1836, and the jury, after conferring together for a few seconds, acquitted both Mrs. Norton and Lord Melbourne of the charges against them. Previous to the trial, her husband had so worked upon her feelings with apparently remorseful letters, that she had returned to him. In her eloquent tract entitled " English Laws for Women in the Nineteenth Century," she shows that this was part of a deeply-laid plot:—" After the trial was over, I consulted whether a divorce, 'by reason of cruelty,' might not be pleaded for me; and I laid before my lawyers the many instances of violence, injustice, and ill-usage, of which the trial was but the crowning example. I was then told that no divorce *I* could obtain would break my marriage; that I could not plead cruelty *which I had forgiven;* that by returning to Mr. Norton I had *condoned* all I complained of."

Her lot was certainly a hard one; and we shall

pass over these unhappy episodes as quickly as possible. Her husband continued to annoy her: reduced her annual allowance, and again publicly assailed her character. One more extract from her own eloquent appeal to the English public, will best tell her tale :—

"My husband being desirous to raise money settled on me and my sons, to employ on his separate estate, and requiring my consent in writing before that could be done, gave me in exchange for such consent a written contract drawn up by a lawyer, and signed by that lawyer and himself. When he had obtained and employed the money he was desirous to raise, like Mr. Patton, of Virginia, he resolved to '*rescind the contract.*'* When I, like the slave Norris, en-

---

* The *Cincinnati Gazette* for November, 1853, mentions a case tried in the Covington Circuit Court, and "by the report it appears that a slave named Sam Norris, belonging to a Mr. J. N. Patton, of Virginia, had been permitted to work in Covington, on condition of paying each year a certain sum to his master, which sum was accordingly paid; that two years ago Mr. Patton proposed that the slave should purchase his freedom by the payment of a certain additional sum, which sum was nearly paid up, when Mr. Patton changed his mind, rescinded the contract, and claimed Sam Norris as his slave. The case was argued with much ability, but at the close of the argument the judge decided for Mr. Patton against Sam Norris, on this principle, that, by the law of Kentucky, '*a slave cannot make a contract, nor can he have moneys of his own.*' The contract, therefore, was null and void; and the money, though received and expended by the master, could not be held *legally* to have been paid." It is to this case that reference is made.

deavoured to struggle against this gross breach of faith, I was informed that by the law of England, '*a married woman could not make a contract or have moneys of her own.*' When I complained of it, I was punished by a flood of libellous accusations, published in all the English newspapers; libels for which, though *proved* falsehoods, I could obtain no redress, because they were published by my husband. The circumstance that Mr. Norton, like Mr. Patton, had obtained all the advantage he sought when he went through the formality and pretence of making a contract with me, made no difference; and as to money, even that which I earned by literature was subject to the claim of my husband, as the manual labour of the slave was subject to the claim of his master—because a married woman is, by the code of England (as Sam Norris by the code of Kentucky), non-existent in law. It is fit that I should add, in behalf of English hearts and English love of justice, that when I stood, with that vain contract in my hand, in the Westminster County Court (I, an intelligent, educated woman, granddaughter of a man sufficiently distinguished to have obtained sepulture in Westminster Abbey, hard by), and when the law was shown to be for me, what it is for the slave in Kentucky, there was, in the court-room of the Westminster County Court, as there was in the court-room of the Covington Circuit Court, evidence of strong sympathy. My case, which opened up a history of wrong, treachery, libel and injustice, endured for years without redress, was evidently considered like that of Norris, to be '.one of great hardship and cruelty;' and the concluding words with which Mr. Norton vehemently attempted to address the Court were drowned in the groans and hooting of an excited crowd. But sympathy could do no more for me than for Mr. Patton's slave. It could not force open for me the iron gates of the LAW which barred out justice. It could not prevent libel and torment and fraud; the ripping up of old wounds, or the infliction of new."

At intervals Lady Stirling-Maxwell renewed the controversy; pathos and sarcasm being skilfully combined by her brilliant pen. At length it ceased, and it is gratifying to know that this beautiful and bitterly-wronged woman, in her latter years, met with the affectionate appreciation which had been denied to her in the bloom of her youth and beauty.

Lady Stirling-Maxwell early commenced her career as a writer, when—as has been stated in the previous notice of Lady Dufferin—she was one of the authors of "The Dandie's Rout," being then but thirteen years of age. Then followed, when she was about seventeen, "The Sorrows of Rosalie," written with a depth of power and a warmth of colouring that drew extravagant praise from James Hogg. Lady Stirling-Maxwell, even in her more matured literary career, never produced anything fuller of the blended fire and pathos with which all her poetry is characterised, than this her first important poem. "The Undying One" followed shortly after, in 1830, and was well received. It was a version of "The Wandering Jew," and the poetess treated the subject in an entirely new and original manner. "If one or two poems," says the reviewer of the *New Monthly Magazine*, "of equal grace and originality with this were produced, we think that it would go far to recover the public from the apathy into which it has fallen with regard to poetry. In the conception of the plot, and in general treatment, the metrical romance before us is an honour to the modern literature of the country, and is the more interesting as being the work of a woman."

In all her writings, whether in prose or in verse, Lady Stirling-Maxwell eloquently pleaded for the poor and for the oppressed. Perhaps a fellow-feeling with the latter class urged her to do so Whatever was weak and helpless and in the right, claimed her ready sympathy. In her "Voice from the Factories," published in 1836, and her letters to the *Times*, in 1841, and in the stirring eloquence of immortal verse at various times and seasons, she had pleaded on behalf of the poor and the desolate, the criminal and the outcast, the miserable and the forsaken.

"The Child of the Islands" is an impassioned, eloquent poem upon the condition of the poor in England. The subject was not an easy one to treat in the manner proposed, and carried out by Lady Stirling-Maxwell. All previous writers had presented an ideal picture, and had recommended ideal modes of redress; but in this grand poem we have a picture of the social condition of the English poor told with pathos, fervour, and *truth*, hitherto unattempted. "The Child of the Islands" is the then baby Prince of Wales, to whom the poem is dedicated; and was written with the ambition of eventually impressing the future "Ruler of the Islands" with a due sense of the wants, trials, and temptations of his humbler fellow-creatures.

In the *Quarterly* for June, 1845, appeared a masterly review of this poem from the pen of J. G. Lockhart. He thinks Lady Stirling-Maxwell exaggerated the condition of the poor, and considers its poetical power, and not its object, is its chief claim to consideration. This poem is divided into four sections, called respectively

"Spring," "Summer," "Autumn," "Winter," and closes with the couplet :—

> BROTHERS! be gentle to this one appeal,
> WANT is the only woe God gives you power to heal!

One extract from this exquisite poem we cannot forbear giving. It is from "Summer"—

> Wild Nomades of our civilised calm land!
> Whose Eastern origin is still betrayed
> By the swart beauty of the slender hand,—
> Eyes flashing forth from over-arching shade,—
> And supple limbs, for active movement made;
> How oft, beguiled by you, the maiden'looks
> For love her fancy ne'er before portrayed,
> And, slighting village swains and shepherd-crooks,
> Dreams of proud youths, dark spells, and wondrous magic books!
>
> Lo! in the confines of a dungeon cell,
> (Sore weary of its silence and its gloom!)
> One of this race: who yet deserveth well
> The close imprisonment which is her doom:
> Lawless she was, ere infancy's first bloom
> Left the round outline of her sunny cheek;
> Vagrant, and prowling Thief;—no chance, no room
> To bring that wild heart to obedience meek;
> Therefore th' avenging law its punishment must wreak.
>
> She lies, crouched up upon her pallet bed,
> Her slight limbs starting in unquiet sleep;
> And oft she turns her feverish, restless head,
> Mourns, frets, and murmurs, or begins to weep:
> Anon, a calmer hour of slumber deep
> Sinks on her lids, some happier thought hath come;
> Some jubilee unknown she thinks to keep,
> With liberated steps, that wander home
> Once more with gipsy tribes a gipsy life to roam.

But no, her pale lips quiver as they moan :
What whisper they ? A name, and nothing more ;
But with such passionate tenderness of tone,
　　As shows how much those lips that name adore.
She dreams of one who shall her loss deplore
With the unbridled anguish of despair !
Whose forest-wanderings by her side are o'er,
But to whose heart one braid of her black hair
Were worth the world's best throne, and all its treasures rare.

The shadow of his eyes is on her soul—
　　His passionate eyes, that held her in such love !
Which love she answered, scorning all control
　　Of reasoning thoughts, which tranquil bosoms move.
No lengthened courtship it was his to prove,
　　(Gleaning capricious smiles by fits and starts)
Nor feared her simple faith lest he should rove :
Rapid and subtle as the flame that darts
To meet its fellow flame, shot passion through their hearts.

And though no holy priest that union blessed,
　　By gipsy laws and customs made his bride ;
The love her looks avowed, in words confessed,
　　She shared his tent, she wandered by his side,
　　His glance her morning star, his will her guide.
Animal beauty and intelligence
　　Were her sole gifts,—his heart they satisfied,—
Himself could claim no higher, better sense,
So loved her with a love, wild, passionate, intense !

And oft, where flowers lay spangled round about,
　　And to the dying twilight incense shed,
They sat to watch heaven's glittering stars come out,
　　Her cheek down-leaning on his cherished head—
　　That head upon her heart's soft pillow laid
In fulness of content ; and such deep spell
　　Of loving silence, that the word first said
With startling sweetness on their senses fell,
Like silver coins dropped down a many-fathomed well

Look! her brows darken with a sudden frown—
She dreams of Rescue by his angry aid—
She dreams he strikes the Law's vile minions down,
And bears her swiftly to the wild-wood shade!
There, where their bower of bliss at first was made,
Safe in his sheltering arms once more she sleeps:
Ah, happy dream! She wakes; amazed, afraid,
Like a young panther from her couch she leaps,
Gazes bewildered round, then madly shrieks and weeps!

For, far above her head, the prison-bars
Mock her with narrow sections of that sky
She knew so wide, and blue, and full of stars,
When gazing upward through the branches high
Of the free forest! Is she, then, to die?
Where is he—where—the strong-armed and the brave,
Who in that vision answered her wild cry?
Where is he—where—the lover who could save
And snatch her from her fate—an ignominious grave?

Oh, pity her, all sinful though she be,
While thus the transient dreams of freedom rise,
Contrasted with her waking destiny!
Scorn is for devils; soft compassion lies
In angel-hearts, and beams from angel-eyes.
Pity her! Never more, with wild embrace,
Those flexile arms shall clasp him ere she dies;
Never the fierce sad beauty of her face
Be lit with gentler hope, or love's triumphant grace!

Lonely she perishes; like some wild bird
That strains its wing against opposing wires;
Her heart's tumultuous panting may be heard,
While to the thought of rescue she aspires;
Then, of its own deep strength, it faints and tires:
The frenzy of her mood begins to cease;
Her varying pulse with fluttering stroke expires,
And the sick weariness that is not peace
Creeps slowly through her blood, and promises release.

Alas, dark shadows, press not on her so!
Stand off, and let her hear the linnet sing!
Crumble, ye walls, that sunshine may come through
Each crevice of your ruins! Rise, clear spring,
Bubbling from hidden fountain-depths, and bring
Water, the death-thirst of her pain to slake!
Come from the forest, breeze with wandering wing!
There dwelt a heart would perish for her sake,—
Oh, save her! No! Death stands prepared his prey to take.

But, because youth and health are very strong,
And all her veins were full of freshest life,
The deadly struggle must continue long
Ere the freed heart lie still, that was so rife
With passion's mad excess. The gaoler's wife
Bends, with revolted pity on her brow,
To watch the working of that fearful strife,
Till the last quivering spark is out. And now
All's dark, all's cold, all's lost, that loved and mourned below.

"The Dream," published in 1840, is one of the longer of Lady Stirling-Maxwell's poems, and certainly one of the most beautiful. It is the one, we think, of all this poetess's productions in which personal feeling is most betrayed. It bears the impress of the fiery ordeal which she had undergone for some years previously. "The Dream" is dedicated to the Duchess of Sutherland, the staunch friend of the writer. The following dedicatory verses, simple in their cruel truth, sensuous in their vivid colouring, and impassioned in their fervour and grateful tenderness, have never been surpassed in their own peculiar style:—

Once more, my harp, once more, although I thought
Never to wake thy silent strings again,
A wandering dream thy gentle chords have wrought,
And my sad heart, which long hath dwelt in pain,
Soars like a wild bird from a cypress bough,
Into the poet's Heaven, and leaves dull grief below!

And unto Thee—the beautiful and pure—
Whose lot is cast amid that busy world
Where only sluggish dulness dwells secure,
And Fancy's generous wing is faintly furled;
To Thee—whose friendship kept its equal truth
Through the most dreary hour of my embittered youth—

I dedicate the lay. Ah! never bard,
In days when poverty was twin with song;
Nor wandering harper, lonely and ill-starred,
Cheered by some castle's chief, and harboured long;
Not Scott's Last Minstrel, in his trembling lays,
Woke with a warmer heart the earnest meed of praise.

For easy are the alms the rich man spares
To sons of Genius, by misfortune bent,
But thou gavest me, what woman seldom dares,
Belief—in spite of many a cold dissent—
When, slandered and maligned, I stood apart
From those whose bounded power had wrung, not crushed,
my heart.

Thou, then, when cowards lied away my name,
And scoffed to see me feebly stem the tide;
When some were kind on whom I had no claim,
And some forsook on whom my love relied,
And some, who *might* have battled for my sake,
Stood off in doubt to see what turn the world would take.

Thou gav'st me that the poor do give the poor,
Kind words and holy wishes, and true tears—
The loved, the near of kin, could do no more,
Who changed not with the gloom of varying years,
But clung the closer when I stood forlorn,
And blunted slander's dart with their indignant scorn.

> For they who credit crime are they who feel
>   Their own hearts weak to unresisted sin;
> Memory, not judgment, prompts the thoughts which steal
>   O'er minds like these, an easy faith to win;
> And tales of broken truth are still believed
> Most readily by those who have *themselves* deceived.
>
> But like a white swan down a troubled stream,
>   Whose ruffling pinion hath the power to fling
> Aside the turbid drops which darkly gleam,
>   And mar the freshness of her snowy wing,—
> So Thou, with queenly grace and gentle pride
> Along the world's dark waves in purity dost glide;
>
> *Thy* pale and pearly cheek was never made
>   To crimson with a faint false-hearted shame;
> *Thou* didst not shrink—of bitter tongues afraid,
>   Who hunt in packs the object of their blame;
> To thee the sad denial still held true,
> For from thine own good thoughts thy heart its mercy drew.
>
> And though my faint and tributary rhymes
>   Add nothing to the glory of thy day,
> Yet every poet *hopes* that aftertimes
>   Shall set some value on his votive lay;
> And I would fain one gentle deed record
> Among the many such with which thy life is stored.
>
> So when these lines, made in a mournful hour,
>   Are idly opened to the stranger's eye,
> A dream of Thee, aroused my fancy's power,
>   Shall be the first to wander floating by;
> And they who never saw thy lovely face
> Shall pause, to conjure up a vision of its grace!

The framework of "The Dream" is simply that of a lovely mother watching over a lovely daughter asleep: "which daughter," says Lockhart, "dreams, and when awaked tells her dream; which dream depicts the bliss of a first love and an early union, and is followed by the mother's admonitory comment, importing the many accidents to which wedded happiness is liable, and exhorting to moderation of hope, and preparation for severer duties." It is in the latter portion of the poem that the passion and interest assume a personal hue ; some passages occur which sound like javelins hurled by an Amazon. For example :—

> Heaven give thee poverty, disease, or death,
> Each varied ill that waits on human breath,
> Rather than bid thee linger out thy life
> In the long toil of such unnatural strife.
> To wander through the world unreconciled,
> Heart-weary as a spirit-broken child,
> And think it were an hour of bliss like Heaven
> If thou couldst *die*—forgiving and forgiven,—
> Or with a feverish hope, of anguish born,
> (Nerving thy mind to feel indignant scorn
> Of all the cruel foes that twixt ye stand,
> Holding thy heartstrings with a reckless hand,)
> Steal to his presence, now unseen so long,
> And claim his mercy who hath dealt the wrong!
> Into the aching depths of thy poor heart
> Dive, as it were, even to the roots of pain,
> And wrench up thoughts that tear thy soul apart,
> And burn like fire through thy bewildered brain.
> Clothe them in passionate words of wild appeal
> To teach thy fellow-creature *how* to feel,—
> Pray, weep, exhaust thyself in maddening tears,—
> Recall the hopes, the influences of years,—
> Kneel, dash thyself upon the senseless ground,
> Writhe as the worm writhes with dividing wound,—
> Invoke the Heaven that knows thy sorrows' truth,
> By all the softening memories of youth—
> By every hope that cheered thine earlier day—
> By every tear that washes wrath away—

By every old remembrance long gone by—
By every pang that makes thee yearn to die;
And learn at length how deep and stern a blow
Man's hands can strike, and yet no pity show.

Lady Stirling-Maxwell has been called the Byron of her sex. Lockhart says: "She has much of that intense personal passion by which Byron's poetry is distinguished from the larger grasp and deeper communion with man and Nature of Wordsworth. She has also Byron's beautiful intervals of tenderness, his strong practical thought, and his forceful expression."* At the same time, although she resembles Byron in her intensity and in her mournfulness, it would be erroneous to confound her sorrowful craving for sympathy, womanly endurance, resignation, and religious trust, with the refined misanthropy of Childe Harold. "She feels intensely, and utters her thoughts with an impassioned energy; but they are not the vapourings of a sickly fancy, nor the morbid workings of undue self-love; they are the strong and healthful action of a noble nature abounding in the wealth of its affections, outraged and trampled upon, and turning from its idols to God when the altar at which it worshipped has been taken away."*

"The Lady of La Garaye" is the most polished

---

* *Quarterly Review*, July, 1840. † R. W. Griswold.

and classic of all Lady Stirling-Maxwell's longer poems. It is one of the later efforts of her genius, and is a good example of the finish and polish which have characterised the works of her more mature years. The poem is founded upon a true story, concerning which the poetess says in her preface :—" I have added nothing to the beautiful and striking simplicity of the event it details. I have respected that mournful 'romance of real life' too much to spoil its lessons by any poetical licence. Nothing is mine in this story but the language in which it is told."

And very choice that language is. The tale is as a beautiful gem, skilfully and exquisitely set by a true and appreciative artist.

But we must not forget her shorter poetical pieces. Like the majority of the shorter poems of her gifted contemporary, Mrs. Hemans, the fugitive pieces of Lady Stirling-Maxwell have gained world-wide popularity. "The Arab's Farewell to his Horse," the well-known song " We have been Friends together," and many others too numerous to mention, divide the palm for popularity with " The Graves of a Household," and other proved favourites by Mrs. Hemans. Unlike her sister, Lady Dufferin, there is seldom a humorous strain in Lady Stirling-Maxwell's poetry. Irony and sarcasm are there in perfection; but humour, in the common acceptation of the word—the broad humour of the Celtic race from which she sprung —is totally absent, save in one or two of her earlier and least meritorious poems. One couplet from "The Recollections of a Faded Beauty" is a good specimen—and one of the best—of the whole. Speaking of one of her discarded lovers, she says—

> Squint it was *not!*—but one eye sought the other
> With tenderness, as 'twere a young twin brother.

All her poems have a spirit of yearning melancholy.

> How my heart yearns for joys for ever flown—
> My mother's hand, my sister's gentle tone!
> And wishes wild within my bosom swell,
> In sorrow's broken tones to bid farewell!

The date of the volume whence the foregoing is taken is 1833, just the time when the unhappy wife was beginning to realise how much happier her maiden days had been. "The Mother's Heart" could only have been written by a loving mother :—

* * * * *

> And thine was many an art to win and bless,
> The cold and stern to joy and fondness warming;
> The coaxing smile—the frequent soft caress—
> The earnest tearful prayer all wrath disarming!
> Again my heart a new affection found,
> But thought that love with *thee* had reached its bound!
> At length THOU camest; thou, the last and least;
> Nicknamed "The Emperor" by thy laughing brothers,
> Because a haughty spirit swelled thy breast,
> And thou didst seek to rule and sway the others;

Mingling with every playful infant wile
A mimic majesty that made us smile :

And oh! most like a regal child wert thou!
 An eye of resolute and successful scheming!
Fair shoulders—curling lip—and dauntless brow—
 Fit for the world's strife, not for poet's dreaming:
And proud the lifting of thy stately head,
And the firm bearing of thy conscious tread.

Different from both! Yet each succeeding claim,
 I, that all other love had been forswearing,
Forthwith admitted, equal and the same;
 Nor injured either, by this love's comparing;
Nor stole a fraction for the newer call—
But in the mother's heart, found room for all!

Amongst the most pathetic of Lady Stirling-Maxwell's poems may be particularised "The Blind Man to his Bride," "The Widow to her Son's Betrothed," and "The Child of Earth." The latter is one of the most touching of those mentioned, and is a good example of Lady Stirling-Maxwell's tenderly passionate style of writing:—

Fainter her slow step falls from day to day,
 Death's hand is heavy on her darkening brow;
Yet doth she fondly cling to earth and say:
 "I am content to die, but oh! not now!
Not while the blossoms of the joyous spring
 Make the warm air such luxury to breathe;
Not while the birds such lays of gladness sing;
 Not while bright flowers around my footsteps wreathe.
Spare me, great God, lift up my drooping brow!
I am content to die—but, oh! not now!"

The spring hath ripened into summer-time,
　　The season's viewless boundary is past;
The glorious sun hath reached his burning prime—
　　Oh! must this glimpse of beauty be the last?
"Let me not perish while o'er land and lea,
　　With silent steps the lord of light moves on;
Nor while the murmur of the mountain bee
　　Greets my dull ear with music in its tone!
Pale sickness dims my eye, and clouds my brow;
I am content to die—but, oh! not now!"

Summer is gone, and autumn's soberer hues
　　Tint the ripe fruits, and gild the waving corn;
The huntsman swift the flying game pursues,
　　Shouts the halloo, and winds his eager horn.
"Spare me awhile to wander forth and gaze
　　On the broad meadows and the quiet stream,
To watch in silence while the evening rays
　　Slant through the fading trees with ruddy gleam!
Cooler the breezes play around my brow;
I am content to die—but, oh! not now!"

The bleak wind whistles, snow showers, far and near,
　　Drift without echo to the whitening ground;
Autumn hath passed away, and cold and drear
　　Winter stalks on, with frozen mantle bound.
Yet still that prayer ascends:—"Oh! laughingly
　　My little brothers round the warm hearth crowd,
Our home-fire blazes broad, and bright, and high,
　　And the roof rings with voices glad and loud;
Spare me awhile, lift up my drooping brow!
I am content to die—but, oh! not now!"

The spring is come again—the joyful spring!
　　Again the banks with clustering flowers are spread;
The wild bird dips upon its wanton wing—
　　The child of earth is numbered with the dead!
"Thee never more the sunshine shall awake,
　　Beaming all readily through the lattice-pane;

The steps of friends thy slumbers may not break,
Nor fond familiar voice arouse again!
Death's silent shadow veils thy darkened brow;
Why didst thou linger?—thou art happier now!"

Truly, as of Mrs. Hemans, it may be said of Lady Stirling-Maxwell, that "she learned in sorrow what she taught in song." In R. D. Horne's *New Spirit of the Age,* he thus compares her with Mrs. Browning :—

"The prominent characteristics of these two poetesses may be designated as the struggles of woman towards happiness, and the struggles of a soul towards heaven. The one is oppressed with a sense of injustice, and feels the need of human love; the other is troubled with a sense of mortality, and aspires to identify herself with ethereal existences. The one has a certain tinge of morbid despondency, taking the tone of complaint and the amplification of private griefs; the other too often displays an energetic morbidity on the subject of death, together with a certain predilection for 'terrors.' The imagination of Mrs. Norton is chiefly occupied with domestic feelings and images, and breathes melodious plaints or indignations over the desecrations of her sex's loveliness; that of Miss Barrett often wanders amidst the supernatural darkness of Calvary, sometimes with anguish and tears of blood, sometimes like one who echoes the songs of triumphal quires. Both possess not only great mental energies, but that description of strength which springs from a fine nature, and manifests itself in productions which evidently originated in genuine impulses of feeling. The subjects they both choose appear spontaneous, and not resulting from study or imitation, though cast into careful moulds of art. The one records and laments the actual; the other creates and exults in the ideal. Both are excellent artists: the one dealing with subjects of domestic interest, the other in designs from sacred subjects, poems of religious tendency, or of the supernatural world. Mrs. Norton is beautifully clear and intelligible in her narrative and course of thought and feeling; Miss Barrett has great inventiveness, but not an equal power in construction. The one is all womanhood, the other all wings."*

It is upon her poetry that Lady Stirling-Maxwell's literary fame chiefly rests, the general public being less accustomed to regard her as a prose writer; yet in the latter department of literature she also excelled. "Like all her family," says one of her anonymous critics, "she had the gift of good English." She wrote well, and she wrote fearlessly, no matter what the subjects were. The first of Lady Stirling-Maxwell's prose works

---

* *New Spirit of the Age*, vol. ii. pp. 139, 140.

of fiction which attracted attention was her novel of "Stuart of Dunleath," concerning which there were many conflicting opinions. She had previously edited a work called "A Residence in Sierra Leone: described from a Journal kept on the Spot, and from Letters written to Friends at Home." "A most animated and sprightly picture of the state of society at Sierra Leone," says *John Bull*, "the point and cleverness of which is, we apprehend, to be placed to the credit of the talented editor fully as much as to that of the original writer of the letters."

When "Stuart of Dunleath" appeared, in 1851, the *Athenæum* criticised it in no very measured terms. It professed to be overcome by the complicated horrors of the plot.

"Can fable be imagined more dismal than this?" asks the reviewer in the *Athenæum*. "We may further ask, whether such a remorseless persecution of the truthful, the gifted, and the loving by destiny, is either veritable or wholesome as the argument of a fiction? To ourselves the answer comes readily. We do not shrink from the discipline of pain in imaginative creation any more than in daily life; but we revolt against the conviction that the brightest and best are marked out for such discipline exclusively, which must be received were we to accept 'Stuart of Dunleath' as a work of Art which is a copy from Nature.

Ours, however, is an objection more likely to attract than to distance readers. The young who 'love the luxury of woe,' are here treated to a sorrow which is Oriental in the amount of its extravagance, and may take to the book accordingly."*

Very different was the verdict of the *Examiner*. "Like the crystal fountain among the fountains of the Crystal Palace, this novel shines among the new novels of the year, pre-eminent and peerless. No prose work of equal power has yet come from the pen of Mrs. Norton, and we are glad to announce her return to a field of composition which she has already so successfully cultivated, by a notice of the present contribution of her genius to the vast wilderness of novelty, instruction, and delight which May has opened to our metropolis."†

The *Critic* did not take the same view of the subject:—

"We cannot quite share the enthusiasm of some of our contemporaries so as to term this novel 'pre-eminent and peerless.' It is a very clever novel, but it is not what the *Examiner* calls it. Mrs. NORTON possesses a great deal of descriptive power and much pathos; her writings are always pleasant to read; she appeals strongly to our sympathies, and her composition is remarkable for a

---

* The *Athenæum*, May 3rd, 1851.
† The *Examiner*, May 3rd, 1851.

certain *glow* of eloquence, felt, though it cannot be described. She has many superiors: she is defective in the two most important features of the *great novelist*—she cannot *create* characters, nor can she construct an ingenious plot."*

A paragraph of "faint praise" follows; but notwithstanding these criticisms, the book met with a deservedly popular reception from the reading public. It was a good novel, written in a clear and forcible style, perhaps too diffuse occasionally, but it had many merits to make amends for so trifling a fault.

Lady Stirling-Maxwell's next novel was "Lost and Saved," which appeared in 1863. It was written with a purpose. "Its purpose," says the *Saturday Review*, "is to show how very harshly and wrongly society treats women, and how leniently and wrongly it treats men. It is an old grievance, and Mrs. Norton evidently feels it keenly. There is no affectation of warmth or depth in her indignation. She writes from the fulness of her heart, and is moved to genuine anger and pity by observing how lightly bad men are censured, and how cruelly good women are treated. But, as in most novels with a purpose, the story in 'Lost and Saved' is sacrificed to the elucidation of the writer's views, and the purpose

---

* The *Critic*, May 15th, 1851.

is only very imperfectly attained through the medium of a story."*

Certainly we do not care so much for this novel as for "Stuart of Dunleath." The latter had passion and pathos; "Lost and Saved" has not much passion, and is quite wanting in pathos. Lady Stirling-Maxwell always wrote eloquently when injured woman was the theme, and the remembrance of her own bitter wrongs gave a zest to her pen. But she had almost exhausted the subject, which accounts for much that is colourless in her pictures, and a great deal that is mechanical in the action of the story. The *Times* praised it, and the *Athenæum* considered it superior to "Stuart of Dunleath;" but we cannot agree with the latter. Lady Stirling-Maxwell could not have written anything that did not bear the impress of genius, but in "Lost and Saved" she has not done justice to that genius.

It may have been that Lady Stirling-Maxwell recognised this herself, for in her next and last novel, published in 1867, we find a marked improvement. "Old Sir Douglas" is one of the most original novels that this age has produced. In common with all her novels, it possesses a keen insight into character and clever pictures of

---

* The *Saturday Review*, May 30th, 1863.

society. Lady Stirling-Maxwell pursued a most unhackneyed course in selecting an elderly gentleman for her hero, and she carried out her conception with much skill. With hereditary eloquence, she denounces the sham propriety which strains at gnats and swallows camels; and "the social Pharisee," says the *Saturday Review*, "is typified in the Dowager Countess of Clocknaben, a gaunt and grim Presbyterian lady, with two pet 'dictums' for ever in her mouth—'Temptations are just simply the sauce the devil serves up fools with,' and 'God's mercy is a great encouragement to obstinate offenders.'"

Notwithstanding defects, Lady Stirling-Maxwell's novels met with very great and deserved success; for the public knew that from the writer was to be expected subtle satire, delicate analysis of character, pathos, and passion. Taken on the whole, her prose works have not disappointed these expectations; but there was one quality the public did not expect, and that was a rare strain of ironical humour which characterises many of her scenes.

Her novels are good, but her poetry is better; and it is as a poetess that Lady Stirling-Maxwell will be remembered when her fame as a novelist will be forgotten. During her latter years she wrote much anonymously, "and took as much pains with a critique of pictures or the review of a new book as if her name had been prefixed at the beginning, or her well-known initials had been appended at the close. She had survived the zest for popularity, and sometimes seemed almost as if she had learned to enjoy, or at all events to provoke, its opposite. One fine quality she evinced in all her ways of thinking, acting, and writing—an unaffected disdain of affectation. Nothing could be simpler or more direct, nothing more tender or noble, than her ordinary conversation; but the iron had entered her soul, and every now and then there was a spice of mockery or scorn bitter as wormwood."*

Caroline Elizabeth Sarah, Lady Stirling-Maxwell, has been celebrated alike for her genius, her beauty, and her misfortunes, all so exceptional that any one of them would have been sufficient to have kept her name from sinking into oblivion. A certain section of the world was inclined to think harshly of her; but she had a staunch clique of true friends who knew and appreciated her, and who always stood by her. Amongst these was Rogers, the poet. In his gossiping "Diary"—which, by the way, is not as popularly known as it deserves to be—Henry Crabb Robinson thus describes a dinner at Rogers's :—

---

* The *Athenæum*, June 23rd, 1877.

"30, Russell Square, 31st January, 1845.

"I dined this day with Rogers, the Dean of the poets. We had an interesting party of eight: Moxon, the publisher; Kenny, the dramatic poet (who married Mrs. Holcroft, now become an old woman), himself decrepit without being very old; Spedding, Lushington, and Alfred Tennyson, three young men of eminent talent belonging to literary young England; the latter, Tennyson, being by far the most eminent of the young poets. His poems are full of genius, but he is fond of the enigmatical, and many of his most celebrated pieces are really poetic riddles. He is an admirer of Goethe, and I had a long *tête-à-tête* with him about the great poet. We waited for the eighth —a lady who, Rogers said, was coming on purpose to see Tennyson, whose works she admired. He made a mystery of this fair devotee, and would give no name.

"It was not till dinner was half over that he was called out of the room, and returned with a lady under his arm. A lady, neither splendidly dressed nor strikingly beautiful, as it seemed to me, was placed at the table. A whisper ran along the company, which I could not make out. She instantly joined our conversation, with an ease and spirit that showed her quite used to society. She stepped a little too near my prejudices by a harsh sentence about Goethe, which I resented. And we had exchanged a few sentences when she named herself, and I then recognised the much eulogised and calumniated Honourable Mrs. Norton, who, you may recollect, was purged by a jury finding for the defendant in a *crim. con.* action by her husband against Lord Melbourne. When I knew who she was, I felt that I ought to have distinguished her beauty and grace by my own discernment, and not waited for a formal announcement. You are aware that her position in society was, to a great degree, imperilled."*

Lady Stirling-Maxwell was always one of the most courted and esteemed of Rogers's guests ; and she gives the following tribute to her host's proverbial taste and refinement :—

> Who can forget, who at thy social board
> Hath sat, and seen the pictures richly stored,
> In all their tints of glory and of gloom,
> Brightening the precincts of thy quiet room,
> With busts and statues full of that deep grace
> Which modern hands have lost the skill to trace,
> Fragments of beauty, perfect as thy song
> On that sweet land to which they did belong,—†
> Th' exact and classic taste by thee displayed,
> Not with a rich man's idle, fond parade,
> Not with the pomp of some vain connoisseur,
> Proud of his bargains, of his judgment sure ;

---

* Diary of H. C. Robinson, vol. iii. p. 261.
† In allusion to the poet's " Italy."

> But with the feelings, kind and sad, of one
> Who thro' far countries wandering hath gone,
> And brought away dear keepsakes, to remind
> His heart and home of all he left behind ?*

Like her sister, Lady Dufferin, Lady Stirling-Maxwell married again late in life. The former married a man when he was on *his* deathbed, the latter married when she was almost on *hers*. Early in the spring of the present year, Mrs. Norton was married in her own drawing-room, Queen Street, Mayfair, to Sir William Stirling-Maxwell, a man distinguished in letters and politics. Their friendship had been long and affectionate, and the wrongs and bitter griefs of her early womanhood found a balm in the respect and love which was shown to her in her old age. Lady Stirling-Maxwell did not long enjoy her new dignity: she died a few weeks after her marriage, at the age of sixty-nine. The fitful fever of her life is over, but the story of this misjudged and gifted daughter of a gifted race must ever provoke the tear of sympathy, whilst her brilliant genius must compel the admiration of all. It is much to be regretted there is no collected and popular edition of Lady Stirling-Maxwell's poems. The majority of them are not as well

---

* From "The Dream."

known as they deserve to be, and for that reason we have quoted largely from them. We trust that at no distant day we shall see the announcement of this valuable addition to our modern poets.

PART V.

MISCELLANEOUS.

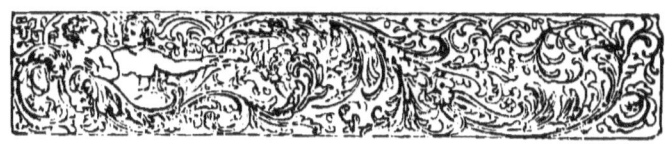

THE LADY FREEMASON.
(HONOURABLE Mrs. ALDWORTH.)
Born 1713.

THE Hon. Elizabeth St. Leger claims a place in the annals of noted Irishwomen, from the strange circumstances which have concurred to hand down her name to posterity. In the only portrait of her ever known to have been taken, she is represented as wearing her Masonic jewels and apron. The face is that of a woman of about five-and-thirty, with a pleasing Madonna-like cast of countenance. Benevolence and strength of character are striking features in what—considering the details we have of her life—must be a faithful likeness.

The subject of this memoir was the youngest child and only daughter of the Right Honourable Arthur St. Leger, created first Viscount Doneraile, June 23rd, 1703, and of his wife Elizabeth, the daughter and heiress of John Hayes, Esq., of Winchilsea. She was married to Richard Aldworth, Esq., of Newmarket, County Cork, who was the son of Sir Richard Aldworth, Provost Mareschal of Munster; but the date of the marriage is uncertain.

Lord Doneraile, the father of the Hon. Elizabeth St. Leger, was a zealous Freemason. He held a warrant, which empowered him occasionally to open Lodge at his own residence, Doneraile House, where, it is recorded, the duties of Freemasonry were never more rigidly performed than by the Masonic brethren of Lodge 150—the number of the warrant.* In the performance of these rites, Lord Doneraile was usually assisted by his son and by some intimate friends. The meetings were sometimes held in the town of Doneraile, but more frequently at Doneraile House, as in the instance about to be related.

Either in the year 1732 or 1733, when Elizabeth St. Leger was about nineteen or twenty years of age, the Lodge was held one night at her father's residence. Whether by design or accident cannot be confidently affirmed, but the fact remains that she certainly was in the room adjoining the one where the Lodge was being held on this particular occasion. This room was at the time undergoing some alterations. Amongst other things, the wall had been considerably reduced in

---

* Another account says the number of the warrant was "44."

one part, for the purpose of making a saloon. The young lady, having heard the voices of the Freemasons, and being giddy and thoughtless, felt a most intense desire to gratify her curiosity, and to witness this mystery so long, so faithfully, and so secretly locked up from public view. She made her arrangements accordingly, and, with a pair of scissors, removed a portion of a brick from the thin part of the wall, placing herself so as to command a full view of everything that passed in the next room. So situated, she witnessed the two first steps in Masonry, which was the extent of the proceedings of the Lodge for that night. Curiosity satisfied, fear now took possession of her mind; for, from what she heard, she concluded that the brethren were about to separate. For the first time she became tremblingly aware of the awkwardness and danger of her situation, and hastily began to consider how she could retire without observation.

There was no mode of escape except through the very room where the concluding portion of the second step was being performed. The apartment was a very large one; the ceremony was being performed at the very far end of it, and the brethren were all deeply engaged. Quick as thought, Miss St. Leger had resolution enough to attempt her escape. She glided along unobserved, laid her hand on the handle of the door, and gently opening it, to her dismay saw, standing on the lobby outside, a grim and surly "tiler," with his long sword unsheathed. With a shriek that pierced through the apartment, the terrified girl fainted, whilst the indignant brethren gathered around her.

Their first care was to resuscitate Miss St. Leger without alarming the house, and then to endeavour to learn from her how much she had witnessed. She confessed the whole truth, and, many of the members being furiously enraged at the transaction, she was placed under guard of the tiler and a member, in the very room where she had lain hidden. The members of the Lodge reassembled, and deliberated as to what, under the circumstances, was to be done. For two long hours the wretched girl listened to the angry discussion, and heard her death deliberately proposed and seconded. It is said that she was only saved from immediate death by the moving and earnest supplication of her younger brother. At length the good sense of some succeeded in calming, in some measure, the irritated feelings of the majority. When, after much more had been said, and many things had been proposed, she was given the option of submitting to the Masonic ordeal to the extent she had witnessed; and, if she refused, the brethren were again to consult. Being waited upon to decide, Miss St. Leger, exhausted and terrified by the storminess and earnestness of the debate, gladly and unhesitatingly accepted the offer.

She was accordingly initiated, and went through the ordeal, without any of the inmates of the house, save those present, being aware of the transaction. Thus vanishes the traditional story that the lady had hidden herself in a clock-case, her presence being betrayed by the whirring of the works, which she had inadvertently set in motion, and was unable to stop.

As Miss St. Leger, and as Mrs. Aldworth, she never made any secret of belonging to the Masonic body. On the contrary, she was rather proud of the distinction, and it is equally certain that the brethren held her in the highest esteem. By her marriage with Mr. Aldworth she had unlimited command of money, and the poor in general—and the Masonic poor in particular—had good reason to record her numerous and unostentatious acts of kindness.

The *Dublin Evening Post* and the *Dublin Weekly Oracle*, the two chief papers of the period, have some quaint advertisements respecting the performances given at the Smock Alley and the Aungier Street Theatres, for the benefit of the

Dublin Masonic Orphan Schools. Upon these occasions the brethren walked in procession to the theatres, with Mrs. Aldworth at their head, wearing her apron and other Masonic insignia. Performers such as Mrs. Woffington, George Anne Bellamy, Barrington, Sheridan, or Garrick, usually gave their services for the sake of the charity; but they were scarcely noticed upon these nights, the Lady Freemason seated in the front of the stagebox being the chief attraction of the evening. The house was always crowded when it was announced she would attend.

In the annals of the craft there is not a more esteemed name than that of Elizabeth Aldworth. Her conduct was unimpeachable in every relation of life. She was an excellent practical Christian, and most punctual and scrupulous in the performance of her Masonic duties. The brethren generously admit her many admirable qualities, and are unanimous in declaring that far from regretting her admission into their society, they consider her name and good deeds reflect a lustre upon the Masonic body.

THE BEAUTIFUL GUNNINGS.

MARIA GUNNING.
BORN A.D. 1733. DIED A.D. 1761.

ELIZABETH GUNNING.
BORN A.D. 1734. DIED A.D. 1790.

"AY the luck of the Gunnings attend you!" was the blessing of an Irish beggar-man in Dublin; and so apposite was the ejaculation that it passed into a proverb. Their social career was as rapid and as brilliant as extraordinary. They came to London in 1750, and by their beauty at once took society by storm. Their intrigues supplied Horace Walpole and the charming Berrys with plenty of food for gossip; one cannot help fancying there is a touch of contemptuous spite in the way in which Miss Berry speaks of them—just that spice of feminine jealousy which gives a piquancy to her letters :—" They have an idea that Lord Blandford is to marry Miss Gunning—an idea so improbable that even the luck of the Gunnings cannot make one believe it." But the beautiful Irish girls did even better than that in the matrimonial market, for they were "Countessed and double-Duchessed."

Well-born and of surpassing loveliness, only equalled by their poverty, Maria and Elizabeth Gunning were the daughters of John Gunning, Esq., of Castle Coote, County Roscommon, and of Bridget, daughter of Theobald Burke, sixth Viscount Mayo. An Irish gentleman of the rollicking duelling old school, Mr. Gunning died about the year 1747, leaving his widow and two daughters quite unprovided for. The estate of Castle Coote was deeply burdened with debt, so that immediately upon the death of her husband Mrs. Gunning was obliged to leave the place. She removed to Dublin in company with her two daughters, and here they resided for some time, existing chiefly upon the bounty of their uncle, Viscount Mayo. Their house was in Great Britain Street—a fashionable locality in that day. George Anne Bellamy, in her voluminous Memoirs, gives the following account of her first meeting with them:—

"As I was returning one day from rehearsal at the bottom of Britain Street, I heard the voice of distress. Yielding to an impulse of humanity, I overleaped the bounds of good-breeding, and entered the house from whence it proceeded. When I had done this, led by an irresistible attraction, I entered without ceremony the parlour, the door of which appeared to be guarded by persons not at all suited to those within. I here found a woman of a most elegant figure, surrounded by four most beautiful girls, and a sweet boy of about three years of age. After making the necessary apologies for my abrupt intrusion, I informed the lady that, as the lamentations of her little family had reached my ears as I passed by, I had taken the liberty of a neighbour to inquire if I could render her any assistance.

"Mrs. Gunning (for that was the lady's name) arose immediately from her seat, and calling me by my name, thanked me for the offer of my assistance, complimenting me at the same time upon possessing such humane sensations. She then informed me that, having lived beyond their income, her husband had been obliged to retire into the country to avoid the disagreeable consequences that must ensue. That she had been in hopes that her brother, Lord Mayo, listening to the dictates of fraternal affection, would not suffer a sister and her family to be reduced to distress; but that his Lordship remained inflexible to her repeated solicitations. The ill-looking men, 1 now found, had entered the house by virtue of execution, and were preparing to throw her and her children out of doors."

George Anne Bellamy introduced Mrs. Gunning and her beautiful daughters to some members of her own profession, and at one time, it is said, the girls had thoughts of acting on the stage as a profession. They became acquainted with Garrick and Peg Woffington. The former advised their mother to have them presented at the Viceregal Court, where their beauty could not fail to attract attention. Mrs. Gunning took the manager's advice, and the future fine ladies of fashion made their curtsies before the representatives of Royalty at Dublin Castle, clad in clothes from the theatrical wardrobe, lent by good-hearted Peg Woffington. They forgot a good deal of Peg Woffington's and of Mrs. Bellamy's kindness in after years. The latter even lent Maria Gunning a good deal of money, which she had no little difficulty in having repaid in after years, when the beautiful Countess snubbed the popular actress.

They went to London, and in 1751 Horace Walpole writes thus of the beautiful Gunnings :—
" There are two Irish girls of no fortune, who are declared the handsomest women alive. I think their being two so handsome, and both such perfect figures, is their chief excellence, for, singly, I have seen much handsomer figures than either; however, they can't walk in the Park or go to

Vauxhall but such mobs follow them that they are therefore driven away."

Their marriages were the great public events of 1752. Maria married the Earl of Coventry, and Elizabeth took for her first husband, on St. Valentine's Day, 1752, the sixth Duke of Hamilton. The elder sister was eighteen, the younger seventeen, when the marriages took place. The beauty and the luck of the Gunnings was the theme of conversation in coffee-room and drawing-room. Politics were only a bad second in public estimation, for before *them* even ranked Miss Jeffries and Miss Blandy, two murderesses, who were hanged at Newgate the same year. "The general attention," says Sir Joshua Reynolds, "is divided between the two young ladies who were married and the two young ladies who were hanged."

In 1754 Mrs. Mary Delany wrote thus of Maria :—" Yesterday, after chapel, the Duchess brought home Lady Coventry to feast me, *and a feast she was!* She is a fine figure and vastly handsome, notwithstanding a silly look sometimes about her mouth ; she has a thousand airs, but with a sort of innocence that diverts one! Her dress was a black silk sack, made for a large hoop, which she wore without any, and it trailed a yard on the ground ; she had on a cobweb-laced handkerchief, a pink satin long cloak, lined with ermine, mixed with squirrel skins; on her head a French cap that just covered the top of her head, of blond, and stood in the form of a butterfly with its wings not quite extended; frilled sort of lappets crossed under her chin, and tied with pink and green ribbon—a head-dress that would have charmed *a shepherd!* She has a thousand dimples and prettinesses in her cheeks, her eyes a little drooping at the corners, but fine for all that.*

These beauties had a brother, a General Gunning, of whom we do not hear much, save that he seemed to be a kind of factotum for his sisters. We hear of one of them giving her name as a surety for the rent, when he wanted to hire the Marchioness of Tweeddale's house on Twickenham Common. Another account gives an amusing picture of him at a masquerade given by the Duke of Richmond at Priory Gardens on June 6th, 1763 :—" There was old General Gunning in a running footman's habit, with Lady Coventry's picture at his button-hole, like a Croix de St. Louis." This erratic elderly gentleman was a constant source of annoyance to his sisters. Finally, he ran away with his tailor's wife, and henceforward society knew him no more.

---

* Memoirs of Mrs. Delany, by Lady Llanover, vol. iii. p. 300.

Notwithstanding her exceeding beauty, Maria Gunning, Countess of Coventry, was accustomed to use cosmetics to such an extent that she seriously affected her health thereby. In 1752, the year in which she was married, and when the "Gunninghiad" was at its height, she had already had the seeds of disease sown in her constitution by this most pernicious habit. In 1759 she died suddenly of rapid consumption and paralysis. She was the elder and more beautiful of the two sisters, and the very year she died her portrait was painted by Sir Joshua Reynolds. In one of her gossiping letters, Mrs. Mary Delany says:—

"And what a wretched end Lady Coventry makes after her short-lived reign of beauty! Not contented with the *extraordinary share* Providence had bestowed on her, she presumptuously and vainly thought to mend it, and by that means they say has destroyed her life; for Dr. Taylor says the white she made use of for her face and neck was rank poison; I wish it may be a warning to her imitators."*

The chief rival of the Countess of Coventry was Lady Caroline Petersham. When the former died, Lady Caroline contrived, with the help of the Viscountess Townshend and the Duchess of Devon-

---

* Memoirs of Mrs. Delany, by Lady Llanover, vol. iii. p. 584.

shire, to keep the town in talk; the first by her beauty and oddity, the second by her cleverness, and the third by her meanness and vulgarity. Up to the very last Lady Coventry kept up an appearance of gaiety, and gave her little dinners as usual.

In the same year, 1759, Sir Joshua Reynolds also painted the portrait of the Duchess of Hamilton, who had now the field all to herself, and reigned supreme Queen of Beauty. She went on a visit to Yorkshire about this time, and seven hundred people sat up all night to see her get into her postchaise in the morning; whilst a shoemaker in Worcester turned an honest penny by exhibiting her Grace's shoe.

Elizabeth Gunning, Duchess of Hamilton, took for her second husband Colonel John Campbell, Lord Lorne, afterwards fifth Duke of Argyll, for whom she had refused the Duke of Bridgewater, the father of British inland navigation. About the time of her marriage there was some scandal afloat concerning the conduct of General Gunning towards *his* wife, but it was hushed up. This brother was always a *mauvais sujet*. The fastidious Horace Walpole especially disliked him, and lampooned him as follows :—

Berkeley Square, June 2, 1791.
TO THE TUNE OF "THE COW WITH THE CRUMPLED HORN," &c.
This is the note that nobody wrote.
This is the groom that carried the note that nobody wrote.
This is Ma'am Gunning, who was so very cunning, to examine the groom that carried the note that nobody wrote.
This is Ma'am Bowen, to whom it was owing, that Miss Minify Gunning was so very cunning, to examine the groom that carried the note that nobody wrote.
These are the Marquises, shy of the horn, who caused the maiden all for-*lorn*, to become on a sudden so tattered and torn, that Miss Minify Gunuing was so very cunning, to examine the groom, &c.
These are the two Dukes, whose sharp rebukes made the two Marquises shy of the horn, and caused the maiden all for-*lorn*, &c.
This is the General, somewhat too bold, whose head was so hot, though his heart was so cold ; who proclaimed himself single before it was meet, and his wife and his daughter turned into the street, to please the two Dukes, whose sharp rebukes, &c.

Indeed, "trim Horace" does not seem ever to have forgiven the beautiful Gunnings for being "Countessed and double-Duchessed," and never fails to give a sidelong sneer at them whenever he can. The coterie at Teddington had little in common, save rank, with the fast gay ladies of the capital.

Whilst Duchess of Argyll, she was sent to bring over the Princess Charlotte, that notable little lady who packed her own things before starting, and arrived in London with several huge cases filled with house-linen, and one small hair-covered trunk containing her modest wardrobe. The Princess preserved her equanimity until she came in sight of St. James's, when she became frightened, and almost began to cry. The experienced Duchess smiled. "Yes," said the Princess, rather angrily, "*you* may laugh, Duchess, *you* have been married twice, but to me it is no joke!" It has been hinted that, after the Princess became Queen of England, she had very good reason to be jealous of His Majesty's attentions to the Duchess of Argyll.

After a brilliant career, Elizabeth, Duchess of Argyll, died, on May 27th, 1790, aged sixty-six. She was the cleverer of the two sisters, and a woman possessed of much common sense and business capacity. Although fond of money and of power, she used the former charitably and she did not abuse the latter.

THE LADIES OF LLANGOLLEN.

LADY ELEANOR CHARLOTTE BUTLER.
BORN 1739.   DIED 1829.
MISS SARAH PONSONBY.
BORN 1755.   DIED 1831.

MANY have been the conjectures as to why these two eccentric ladies should have left family and friends, and have lived for so many years together in perfect friendship. The world made free with their names, but they lived down all scandal, and the highest in the land were proud to call them friends. Their original idea had been to retire from the world—

The world forgetting, by the world forgot;

and to find a solace for all worldly ills in mutual friendship. But the world would not permit them to do this. The fame of their romantic friendship spread far and wide, and the cottage at Llangollen became the scene of a succession of coteries as brilliant as those of Mrs. Garrick, and as learned as those of Mrs. Montagu. For in the Llangollen cottage the events and scandals of the great world were as well known as in the *salons* of London and Paris.

The following letters and details of the lives of these two ladies—which have never before been published—have been supplied by their relative and executor, C. W. Hamilton, Esq., of Hamwood, County Meath. These details include extracts from the Diary of a Mrs. Goddard, a manuscript remarkable not alone for the light which it throws upon this curious friendship, but also as being an excellent picture of the social life of the age wherein it was written.

Lady Eleanor Butler, who was born about the year 1739, was the daughter of Walter, sixteenth Earl of Ormond. She had been educated in France, and it is conjectured that she there acquired habits of taste and refinement which rendered the society of Kilkenny, where she resided with her mother and sisters, very distasteful to her. She is also supposed to have had some love affair when in France, and to have been disappointed, for the recollections of France seem to have been strongly rooted in her mind, and amongst the pleasantest of her associations. When she was on her deathbed, she insisted upon Miss Ponsonby, who was then seventy-four years old, sitting on her bed and quavering forth *Malbrook s'en va't en guerre*.

Her home was not a happy one, for her mother was of a violent and eccentric temper. When this old lady died, there was some confusion at her funeral, and the people of Kilkenny said they expected her to rise in her coffin and abuse them! Thus, disappointed in love and with an uncongenial home, Lady Eleanor Butler conceived the idea of forming this romantic friendship with Miss Ponsonby, of retiring from the world, and of their living for each other in some secluded spot.

The idea first took possession of her mind in 1778, when she was thirty-nine years old. Miss Ponsonby was but twenty-three, and sixteen years her junior.

Miss Sarah Ponsonby was the daughter of Chambre Ponsonby, and niece of Lady Betty Fownes. The latter was the daughter of the first Lord Bessborough. Miss Ponsonby was adopted by Sir William and Lady Betty Fownes, and lived with them at Woodstock, in the County Kilkenny, and also at No. 40, Dominick Street, Dublin, during the Parliamentary session. Sir William and Lady Betty always treated her as their daughter, and gave her every advantage. She was very highly educated, was a good linguist, and sketched well from Nature. Apparently she had every comfort and blessing that wealth and affection could bestow upon her, so that it was with no slight degree of consternation her adopted mother and friends heard of her determination to share the fortunes of Lady Eleanor Butler.

Their friends were in despair at their strange decision, and did all in their power to dissuade them from it. But all to no purpose; they had made up their minds to go away, and nothing could turn them from it. They were questioned as to their motives, but preserved silence, giving no satisfaction beyond saying that they wished to spend the remainder of their lives in the society of each other. Finding their relatives and friends obdurate, they determined to run away.

The first attempt was a failure, in consequence of Miss Ponsonby breaking her leg in trying to get over the park wall, at an early hour of the morning. Lady Eleanor (then Miss) Butler had made an appointment to meet her at a ruined abbey near Thomastown, and there they were obliged to spend the night.

The fugitives were brought back in disgrace, but made a second attempt at the end of March, 1778. This time they got as far as the quay at Waterford, when they were again captured, and Miss Ponsonby brought back by Lady Betty Fownes, whilst Miss Butler was sent to her sister Elizabeth, Mrs. Kavanagh, of Borris.

The following letter is from Mrs. Tighe, Lady Betty Fownes's only daughter. It is addressed to Mrs. Goddard, the valued friend of the family, before referred to, extracts from whose Diary must form the staple of this memoir.

"MY DEAR MRS. GODDARD,—The runaways are caught, and we shall soon see our amiable Friend again, whose conduct, though it has an appearance of imprudence, is, I am sure, void of any serious impropriety. There were no gentlemen concerned ; nor does it appear to be anything more than a scheme of romantic friendship. My mother is gone to Waterford for Miss Butler and her, and we expect to see them to-night. I am happy at having this opportunity of giving my dear Mrs. Goddard pleasure, and of assuring her I am her affectionate friend and servant,

"S. TIGHE.

" Woodstock, 2 April, 1778."

That these two eccentric ladies had each a secret reason for wishing to fly from the world, and were equally determined not to disclose that secret, is quite clear. The following letter from Lady Betty Fownes shows plainly that even their most intimate friends had no idea of the real causes which actuated their movements.

"My D' G.,—Sally* is much better, but very weak, low, and dejected. She made me watch the windows all day yesterday, she was so sure you would have come, and told me to-day she would write you a line. Sure you will lose no time. She was most anxious to see your letter to me. I did not read it all, as anything against Miss B. is death to her. Be very cautious till we meet. Stories, to be sure, there must be in plenty. I can't help giving credit to S. P.'s, which is that they were to live together. A convent, I used to think, but she now says that is what she flew from, and that we were all much mistaken, and that if we knew Miss B. we would love her as well as she did. Altogether, it is a most extraordinary affair. I sometimes can hardly think the cause is known by any but themselves. God knows how it is, or how it will end. I know she is very ill. I am sure nothing could be of so much use to her as seeing you, and hearing you talk to her. I think you will soon come now, my dear. She has taken my little senses away. I sometimes sit for hours and can't speak to her. Sally Tighe has been of infinite use to her; if she had not been here I must have died, I really think. She is so clever at preaching to her. I fear they must very

---

* Miss Pousonby was always called "Sally" in the family.

soon leave me, and then indeed, if you don't come, I shall give myself up at once. God bless you. Ever yours.

"Write, if it be but a line every day. Enclose to Sir W^m."

The following letter is also from Lady Betty Fownes, and shows conclusively both her affection for Miss Ponsonby and her distress at her unaccountable conduct. It was written the Sunday after the preceding one.

"SUNDAY.

"A very bad night; her throat much inflamed; her fever not so great. If she forgets herself for a little, she starts and seems in such a way that I dread her sleeping. I think her in very great danger. I seldom leave her. God's will be done. Miss B. has wrote her a letter every day, which distressed her to read. I am astonished she will do it. This day I write to Mrs. Kavanagh, of Borris, to beg Miss B. might not write volumes to her till she was better, and this day a letter to me from Mrs. K., but none from her. Dr. Baker is here, does all he can, and she seems to like him. It is a most extraordinary affair. Nobody could behave with more good sense or prudence than Mrs. Hamerton, who was sent for her, and never quit her till she brought her back to Ballyhail. She is now at Borris, and, by all we can learn, very well—dines with the family, and seems hearty; but I can scarcely believe it. This poor creature, I am sure, could not. Shall we see you? God grant it! She has raved of you; and yesterday I told her I had written to press you. She seemed quite delighted, and said that would be the thing. We hear the Butlers are never to forgive their daughter, and that she is to be sent to France to a convent. I wish she had been safe in one long ago; she would have made us all happy. Many an unhappy hour she has cost me, and, I am convinced, *years* to Sally. It is happy for you you were not here at the time. Now is the time to show friendship to her, which I think you will, and to your very affectionate friend,

"E. FOWNES."

Yet one letter more upon this subject. It is from Miss Ponsonby, and shows how fully she had made up her mind to accompany Miss Butler.

"I thank you, my dear friend, for the good opinion of me expressed in your letter received this day by Lady Betty. I am not yet recovered, although I made a visit to Borris the day before yesterday. A constant head and heart ache. I have much to tell you; but as it is not, I hope, many days ere I shall have an opportunity of *speaking*, I defer writing, being particularly weak to-day. They propose great terms to Miss B. if she will reside in a convent *some years*, and give me up for ever. I am not heroic enough to wish she should accept them, nor is she, I believe, to listen to them. Worn out by misfortunes, I have still the comfort of self-approbation. Were it to do again, I would act as I have done. If it is any satisfaction to you to know that you possess a third place, at least, in an almost broken heart, be assured of it. God bless you.

"Lady Betty, just returned from *Kilkenny, desires you will excuse her writing. Her head very bad. Thanks you for your letter."

Mrs. Goddard, the lady from whose Diary the following extracts are taken, seems to have been a trusted mutual friend. The entries commence with June 15th, 1774, before which date Mrs. Goddard had become a widow. She appears to have played no unimportant part in the brilliant Dublin society of the time, and was constantly paying visits in the country. The accounts of these visits; of the company she met with at the various country houses, and the modes of loco-motion, are as graphic and interesting as they are

---

* Not from the Castle.

amusing. Even the expenses of her journeys are recorded—documents now valuable as showing the way in which a gentlewoman travelled a hundred years ago. Mrs. Goddard was an indefatigable letter-writer, and her correspondence was most voluminous. Evidently the confidante of many, she heard everything and said nothing. She understood the motives of actions which the world wondered at, and in no case more clearly than in that of the romantic friendship between the ladies of Llangollen.

Mrs. Goddard, as we gather from her journal, was in constant correspondence with Sir William and Lady Betty Fownes, and also with Miss Ponsonby, their adopted daughter. Their names are frequently mentioned in the Diary; and we find she also visited them occasionally, both in Dominick Street, Dublin, and at Woodstock. An entry respecting one of her visits to Lady Betty is rather amusing :—

"*Friday, 4th.*—Play'd cribbage with Mr. Z. He asked me was I well; feared I was not, as I hardly eat anything. I s^d I was very well, and eat as much as I cou'd.

"*Sunday, 6th.*—The rest of the family went to Kilkenny; Mr. Z. and I to Woodstock, where I spent a most agreeable fortnight. Lady Betty sometimes made me nervous by her violent attacks on Mr. Z. to marry me, and her continually urging me to do the same, though neither of us had the least thought of each other. She went so far as to say I ought, and it wou'd be a praiseworthy thing of me to offer myself to him, for that she was sure the proposal would be accepted with transport. He would live at least ten years the longer for it, and both of us much happier than we are."

Mrs. Goddard did not take Lady Betty's advice. She remained a widow, going about amongst her friends and enjoying life. It would seem that to her alone Miss Ponsonby revealed her true reason for wishing to go off with Miss Butler. That reason was none less than that the old Sir William Fownes had made love to his adopted daughter. Miss Ponsonby could no longer remain under his roof; and she evidently shrank from wounding the feelings of her kind adopted mother by revealing the true cause of her wishing to leave Woodstock. Unfortunately, it was whispered abroad, although nothing definite was known, and there is very little doubt but that the fear of exposure hastened Sir William Fownes's death.

So for more than half a century Miss Ponsonby kept her secret, and the busy world employed itself in conjectures respecting this romantic friendship—conjectures all of them wide of the truth. The following extracts from Mrs. Goddard's Diary tell the whole story:—

1778.

"*April. Thursday, 2nd.*—Got a letter from L. B. F.* and Mrs. Medows to tell me that Miss Butler and Miss Pons. had run away the Monday before. Wrote to both that day, and with a fretting heart. Went with B. B.†, Nancy, Kitty, and Anne to masquerade it at Fall's.

"*Friday, 3rd.*—Having no account of their being found, staid at home to think of them. Wrote to Mrs. Medows.

"*Saturday, 4th.*—Got a letter from Mrs. Tighe;‡ another from Sr William to tell me they were catched and in safety. Wrote to my two intelligencers, and went with Mrs. Rochfort to the Italian Opera, where we were well frightened with the riot between the army and mob, and did not come home until past one.

"*Sunday, 5th.*—At the Magdalen;§ drank stupid tea with the Newcomens.

"*Monday, 6th.*—Got letters from Lord S. Z.,∥ with the news of Miss P.'s flight, and L. B. F.,¶

---

* Lady Betty Fownes.
† Either Barbara or Betty Bennett.   ‡ Already given.
§ The Church attached to the *Magdalen Asylum*, Lower Leeson Street, Dublin.
∥ Lord Shuldham Izod.   ¶ Letter already given.

telling me she (Miss P.) was very ill. Went with Beck and Mrs. Rochfort to 'School for Scandal;' saw L^d (Shuldham Izod) there, who wished to talk with me on the runaways, but we were too much surrounded."

Later on the subject is resumed.

"*Wednesday, 22nd.*—Got a letter from L. B. F. to tell me Miss Butler had again absconded from Borris* on Sunday night. Wrote to L. B. F., Miss Pons., and Z.

"*Thursday, 23rd.*—F. H. came. Got another letter to tell me Miss Butler was and had been at Woodstock, conceal'd by Miss P. from Sunday till Monday night without their privity. Wrote to L. B. F. At Mrs. Radcliffe's in the evening to speak to the Bishop of Elphin.

"*Friday, 24th.*—Set out with Jane. Dined at Mrs. Eustace's, Naas, upon excellent mutton-chops. Slept at O'Brien's, Timolin.

"*Saturday, 25th.*—Stop'd at Carlow; saw Mrs. Best, the little Warrens. Dined at the Royal Oak, and got to Woodstock at nine; a most terrible long jaunt it was. Found them all in distraction. Saw my poor Miss Pons., but Miss B. did not appear.

"*Sunday, 26th.*—Saw Miss Pons. again, who

---

* The residence of her sister Elizabeth, Mrs. Kavanagh.

came down to dinner; but Miss B. not till evening, when she came in to tea, but did not speak to me.

"*Monday, 27th.*—Spoke to them both. Gave them my best advice, which they seemed to take well, and I hoped from their manner wou'd have been followed. They both dined with us.

"*Tuesday, 28th.*—L. B. F. made me go with her to talk to them. They seem'd to have grown hardened in their resolution of going together. Mr. Park came with Mr. Butler's permission that they should go together, and talk'd in vain to dissuade them from it. They w^d not show themselves below to-day.

"*Wednesday, 29th.*—Sr William wrote to Sr W. Barker and Coll. Lyons, to acquaint them of their resolution, and to Mr. Butler, entreating he w^d come for his Daughter. F. H. staid with me until this day.

"*Thursday, 30th.*—The Ladies did not come down to dinner, for fear Mr. Park should be questioned about Miss P.

"*Friday, May the 1st.*—L. B. and I set out with Mr. Park, who was going to Kilkenny, at eight in the morning. We parted him on the road, and then breakfasted with Mr. Z., to whom, by Miss Pons' desire, I told the secret transaction between her and Sr William. Returned to dinner, when the ladies joined us, and Miss P. play'd cards in the evening.

"*Saturday, the 2nd.*—I talk'd again to Miss Pons., and to dissuade her from her purpose, but to discharge my conscience of the duty I owed her as a friend by letting her know my opinion of Miss Butler, and the certainty I had they would never agree living together. I spoke of her with harshness and freedom; said she had a debauch'd mind; no ingredients for friendship, that ought to be founded on Virtue, whereas hers every day more and more showed me was acting in direct opposition to it, as well as to the interest, happiness, and reputation of the one she professed to love. Sr W. joined us, kneel'd, implored, swore twice on the Bible how much he lov'd her, would never more offend, was sorry for his past folly, that was not meant as she understood it, offered to double her allowance of 30*l.* a year, or add what more she pleas'd to it, even tho' she did go. She thank'd him for his past kindness, but nothing c'd hurt her more, or w^d she ever be under other obligation to him, said if the whole world was kneeling at her feet it should not make her forsake her purpose—she w^d live and die with Miss B.; was her own mistress, and if any force was used to detain her she knew her own temper so well it w^d provoke her to an act that w^d give her friends more trouble than anything she had yet done. She, however, haughtily, and, as it were, to get rid him, made Sr W. happy by telling him if ever she was in distress for money he should be the first she would apply to. They dined with us, and I never saw anything so confident as their behaviour. Wrote to Burton and Mrs. Medows.

"*Sunday, 3rd.*—Sr W. read prayers at home; Miss P. one of the congregation. The fact of their carriage being come was known to all but L. B. We played 'The Game of the Goose,' Mr. Bowers looking on. All dull but the girls. At night, Miss P. going to bed gave me an embrace.

"*Monday, 4th.*—She call'd at my door. I w^d not open it. (Wrote to Z. Beck and Lord Shuldham of these matters.) At six in the morning they set out, merry as possible. *Mem.* It was at Miss P.'s desire I went to and told Mr. Z. of what had pass'd between her and S^r W.

"*Tuesday, 5th.*—Wrote to Beck.

"*Wednesday, 6th.*—Wrote to Beck and Mrs. Taylor.

"*Thursday, the 7th.*—Wrote to Burton and Z. Park came.

"*Friday, 8th.*—Nothing.

"*Saturday, 9th.*—Mr. Park went, but left Miss Blunt, that he brought with him, behind.

"*Sunday*, 10*th.*—Went to Church. Mr. Hickson pray'd and preach'd for the first time.

"*Monday*, 11*th.*—We all drank tea with Long.

"*Tuesday*, 12*th.*

"*Wednesday*, 13*th.*

"*Thursday*, 14*th.*—Nothing.

"*Friday*, 15*th.*—All went to Kilkenny. The family at Woodstock dined at Mr. Park's; I at Mr. Ham's, where I heard Sr William's gallantry to Miss P. was beginning to be whispered. I paid a visit to the castle, and not a word was said to me of Miss B."

The Diary contains nothing very particular for the next few days, until Friday, the 22nd, when the chronicler records,—

"L. B. very rude to me at breakfast."

On that day week she went with Miss Blunt to see "the barn the ladies had taken shelter in for a day and near two nights." She also says that Mrs. Tighe and her family had come to stay at Woodstock.

"*Sunday*, 31*st.*—At 3 in the morning was waked by Sr William's roars, who said, and the whole house thought, was dying of a strangallion or gout in the stomach. He was bled, bathed in warm water. I took an opportunity to tell him the cause was in his mind, fell asleep at 5, and waked pretty well at 11, when he saw Tom

Butler, who had been here two hours, come down stairs.

"*Monday, June the 1st.*—Sr W. not so well as he was; came down.

"*Tuesday, 2nd.*—The same, but did not come down; wrote to Burton. Boyde came; blister'd, glister'd, and physick'd S^r W^m in the space of half an hour.

"*Wednesday, 3rd.*—T. Butler came; put on fresh blisters; his pulse grew better.

"*Thursday, 4th.*—The same.

"*Friday, 5th.*—The same.

"*Saturday, 6th.*—T. B. came for him; better; went away with Boyde. Sr W. told me before Mrs. Tighe, his illness was his own fault that he was punished for, and at eleven at night we all went to bed, leaving him with every symptom of returning health.

"*Sunday, 7th.*—At two in the morning he was seized with a paralytic stroke, lost the use of his right side, and his speech, and c^d not swallow. Expresses sent for T. B., that with Boyde came at ten. They cupp'd, blistered, and glister'd him. Toward evening he c^d swallow.

"*Monday, 8th.*—The same.

"*Tuesday, 9th.*—A blister on his head made the fourteenth he had on him. This night he grew better.

"*Wednesday, 10th.*—Dr. Young and Mr. Bowers

gave out he was so much better that I walk'd to Inistiogue to communicate the good news there. On my return found T. Butler here, who thought differently, and contrary to his intention when he came, not meaning to go till evening, left us at one o'clock. Soon after Sr W. grew worse, and continued to do so till Thursday, the 11th, at eight o'clock, when he died, after an agony of twelve hours.

"*Friday*, 12*th*.—Everything dismal.

"*Saturday*, 13*th*, at near eight in the morning, he was carried on men's shoulders to Inistiogue, and there interred."

So upper earth has done with the chief agent in causing the expatriation of Miss Ponsonby.

Their friends and relatives, seeing Miss Ponsonby and Miss Butler were so decided in their determination to leave Ireland and to live together, at length gave an unwilling consent. They set out from Waterford, and arrived at Milford Haven on the 16th of May, 1778, accompanied by their faithful maid, Betty Carroll. A suitable allowance was settled upon them, and as they had not yet decided upon a residence in any place in particular, they went for a tour throughout the Principality.

Eventually they settled down in a small farmhouse, close to the village of Llangollen, which, under their care, became a celebrated cottage *ornée*.

Every spot of the small grounds surrounding it was made the subject of some special interest in gardening or rustic ornamentation. The kitchen and two sitting-rooms joined the basement story, and were kept in beautiful order. The walls were adorned with prints and small pictures, and the library was full of the works of the best authors, English and foreign.

Such was the retreat where these two eccentric women lived for more than half a century. At different times, literature, wit, and gossip filled these little sitting-rooms; for one of the most curious features of this friendship was that the world should have so persistently refused to allow the ladies of Llangollen to enjoy the seclusion which they apparently sought.

Their friends kept up a constant correspondence with them, keeping them well informed of the events of the world which they had left. During the disastrous period of the Irish Rebellion of 1798, they received frequent accounts from their friend Mrs. Tighe, of Rosanna, the mother-in-law of "Psyche." Mrs. Tighe's son, Mr. Henry Tighe, took an active part during the disturbances, as the following letters, written by his mother to Miss Ponsonby, will show.

"20 June (1798).

"MY DEAR FRIEND,—As you never heard an account of our dear Harry's escape, I must mention it to you. After the officers were *supposed* to be killed belonging to the Antrim Militia, after Walpole, through vile generalship, had led the troops into the midst of the foe, Harry took the lead of fifteen volunteers and the rest, and had to cut his way through half a mile of the Pikemen and back again, which he effected with only the loss of a few men. He distinguished himself very much, got great applause, and has been pointed out as a person of great bravery. He is safe at Rathdrum, and 'greatly beloved by his corps.' I hasten to tell you of a diabolical plot just discovered at Cork to destroy all the Protestants. The town was divided into 136 sections, a company to each, who were to effect the destruction of all the Protestants in each section. This was afterwards, on a small scale, subdivided so that twelve men had each a part allotted them. One of the expelled collegians, shocked at the brutality of the measure, turned informer. At Waterford, the same plan was formed. The King's troops have had a victory in County Meath, another on the borders of County Wicklow, when 900 of the Rebels were killed, and not one Royalist."

There are many letters upon the same subject;

one more we give, as a graphic picture of the state of the country. It is also from Mrs. Tighe, and addressed to Miss Ponsonby. The beginning, which refers to private affairs, is omitted.

"2nd July (1798).

"My dearest Friend,—

* * * *

* * * *

"In letters which have arrived from the County Wicklow to-day, I heard from one who had met a man the day before, who, along with his brother, had been forced from their own home by the Rebels. They had been tried for their lives on account of being Protestants, and had made their escape when just going to be put to a miserable death; he heard them declare it to be their determined intention not to suffer one Protestant to live in this Land of Liberty. This was the universal view of the Sovereign People, &c. &c. Another, whose advice I asked about returning to Rosanna, writes :—' I cannot bid you come ; nor do I know when this country will be quiet.' Some think Lord Cornwallis will not do much good by kindness. The Rebels say they will not come in, and submit to slavery. They will not submit without a proper peace. Mrs. Eccles, likewise, advises me to wait for fourteen days the result of the Proclamation before I think of moving. Harry heard a report of a rising in Dublin. He hastened to town, stayed a day, and made us happy, as his return on Thursday made us the reverse; for he went back *alone*. Since that he has been out with all the troops to engage 2000 Rebels within 5 miles of Rathdrum. The first cannon our troops fired passed over their heads, which encouraged them in such a degree to place faith in the assurances of their Priests that our guns could not hurt them. They made the hills resound with their huzzas, flourishing their hats on the tops of their pikes. However, another shot, better directed, made such a lane through the heart of them that they fled in all directions.

* * * *

" Unite your prayers with mine, my dear friend, that there may soon be an end to civil war. A son killed a father, a brother a brother, near Kilkenny. In the County Kilkenny they are pretty quiet. A few nights ago I went to rest with the firm persuasion that Rosanna was burned, for I was assured that an express had arrived to a gentleman, in which it was said Glynmouth (within a mile of it) had been burned.

* * * *

" Poor Mr. R. Tighe, not only the friend of the

poor, but the defender of Popery, his house has been already destroyed. They have made foes of many, he among the rest, who upon Liberal Principles defended them, and wished to convince others their religion was not so sanguinary as formerly. Sixty families have quitted their communion; others declare they would do so were they not afraid. One man told a friend of mine that if he turned he should be murdered. The Cavan Militia have turned, and gave the body of Murphy, a Priest, to the dogs. They begin to discover the delusion that their Priests have kept them under so long. I hope they may not fly to the other extreme.

* * * *

"I can get no list of the Protestants killed at Enniscorthy, though on Mary's account I have tried to do so; perhaps before I write next I may. The Lord Mayor has a list both of the massacred at Enniscorthy and Wexford. Mrs. Richards, even since her escape at Wexford, has had another, having been taken and put into a house at Enniscorthy to be burned, but escaped out of the window. She is, they hope, in England, never to come back. Tell me *your opinion* of this business, and what you think will be the end. "Ever your affectionate friend."

Mrs. Tighe's letters are most voluminous and accurate, and would, if properly edited, form an excellent *social* history of the state of Ireland in 1798.

"The Ladies," as they were now commonly called, were objects of interest and curiosity to the social world at large. Statesmen, poets, authors, artists, and celebrities of all kinds and classes corresponded with them, and sought the honour of their acquaintance. Amongst the vast mass of correspondence which they left are letters from Lady Mornington, the mother of the Duke of Wellington, and refer to the Duke's first appointment:—

"There are so many little matters to settle for Arthur," says Lady Mornington, "who has just got into the army, and appointed Aide-de-Camp to Lord Buckingham, and must be set out a little for that; in short, *I must do everything* for him; and when you see him you will think him worthy of it, as he really is a very charming young man. Never did I see such a change for the better in anybody. He is wonderfully lucky: in six months he has got two steps in the Army, and appointed Aide-de-Camp to Lord Buckingham, which is ten shillings a day."

The Duke of Wellington was their staunch friend during life, giving good proof of his friendship when, in 1829, he procured for them a pension of 200*l.* a year. This was a piece of gross jobbery, as they had done nothing whatever to entitle them to it. Their means certainly were limited, and from various sources we gather they applied occasionally to their friends for money. Miss Ponsonby's application to her cousin, the Earl of Bessborough, was received with much coldness. He blamed her for leaving her friends, sent her fifty pounds, and requested her not to send him any presents. A letter from Edmund Burke is interesting, as showing "the Ladies" were the subjects of scandalous reports in the newspapers.

"My dear Ladies,—I am very much flattered by being honoured with your commands. You do no more than justice to me and to this family when you suppose us ready to do everything in our power to show our respect to your character, and our grateful remembrance of the polite and hospitable reception you gave us in your elegant retirement at Llangollen. It is, however, a most sensible mortification to us all that our correspondence should begin upon an occasion so disagreeable. They must be the most wicked, probably—certainly the most unthinking—of all wretches, who could make that retirement unpleasant to you. I have not seen the base publications to which you allude. I have spoken to a friend who has seen them, and who speaks of them with the indignation felt by every worthy mind; but who doubts whether that redress can be had by an appeal to the law to which the whole community, as well as you, are entitled. There are offences of this nature, deserving of the severest punishment, but on which it is very difficult, if not impossible, to bring the offenders to justice. My brother is absent on the Circuit, but my son is here; and if on the perusal of those infamous papers it should appear that there is any hope of obtaining a legal sentence on their author or publisher, you may be assured that no pains shall be wanting for that purpose, without trouble or expense to you. I am afraid indeed that this object cannot be compassed. Your consolation must be that you suffer only by the baseness of the age you live in; that you suffer from the violence of calumny for the virtues that entitle you to the esteem of all who know how to esteem honour, friendship, principle, and dignity of thinking; and that you suffer along with everything that is excellent in the world. I do not wonder that minds tenderly sensible to reputation should feel for a moment from this shocking licence; but I should be sorry and ashamed for the independence of virtue if the profligacy of others should shorten, or even embitter in any degree, such valuable lives as yours. I trust that the piety, good sense, and fortitude that hitherto has distinguished you, and made you the mark of envy, even in your retreat, will enable you, on recollection, perfectly to despise the scandals of those whom, if you knew them, you would despise on every other account, and which, I faithfully assure you, make no impressions, except those of contempt, on any person living. The newspapers have overdone their part, and have brought things to such a point by their indiscriminate abuse, that they really contribute nothing to raise or lower any character; so that if you contrive to keep yourselves, in your own persons, where you naturally are, infinitely above the feeling of their malice, the rest of the world will not be in the smallest degree influenced by it, any further than as you, being objects of low, unmerited persecution, will increase their interest in characters in every point so formed to engage it. I do not know one of the persons who are engaged in the conduct of the papers, and have great reluctance in acknowledging their importance so far as to make an application to them; but since you desire it, I will make an inquiry into their connexions, and will take care to have notice given to them to attend to their behaviour in future, rather in the

style of menace than as asking any favour from them. Mrs. Burke desires her most respectful and affectionate compliments; and I shall think myself highly honoured if you continue to believe me, with the most perfect sentiments of respect and regard,
"Ladies,
"Your most faithful
"& most obed^t & oblig^d
"humble servant,
"EDM. BURKE.
"Beconfield, July 30th, 1790."

There are also letters from Viscount Castlereagh, Sydney Owenson (Lady Morgan), Lord Bolingbroke, the Duke de Montpensier, Lady Davy (the wife of Sir Humphry Davy), some lively letters from Miss Harriett Bowdler (a celebrated Bath blue-stocking), from Lady Charlotte Bury, soliciting contributions for her "Journal of the Heart," from Southey the poet, Thomas Moore, and William Wilberforce. The letter of the latter is so interesting, as giving the author's reasons for the publication of his work on "Practical Christianity," that we make no apology for inserting it.

"Barmouth, Sept. 9th, 1823.

"MY DEAR MADAM,—I should have lived in the world as long as I have done to very little purpose, as far as yᵉ chapter of Manners is in question, if I had not learned that if I were to wish a Lady of Rank to do me the honour of accepting any trifling mark of my Respectful Attention, I ought not to dispatch it like a collar of Brawn or a Norfolk Turkey at Xmas, to be brought in by the Porter of the Stage Coach, without other explanation than that of his way-bill. I have just now learned, greatly to my discomposure, that thus unceremoniously has a volume been transmitted to your Ladyship, which I had ordered to be delivered by my amanunsis; who, having been suddenly called to London by yᵉ death of a Brother, was to pass through Llangollen, on his way to this place. Let me beg your Ladyship to allow yʳ imagination to perform the easy, because the kind and candid task of supposing that such was the manner in which my book had the honour of being conveyed to yʳ Ladyship's residence. But yʳ imagination has the farther office imposed on it, of supposing (for such was my intention) that its introduction was attended with an explanatory letter. This desideratum let me now beg leave to supply.

"It pleased God, soon after my becoming Member for Yorkshire, by a careful perusal of the Holy Scriptures, to convince me that the religious system of professed Christians, in the generality of the Higher and Middle Classes of this country, was essentially erroneous and defective; and, therefore, that I could not render a more important service to my countrymen in general, in the higher ranks of life, and more especially to a very numerous body of very kind friends, with whom the goodness of Providence had blessed me, than endeavour to rectify, what appeared to me, the errors in this most serious of all concerns, and at the same time to account for a considerable change which they had witnessed in my conduct. So few, however, were my seasons of leisure, that it was not till 1797 that I was able to finish and lay before the world the result of my reflections. And then, and ever since, I have taken the liberty of presenting my volume to the friendly circle that was around me.

"Permit me to request a place for it in your Ladyship's library, and I would take the liberty of pointing out the table of contents at the Beginning of the volume, which affords the opportunity of selecting the parts which any one may think most likely to claim his perusal. I would hint that for those who are at all instructed, the introduction had been first penned. The 4th & 7th chapters have been, I believe, most generally acceptable.

"I will only indulge the hope, that if yr Ladyship will excuse the very unseemly mode by which the volume was transmitted, and accept it as a testimony of Respect and Regard.

"Mrs. W.—for all our young people are absent from us on a tour—desires me, with my own, to present her best respects to your Ladyship and Miss Ponsonby, & I have the honour to remain, always y^r Ladyship's obliged & faithful servant,

"W. WILBERFORCE.

"The Lady Eleanor Butler, &c. &c."

The cottage at Llangollen became, in time, quite a Museum, from the many curiosities contributed by obliged and admiring friends. It was one of the sights of Wales; and, as years bore on, its eccentric occupants no less so.

In September, 1823, when fulfilling a theatrical engagement at Oswestry, the elder Charles Mathews thus writes of them :—

"The dear, inseparable inimitables, Lady Eleanor Butler and Miss Ponsonby, were in the boxes here on Friday. They came twelve miles from Llangollen, and returned, as they never sleep from home. Oh! such curiosities! I was nearly convulsed! I could scarcely get on for the first ten minutes my eye caught them! Though I had never seen them, I instantly knew them. As they are seated, there is not one point to distinguish them from men; the dressing and powdering of the hair; their well-starched neckcloths; the upper part of their habits, which they always wear, even at a dinner-party, made precisely like men's coats; and regular black beaver men's hats. They looked exactly like two respectable, superannuated old clergymen, one the picture of Borwlaski. I was highly flattered, as they never were in the theatre before. I have to-day received an invitation to call, if I have time as I pass, at Llangollen, to receive in due form from the dear old gentlemen, called Lady Butler and Miss Ponsonby, their thanks for the entertainment I afforded them at the theatre."

Mr. Mathews could not accept the invitation, but, more than a month later, he paid his respects to "the Ladies" at Porkington. The following is his humorous and graphic account of the interview :—

"Well, I have seen them, heard them, touched them! The pets—'The Ladies,' as they are called—dined here yesterday : Lady Eleanor Butler and Miss Ponsonby, the curiosities of Llangollen. . . . I mentioned to you in a former letter the effect they produced upon me in public, but never shall I forget the first burst yesterday upon entering the drawing-room, to find the dear, antediluvian darlings, attired for dinner in the same mummified dress, with the Croix de St.

Louis, and other orders, and myriads of large brooches, with stones large enough for snuff-boxes, stuck in their starched neckcloths. I have not room to describe their most fascinating persons. I have an invitation from them which I much fear I cannot accept. They returned home last night —fourteen miles, after twelve o'clock! They have not slept one night from home for above forty years. I longed to put Lady Eleanor under a bell-glass, and bring her to Highgate, for you to look at."

When "the Ladies" first went to live at Llangollen, they assumed a style of dress which they never afterwards departed from. Their head-covering was a sort of beaver hat, and they always wore long cloth coats, somewhat like ladies' riding habits, but with the upper part cut like a man's coat.

In 1824 they were visited by William Wordsworth and some members of his family. The following is from the pen of the poet:—

SONNET
To Lady Eleanor Butler and the Hon. Miss Ponsonby, composed in the grounds of Plâs-Newydd, Llangollen.

"A stream to mingle with your favourite Dee
Along the Vale of Meditation* flows;
So styled by those fierce Britons, pleased to see
On Nature's face the expression of repose;

---

* Glyn Myvyr.

Or, haply there some pious Hermit chose
To live and die—the peace of Heaven his aim,
To whom the wild sequestered region owes
At this late day its sanctifying name.
Glyn cyfaillgdrwch, in the Cambrian tongue,
In ours the Vale of Friendship, let this spot
Be named, where faithful to a low-roof'd cot
On Deva's banks, ye have abode so long:
Sisters in Love—a love allowed to climb
Even on this earth, above the reach of Time."

The foregoing poem was enclosed in the following note :—

" Mr. W. has more than fulfilled his promise, he fears at the risk of tiring those whom he wished to gratify. This sonnet is a faint expression of his feelings on that interesting spot. Mrs. and Miss W. join him in respectful regards and sincere wishes, in which Mr. Jones unites.

" Plas-yr-Llan, near Rcekin,
" 4th Sept.

" The Lady Eleanor Butler, and
The Honble. Miss Ponsonby,
Plâs-Newydd,
Llangollen."

Amongst these MSS. is also a long poem by Thomas Campbell, author of " The Pleasures of Hope," upon the subject of " The Origin of Painting."

One more letter, and we have done. It is from

the statesman Canning, and is a good example of that popular orator's polished style :—

"Mr. Canning has the honour to apprise the Ladies at Llangollen that his daughter looks forward to the pleasure of being presented to them next week, when Lord Clanricarde carries her to her new country.

"Mr. Canning wishes that he were to be of the party, instead of resuming, as he must do, about the same time, the toils of the House of Commons.

"He has, however, a selfish reason for recalling himself at this moment to the Ladies' recollection. They insisted with him that he should find some occasion for profiting by their kind offer of a specimen of Llangollen *mutton*. Now, he knows no more worthy occasion likely to occur in the whole year than that of the celebration of the King's Birthday, which takes place on Saturday, the 23rd, on which day Mr. Canning entertains the Foreign Ministers.

"He intended therefore to have proved his obedience to the Ladies' commands by a message through Clanricarde, but as, upon calculation, he doubts whether such a message would reach Llangollen in time, he has resolved upon this mode of executing his purpose.

" His address is Foreign Office, *for mutton as well as for letters.*

"Ludbrook, Apr. 13, 1825."

Thus, of the world—but not in it—despite the romantic dreams of youth, these two friends went down the hill of life together. In the winter of 1828, Lady Eleanor Butler caught a severe cold, from which she does not seem ever to have completely rallied. She fought with death throughout the winter and spring, but as the summer advanced her health became worse. She died on the 2nd of June, 1829, at the advanced age of ninety years. The following inscription was placed upon her tomb in the churchyard of Llangollen:—

Sacred to the Memory of

THE RIGHT HONOURABLE

LADY ELEANOR CHARLOTTE BUTLER,

Late of Plâs-Newydd, in this Parish.

Deceased 2nd *June,* 1829.

Aged 90 Years.

Daughter of the Sixteenth, Sister of the Seventeenth

EARLS OF ORMONDE AND OSSORY;

Aunt to the late and to the present

MARQUESS OF ORMONDE.

Endeared to her friends by an almost unequalled excellence of heart, and by manners worthy of her illustrious birth, the admiration and delight of a very numerous acquaintance, from a brilliant vivacity of mind, undiminished to the latest period of a prolonged existence. Her amiable condescension and benevolence secured the grateful attachment of those by whom they had been so long and so extensively experienced. Her various perfections, crowned by the most pious and cheerful submission to the Divine Will, can only be appreciated where it is humbly believed they are now enjoying their Eternal Reward, and by her of whom for more than fifty years they constitute that happiness, which through our Blessed Redeemer she trusts will be renewed when THIS TOMB shall have closed over its LATEST TENANT.

"𝔖orrow not as others, who have no hope."
1 THESS. chap. iv. v. 13.

In a little more than two years that tomb had "closed over its latest tenant:" Miss Ponsonby died on the 9th of December, 1831, at the age of seventy-six. It is thus recorded on the tombstone:—

SARAH PONSONBY
DEPARTED THIS LIFE
On the 9th of December, 1831, aged 76.

She did not long survive her beloved companion, LADY ELEANOR BUTLER, with whom she had lived in this valley for more than half a century of uninterrupted friendship.

"But they shall no more return to their house, neither shall their place know them any more."—JOB, chap. vii. v. 10.

Reader, pause for a moment, and reflect, not on the uncertainty of human life, but upon the certainty of its termination, and take comfort from the assurance that, "As it is appointed unto men once to die, but after this the judgment, so Christ was once offered to bear the sins of many; and unto them that look for Him shall He appear the second time, without sin unto salvation."
HEB. chap. ix. v. 27, 28.

On the same tombstone is also the following inscription to the memory of their faithful servant, who had accompanied "the Ladies" from Ireland:—

In Memory of
MRS. MARY CARRYL,
Deceased 22nd November, 1809.

This monument is erected by Eleanor Butler and Sarah Ponsonby,
of Plâs-Newydd, in this Parish.

Released from earth, and all its transient woes,
She whose remains beneath this stone repose,
Steadfast in faith, resigned her parting breath,
Looked up with Christian joy, and smiled in death.
Patient, Industrious, Faithful, Generous, Kind,
Her conduct left the proudest far behind;
Her virtues dignified her humble birth,
And raised her mind above the sordid earth.
Attachment (sacred bond of grateful breasts)
Extinguished but with life, this Tomb attests.
Reared by Two Friends, who will her loss bemoan,
Till, with her ashes, Here shall rest their own.

After the death of Miss Ponsonby, the contents of the cottage were sold by auction. The sale attracted much attention, from the miscellaneous character of the articles. The cottage, wainscoted with carved oak, still remains, and is worthy of a visit from any pilgrim to the Vale of Llangollen.

LADY LOUISA CONOLLY.

Born, a.d. 1742. Died, a.d. 1821.

AM amazed you did not know that Lord Mornington had made his addresses to Lady Louisa Lennox," says Mrs. Delany in one of her letters,—" young Lady Kildare's sister, a pretty girl, about sixteen. He was well received, and much encouraged by all the family, and no appearance of dislike in the young lady; but before an answer was positively given, Mr. Conolly, with double his fortune (and perhaps about half his merit), offered himself, and was accepted. The answer to Lord Mornington was, that 'the young lady had an insurmountable dislike to him.'"

But Mrs. Delany was wrong in her surmises about Lady Louisa's choice. The Right Hon. Thomas Conolly was a most excellent husband, and a most estimable man in every relation of life. He was one of His Majesty's Privy Councillors, and for forty years represented the County of Londonderry. He died at his residence of Castletown, deeply and sincerely regretted for his public and private worth.

His wife, Lady Louisa Conolly, was the third daughter of Charles, second Duke of Richmond. Her two sisters were Lady Kildare, famous for her wit and sprightliness, and Lady Sarah Lennox, no less celebrated for her beauty. Mrs. Delany calls Lady Louisa "a pretty girl," but makes no special comment upon her appearance; and as the observant old lady invariably noted anything remarkable in the manners or appearance of her acquaintances, we may take it for granted that the charms of Lady Sarah eclipsed those of her afterwards more famous sister. However, we know she was tall, and of a commanding presence.

After the death of her husband, in 1803, Lady Louisa Conolly resided almost entirely at Castletown, near Celbridge, the most princely mansion in Ireland. Here she devoted herself to the education of the poor, and the general improvement of all living upon her estate. The Female Charter School at Celbridge she took under her especial care. It became one of the best female schools in Ireland, and has maintained its character until the present day.

Lady Louisa Conolly's energy of mind and her intellectual acquirements were very great. The demesne at Castletown must have been like a small town or village of the feudal ages, and Lady Louisa the Lady of the Castle. Just within the Celbridge entrance to the demesne she had a church erected, with separate sittings for the girls of the Charter House School. Extensive brewhouses, bakehouses, and buildings of a similar nature were within the boundary of the demesne, and upon the ruined kennels of her late husband's hounds she had built the first Industrial Schools that ever were in Ireland.

These schools were Lady Louisa's especial care, and were destined for both sexes. For the boys there were workshops, having a skilled, practical person at the head of each department; and here they were taught carpentry, tailoring, shoemaking, basket-making, and other trades, in addition to a good practical English education. The girls were taught knitting, sewing, laundry-work, breadmaking, cookery, and other branches of industry. In the welfare and progress of these schools their foundress took a deep interest, and was unremitting in her supervision of every department.

In addition to giving up her fortune to purposes like the foregoing, she also devoted her intellectual acquirements to the needs of her estate; for Lady Louisa Conolly was her own architect. She designed every building that she had erected, not considering the very fences and field-gates beneath her notice.

Everything on her property—animal, vegetable, or mineral—was cared for well, cultivated to the utmost, and worked to the best advantage. Moreover, all the materials used in all the buildings erected by Lady Louisa—such as timber, stones, bricks, lime, sand, &c. &c.—were all the produce of the Castletown estate. As far also as was practicable, all the raw material used in the Industrial Schools was from home sources. She had a personal knowledge of every one employed on her estate. Her clear, vigorous intellect enabled her to comprehend the details of the various branches taught in her schools; and she personally superintended the tradesmen during the erection of the various buildings.

"I have seen her," says one who remembers her during the latter years of her life, "directing the tradesmen in the erecting of a huge press for expressing the oil from beech mast, &c. I remember often seeing her pass out of the garden to the house, dressed in her usual long, light-grey cloth pelisse, or surtout, having huge side pockets, and those pockets stuck full of the largest parsnips and carrots, their small ends appearing above; these being doubtless for the poor, who were permitted to come to the house two or three times a week for food, &c."*

Lady Louisa Conolly lived a life of charity and kindness towards all. She was much beloved and looked up to in her wide circle of distinguished friends and relatives. Amongst the latter may be mentioned her nephews, the gallant Napiers, the sons of her sister, Lady Sarah Lennox.

This wise and good woman was in her eightieth year at the time of her death, which took place in a tent which she had erected on a grass-plot before the house at Castletown. In her last illness she was attended by Sir Philip Crampton, Surgeon-General to the Queen in Ireland, the immediate cause of her death being an abscess in her hip. She died in August, 1821, sincerely beloved and deeply regretted by all classes.

---

* Extract from a letter written by Mark Kelly, an old servant of the Conolly family, who has supplied many of the details contained in this brief memoir.

SARAH CURRAN.

"PERHAPS you could tell me who that pale beauty is? I have seen her once before."

"Seen her, and not know her! She is the youngest daughter of John Philpot Curran."

In the lovely valley of Glendalough, County of Wicklow, the foregoing question was asked by a gentleman, and responded to by Miss Lambart, the true friend of the ill-fated Sarah Curran, the betrothed of Robert Emmet.

A "pale beauty." All writers who have mentioned Sarah Curran have concurred in their praise of her grace and beauty; nevertheless, not one has given any more definite description of her personal attractions. Moreover, there is, unfortunately, no authentic likeness of her extant, so that the reader must finish the portrait as imagination suggests.

"She is kind, she is lovely, and Heaven only knows how good!" exclaimed Robert Emmet, in all the fervour of his enthusiastic love and patriotism. "I must make myself worthy of the woman of my choice, and the glory which sheds its lustre on the husband shall reflect its splendour on the wife!"

Poor Robert Emmet! He gave utterance to these impassioned words but a few weeks before his untimely death. Of all the good men, bad men, and great men engaged in national conspiracies in Ireland, not one has acquired by his patriotism or his death the fame which, from the hour of his rebellion, surrounded and seemed to halo the name of Robert Emmet. His rebellion, "the miniature rebellion of 1803," was an abortion, and its failure may be entirely ascribed to the religious hatreds which the rising of 1798 had evoked. His preparations for it were boyish; he was merely the enthusiastic victim of an idea, and being from his sensitive and visionary nature incapable of organisation on a large scale, he discovered his mistake in five minutes after the firing of the three signals in Thomas Street, Dublin. But, setting these circumstances aside, his youth and his obvious love for Ireland, and his ardent and daring love for Sarah Curran, had about them all the elements which in all ages have sufficed to constitute personal heroism. The story of his fate, and the story of his love, challenged at first pity, then sympathy, and lastly national regard. His friend, Thomas Moore, in wedding immortal verse to national song, has helped to deify and to render immortal the loves of Robert Emmet and Sarah Curran.

The daughter of John Philpot Curran—who was totally opposed to his young countryman in politics—at the house of their mutual friend, Mr. Lambart, of Castle Rath, County of Wicklow, Sarah Curran met with and loved the gifted young student. The attachment was disapproved of by the Curran family, and she was forbidden to have anything to say to the young rebel. But she had given her love unreservedly, and though she dared not mention her lover's name, she yet remained staunch to him. Through the instrumentality of their friend, Miss Lambart, they kept up a secret correspondence; and through evil report and good report the heart of Sarah Curran never swerved from the man she loved.

The story of her passionate and devoted love for Robert Emmet is one of the most pathetic love episodes which has ever been recorded. Soul-tragedies occur, not infrequently, but the world hears nothing of them, for it is woman's nature to prove

> How sublime a thing it is
> To suffer and be strong.

Sarah Curran had suffered and had been strong in her love, but her frail physique was not proof against the grief which weighed upon her heart, and sapped the foundations of her strength. Every instinct of her loving woman's nature was so bound up in the soul of her patriot lover that—

> When his spirit wonned above,
> Hers could not stay for sympathy.

After the execution of her lover for high treason, Sarah Curran left her father's house. Forbidden to mention the name of Robert Emmet, she found the restraint imposed upon her by this mandate too much to endure. Moreover, she had the bitterness of constantly hearing his memory and opinions spoken of with contempt and ridicule. It was too much for her broken heart, and therefore, in company with an elder sister, she one day quitted her father's house, and proceeded to Cork, on a visit to the family of a Mr. Penrose. Whilst staying with this kind Quaker family, she became acquainted with a Captain Sturgeon, who seems to have been a man of singularly refined and delicate feelings. The heart-widowed, friendless situation of the poor girl seems to have touched him deeply, and, convinced that one so true to the dead love could not but be worth winning, even although influenced in her decision merely by esteem, he made her an offer of his hand and heart.

Finally she consented to become his wife. Robert

Emmet's memory was not forgotten, and its prior claim on her heart was fully recognised by the friend and protector who had assumed a husband's title, and proved the generosity of his nature in his loving protection of her.

In the *Hibernian Magazine* for February, 1804, the marriage was announced in the following terms:—

"At Cork, Captain R. H. Sturgeon, of the Royal Staff Corps, and *nephew* of the late Marquis of Rockingham, to Miss Sarah Curran, daughter of J. P. Curran."

Under the title of "The Broken Heart," Washington Irving gives an exquisitely pathetic sketch of the love of Sarah Curran for "young E— —, the Irish patriot." He says:—

"She loved him with the disinterested fervour of a woman's first and early love. When every worldly maxim arrayed itself against him; when blasted in fortune; when disgrace and danger darkened around his name—she loved him the more ardently for his very sufferings. If, then, his fate could awaken the sympathy even of his foes, what must have been the agony of her whose whole soul was occupied by his image! Let those tell who have had the portals of the tomb suddenly closed between them and the being they most loved on earth—who have sat at its threshold, as one shut out in a cold and lonely world, from whence all that was most loving and lovely had departed.

"But then the horrors of such a grave! so frightful! so dishonoured! There was nothing for memory to dwell on that could soothe the pang of separation—none of those tender, though melancholy, circumstances that endear the parting scene—nothing to melt sorrow into those blessed tears, sent, like the dews of heaven, to revive the heart in the parting hour of anguish.

"To render her heart-widowed situation more desolate, she had incurred her father's displeasure by her unfortunate attachment, and was an exile from the paternal roof. But could the sympathy and kind offices of friends have reached a spirit so shocked and driven in by horror, she would have experienced no want of consolation, for the Irish are a people of quick and generous sensibilities. The most delicate and cherishing attentions were paid to her by families of wealth and distinction. She was led into society, and they tried by all kinds of occupation and amusement to dissipate her grief, and wean her from the tragical story of her love. But it was all in vain. There are some strokes of calamity that scathe and scorch the soul—that penetrate to the vital seat of happiness, and blast it, never again to put forth bud or blossom. She did not object to frequent the haunts of pleasure, but she was as much alone there as in the depths of solitude. She walked about in a sad reverie, apparently unconscious of the world around her. She carried with her an inward woe that mocked at all the blandishments of friendship, and 'heeded not the song of the charmer, charm he never so wisely.'

"The person who told me her story had seen her at the masquerade. There can be no exhibition of far-gone wretchedness more striking and painful than to meet it in such a scene. To find it wandering like a spectre, lonely and joyless, where all around is gay—to see it dressed out in the trappings of mirth, and looking so wan and wobegone, as if it had tried in vain to cheat the poor heart into a momentary forgetfulness of sorrow! After strolling through the splendid rooms and giddy crowd with an air of utter abstraction, she sat herself down upon the steps of an orchestra, and looking about for some time with a vacant air, that showed her insensibility to the garish scene, she began, with the capriciousness of a sickly heart, to warble a little plaintive air. She had an exquisite voice; but on this occasion it was so simple, so touching, it breathed forth such a soul of wretchedness, that she drew a crowd mute and silent around her, and melted every one into tears.

"The story of one so true and tender could not but excite great interest in a country remarkable for enthusiasm. It completely won the heart of a brave officer, who paid his addresses to her, and thought that one so true to the dead could not but prove affectionate to the living. She declined his attentions, for her thoughts were irrevocably engrossed by the memory of her former lover. He, however, persisted in his suit. He solicited not her tenderness, but her esteem. He was assisted by her conviction of his worth, and her sense of her own destitute and dependent situation; for she was existing on the kindness of friends. In a word, he at length succeeded in gaining her hand, though with a solemn assurance that her heart was unalterably another's.

"He took her with him to Sicily, hoping that a change of scene might wear out the remembrance of early woes. She was an amiable and exemplary wife, and made an effort to be a happy one; but nothing could cure the silent and devouring melancholy that had entered into her very soul. She wasted away in a slow but hopeless decline, and at length sank into the grave, the victim of a broken heart."

Sarah Curran was the subject of the following lines, composed by Thomas Moore, the friend of her patriot lover:—

She is far from the land where her young hero sleeps,
    And lovers around her are sighing;
But coldly she turns from their gaze, and weeps,
    For her heart in his grave is lying.

She sings the wild songs of her dear native plains,
    Every note which he loved awaking:
Ah! little they think, who delight in her strains,
    How the heart of the minstrel is breaking.

He had lived for his love, for his country he died,
    They were all that to life had entwined him;
Nor soon shall the tears of his country be dried,
    Nor long will his love stay behind him!

Oh! make her a grave where the sunbeams rest,
    Where they promise a golden morrow;
They'll shine o'er her sleep, like a smile from the west,
    From her own loved island of sorrow.

In the life of George Petrie—the eminent Irish antiquary—by Dr. W. J. Stokes, the following touching incident is related:—

"Petrie's father, though a loyalist, was on friendly terms with many of the prominent patriots whose portraits he painted; and after the execution of Emmet he was requested to paint a portrait of him from memory, with the aid of such studies of the head and face as he had by him. One day, just as the portrait was finished, Petrie—then a little boy—was sitting in a corner of the room, when he saw a lady, thickly veiled, enter and walk straight to the easel on which the work rested. She did not notice the child, and thought herself alone. She lifted her veil, stood long and in unbroken stillness gazing at the face; then suddenly turning, she moved with an unsteady step to another corner of the room, and, bending forward, pressed her forehead against the wall, heaving deep sobs, her whole frame shaken with a storm of passionate grief. How long this agony lasted the boy could not tell; it appeared to him to be an hour; and then, with a sudden effort, she controlled herself, pulled down her veil, and as quickly and silently left the room as she had come into it."

It is almost needless to add that the veiled lady was Sarah Curran.

POSTSCRIPT.

IN recording these few brief memorials of noted Irishwomen, it will have been seen that I have quoted largely in many instances. I considered it better to do so, preferring to give generally accepted and valuable tested criticisms, with which I agree, rather than the same sentiments embodied in my own words. In every particular, where it has been at all practicable, original documents have been consulted. Nevertheless, it should be borne in mind, that my information in the majority of cases has been derived from so many varied sources, and so devious have been my wanderings through literature in search of it, that it would be impossible for me to enumerate all the works I have referred to. Some of the details may appear to be scant, yet these volumes represent the result of some years of reading. For the satisfaction of those who may wish to pursue the subject further, I subjoin a list of a few of the chief authorities consulted :—

Manuscripts and documents in the Library of the
  Royal Irish Academy, Dawson Street, Dublin.
Documents in the Library of Trinity College, Dublin.
Original letters, and files of manuscript playbills, in
  Manuscript Room, British Museum Library.
The Lives of the Saints.
Annals of the Four Masters.
O'Curry's Materials.
O'Flaherty's Ogygia.
Keating's History of Ireland.
Miss Cusack's History of Ireland.
Ryland's History of Waterford.
Histories of England.
O'Hart's Irish Pedigrees.
Strype's Ecclesiastical History.
Ware's Annals.
Kilkenny Archæological Journal.
Sir William Wilde's Catalogue of the Royal Irish
  Academy.
Sir Bernard Burke's Vicissitudes of Families, and
  other works by the same writer.
Earls of Kildare.
Encyclopædia Britannica.
Anthologia Hibernica.
Notes and Queries.
Men of the Time.
Ryan's Irish Worthies.
The Quarterly Review.
The Edinburgh Review.
American Review.
Annual Register.
Blackwood's Magazine.
The Gentleman's Magazine.
The European Magazine.
Macmillan's Magazine.

The Scots' Magazine.
Dublin University Magazine.
The Analectic Magazine.
Frazer's Magazine.
Irish Penny Journal.
The Irish Register.
Illustrated London News.
The Newry Magazine.
Liddell's Living Age.
American Monthly Review.
American Quarterly Register.
Bolster's Cork Magazine.
The Critic.
The Examiner.
The Athenæum.
The Times.
Dublin Freeman's Journal.
The Dublin Advertiser, and files of other Dublin papers.
History of Irish Biographical Literature.
Wills's Lives of Celebrated Irishmen.
P. Fitzgerald's Life of Garrick.
  ,, ,, Lives of the Kembles.
  ,, ,, Romance of the English Stage.
Arthur Murphy's Life of Garrick.
The Dramatic Censor.
Geneste's History of the Stage.
Hitchcock's View of the Irish Stage.
Chetwood's History of the Stage.
The Kilkenny Theatre.
O'Keefe's Recollections.
Boaden's Memoirs.
Tate Wilkinson's Memoirs.
George Anne Bellamy's Memoirs.
Mrs. Robinson's Memoirs.

Mrs. Mary Delany's Memoirs.
Miss Berry's Journal.
Pepys' Diary.
Thomas Moore's Memoirs. Edited by Lord John Russell.
Evelyn's Diary.
Horace Walpole's Diary and Correspondence.
Life and Correspondence of Sir Joshua Reynolds.
George Selwyn's Diary and Correspondence.
Lockhart's Life of Scott.
Thomas Moore's Life of Byron.
Lady Blessington's Conversations with Lord Byron.
Ballard's Lives.
Hale's Record of Woman.
Allan Cunningham's Biographical Notes.
Prescott's Biographical Miscellanies.
Doctor Doran's "Their Majesties' Servants," and other works by the same author.
Brookiana.
Brooke's Reliques of Irish Poetry.
Life of R. L. Edgeworth.
Queens of Song. By Ellen Clayton.
Diary and Correspondence of Henry Crabb Robinson.
Griswold's Female Poets.
Rowton's Cyclopædia.
R. D. Horne's " New Spirit of the Age."
F. T. Porter's " Gleanings."
Novels and Novelists. J. C. Jeaffreson.
Friends and Foes of Lady Morgan.
Memoirs and Correspondence of Lady Morgan.
Diary of Lady Morgan.
S. C. Hall's Memories.
Poets and Dramatists of Ireland, by D. F. MacCarthy.
Alibone's Biographical Dictionary.
Obituary of Eminent Persons.

The Georgian Era.
Poole's Index to Periodical Literature.
Works of G. and P. Wharton.
Broadsides and tracts in British Museum Library.

From other sources—chiefly private—much of my information has been gleaned. I regret very much that it was not until the first volume of the work had gone to press that I was able to obtain the necessary information respecting Gormflaith, or Gormley, a famous ancient Irish queen. The reader who feels an interest in her fortunes cannot do better than procure Mr. W. H. Hennessy's notice of this remarkable woman. The memoir was published in the *Hibernian Magazine*, about 1863. The daughter of a king, the sister, wife, and mother of kings, Gormflaith went through many vicissitudes, until she at length begged her bread from door to door.

That which I have chosen to call the "Mediæval Period" is comparatively barren of material for biographies of women. A reason for this may be found in the unsettled state of Ireland at that time. Few records were kept, save what related to the much-vexed question of government. Under the Brehon laws, women enjoyed many privileges, and were considered of far more importance than under the English rule; so, as political matters form the staple of records relating to the

Ireland of this period, we find little concerning Irishwomen, save in a very few instances, where they have been directly associated with the government, as in the cases of the Countess of Desmond and Grace O'Mailly.

Ireland has given to the British stage its chief comedy actresses. The vivacity and versatility of the Celtic temperament, combined with that dash of pathos just sufficient to show up all the more sparkling qualities—attributes which constitute in themselves the very essence of comedy—have seldom been found in greater perfection than in the characters of the Irish actresses enumerated in this book. Tragedy has not been so well represented by them. Some of the comedy actresses have essayed it, but none have excelled in both departments. The grand and gloomy Sarah Siddons has never had a parallel amongst Irish actresses. Maria Pope was the only one of our countrywomen who successfully wore the mantle of tragedy; but death claimed her before her splendid talents were fully matured. Miss O'Neill also claims a high place amongst tragic actresses, but neither attained to the level of the great daughter of the Kembles.

Amongst Irishwomen, British literature has found some of its best representatives. The historical novel and the romantic novel both owe their origin to Irishwomen. Maria Edgeworth inspired Sir Walter Scott with a desire to do for the literature of his country what she was doing for hers, in painting its manners, customs, and abuses. On the other hand, Jane Porter, in her historical romances of "The Scottish Chiefs" and "Thaddeus of Warsaw," gave the Scottish novelist the idea of utilising the legends of war and love with which his brain was stored, and of weaving them into the world-famed Waverley Novels. Sir Walter Scott always generously acknowledged his obligations to these two Irishwomen. The Byron of her sex, Lady Stirling-Maxwell (Hon. Mrs. Norton) takes the highest rank amongst female poets; whilst the career of Lady Morgan affords a striking example of combined talent and perseverance, of which the women of any nation might feel proud.

The unpublished poem by William Wordsworth, which had been announced to appear in the memoir of "The Ladies of Llangollen," I have been unfortunately obliged to omit at the dictation of Mr. William Wordsworth, the son of the poet, who forbids the publication of any hitherto unpublished poem by his father.

In the hope that this book may prove useful as a work of reference, I have prefixed a copious index to each volume.

INDEX

TO

THE SECOND VOLUME.

(*The names of Plays are printed in Italics.*)

ABERCORN, Lady, 179, 183
Academy, Royal Irish, 43, 44
Aldworth, Mrs., 279, 280
Aldworth, Richard, 275, 276
Almacks, 98
Altenberg, Count, 86
Amiens, Peace of, 84
Anglas, Boissy d', 84
Annual Register, 228
Anthologia Hibernica, 49
Antrim Militia, 311
Arab's Farewell to his Horse, the, 257
Archer and Jones, 47
Argyle, Duke of, 288
Argyle, Duchess of, 289, 290
Athenæum, the, 190, 191, 242, 263, 266
Autumn, 249

BAILLIE, Joanna, 126, 150
Ballantyne, James, 100
Ballard, —, 25
Barbauld, Mrs., 146
Barber, Mrs., 24
Barker, Sir William, 304
Barrett, Miss, 261
Barrington, 280
Beattie, Dr. William, 212
Beaufort, Admiral Sir Francis, 77
Beaufort, Miss, 77
Beauty, Queen of, 288
Beck, 306

Behn, Aphra, 4, 9, 15, 19
Bellamy, George Anne, 280, 282, 284
Bentley, Dr., 70
Berkeley, Earl of, 66
Berry, Miss, 281
Bessborough, Lord, 293, 316
Best, Mrs., 303
Bethel, Counsellor, 188
Blachford, Mary, 52, 53, 55
Blachford, Rev. William, 52
Blachford, Theodosia, 52
Blackwood, Captain, 233
Blackwood's Magazine, 121
Blandford, Lord, 281
Blandy, Miss, 285
Blessington, Countess of, 198, 224
Blessington, Earl of, 201, 203, 205, 207, 208, 210
Blunt, Miss, 306, 307
Borris, 294, 298, 303
Bowers, Mr., 306, 308
Bowles, Caroline, 126
Boyle, Charles (Earl of Orrery), 70
Boyle, Henrietta, 70, 72
Boyle, Mary, 64, 69
Boyle and Bentley Controversy, 70
Brehon Laws, 349
Bridgewater, Duke of, 288
Britain Street, 282
British Critic, 81
British Museum, 228
British Stage, 349
Brooke, Arthur, 28

VOL. II.   A A

INDEX.

Brooke, Captain, 44
Brooke, Charlotte, 27, 51
Brooke, Henry, 27, 28, 29, 33
Browne, Felicia Dorothea, 109, 114
Browne, Mr. and Mrs., 48
Browne, Mr., 109, 110
Browne, Mrs., 110, 113
Browning, Elizabeth Barrett, 57
Browning, Mrs., 261
Brownrigg, General, 176
Buccleuch, Duke of, 212
Buck, Miss, 163
Buckingham, Duke of, 12
Buckingham, Lord, 315
Buckingham, James Silk, 190
Budgell, 8
Buller, Mrs. Richard, 106
Burke, 100
Burke, Edmund, 229, 316, 319
Burke, Mrs., 319
Burke, Theobald, 282
Burney, Miss, 166
Burton, 306, 308
Butler, Lady Eleanor Charlotte, 291, 292, 293, 294, 295, 298, 301, 302, 303, 304, 305, 309, 322, 323, 327, 328
Butler, Mrs., 304
Butler, Tom, 307, 308, 309
Byron, Lord, 74, 97, 186, 204

CALLANDER, Colonel, 239
Callander, Lady Elizabeth, 239
Cambridge University, 6
Campbell, John, 288
Campbell, Thomas, 325
Canning, Mr., 201, 326
Canterbury, Viscountess, 199
Carlow, 303
Caroline, Princess of Wales, 17
Carrol, 7
Carryl, Mrs. Mary, 329
Carteret, Lord, 25
"Carwell," 237
Castlereagh, 201
Castletown, 330, 332, 333, 334
Castle Coote, 282
Catholic Emancipation, 189, 192
Cavan Militia, 314
Celbridge, 331, 332
Centlivre, Joseph, 8
Centlivre, Susanna, 3, 15, 27
Charlemont, Earl of, 44, 60

Charles II., 76
Charlotte, Princess, 289, 290
Charter School, Female, 331, 332
Cherry, 160
Christian, of Luneberg, Duke, 150
Cibber, Colley, 4
City, 230
Clanricarde, Lord, 326
Clarke, Dr. Sir Arthur, 177
Clarke, Lady, 184
Clenard, 35
Clocknaben, Dowager Countess of, 267
Colburn, 185, 186, 187, 190, 191
Comerford, 52
Commons, House of, 17, 98, 326
Congreve, 13
Conolly, Lady Louisa, 330, 331, 332, 333, 334
Conolly, Mr., 330
Coote, 282
Cork, 331
Cork, First Earl of, 64, 65
Cork, John, Earl of, 70
Cork, Lady, 187
Cork and Orrery, House of, 70
Cornwall, Barry, 221
Cornwallis, Lord, 312
Cossack, the, 74
Cotton, 98
County Meath, 311
County Wicklow, 311, 312
Court, the, 8, 67, 76
Court of Denmark, 17
Court of Dublin, Viceregal, 53
Coventry, Earl of, 285
Coventry, Lady, 285, 286, 287, 288
Covington, Circuit Court, 246
Cowper, Hon. Charles Spencer, 201
Cowper, Lady, 98
Crampton, Sir Philip, 334
Crawford, Mrs., 171
"Critic," 264
Croker (Quarterly Review), 185
Crossley, Francis, 171
Crystal Palace, 264
Cunningham, Allan, 150
Curran Family, 337
Curran, John Philpot, 335
Curran, Sarah, 335, 336, 337, 338, 339, 342, 344

DAILY NEWS, the, 215
Dandies' Rout, 232, 246

Darnley, Lord, 52
D'Aubray, Madame, 86
Davy, Lady, 74
Davy, Sir Humphrey, 74, 98
Debt of Honour, the, 226
De Foe, 151
Delany, Mary, 285, 287, 330, 331
Dermody, Thomas, 160, 161, 162
Desmond, Countess of, 349
Devonshire, Duchess of, 287
Devonshire, Lord, 65
D'Houdetot, Sophie, 84, 85
D'Israeli, 225
D'Israeli, the Elder, 228
Dick, Quentin, 172
Dickens, Charles, 212
Dilke, Wentworth, 190
Dixon, William Hepworth, 169, 180
Doddridge, Dr., 43
Dodsley, 229
Dominick Doubleface, 226
Dominick Street, 293, 300
Doneraile, Lord, 276
Doneraile House, 276
D'Orsay, Count, 201, 203, 205, 207, 210, 216, 217, 220, 221
D'Orsay, Countess, 210
Dream, the, 252, 254
Down and Connor, Bishop of, 75
Dublin, 299, 313, 336
Dublin, Bay of, 237
Dublin Castle, 284
Dublin Masonic Orphan Schools, 280
Dublin Evening Post, 279
Dublin, Viceregal Court of, 53
Dublin Weekly Oracle, 279
Dumout, 95
Dungarvan, Charles, Viscount, 70

ECCLES, Mrs., 312
Edelcrantz, Chevalier, 86
Eden, Sir Frederick, 147
Edgeworth, Edward, 75
Edgeworth, Francis, 75
Edgeworth, Lady, 75, 76
Edgeworth, Maria, 73, 107, 127, 350
Edgeworth, Mrs., 84
Edgeworth, Richard Lovell, 73, 76, 78, 79, 81, 63
Edgeworth, Abbé, 95
Edgeworth, the Misses, 84, 96, 98
Edinburgh Review, 124

Elers, Miss, 76
Elers, Paul, 76
Elizabeth, Queen, 75
Ellice, Edward, 243
Elwood, Mrs., 148
Elphin, Bishop of, 303
Emmet, Robert, 335, 336, 337, 338
England, 314
England, Queen of, 290
Enniscorthy, 314
Erskine, 202
Ettrick Shepherd, the, 123
Eustace, Mrs., 303
Everard, Richard, 174
Examiner, 264

FARMER, Captain, 200
Farmer, Mrs., 201
Farquhar, 8
Featherstone, Mrs., 164, 168, 170
Firmont, l'Abbé de, 96
Fielding, 11
Fitzpatrick, 74
Flaxman, 63
Fletcher, Mrs., 126
Forrester, Miss, 213
Foundling Hospital, 85
Fownes, Lady Betty, 293, 294, 295, 297, 298, 300
Fownes, Sir William, 293, 300, 301, 302, 304
Fox, 100
Fox, Mr. 7
Fox, Sir Stephen, 7
France, 292
Frazer's Magazine, 154
Freeman, Susanna, 6
Froissart, 228
Fry, Mrs., 98

GARDINER, Lady Harriet Frances, 201, 206
Garrick, 280, 284
Garrick, David, 30, 31
Garrick, Mrs., 291
Genlis, Madame de, 80, 84
George IV., 150
Gifford, Countess of, 232, 233, 235, 238
Gifford, Earl of, 233
Glendalough, 335

INDEX.

Glorvina (*see* Owenson, Sydney, or Morgan, Lady)
Glynmouth, 313
Goddard, Mrs., 292, 295, 299, 300, 301, 302
Goethe, 270
Good Hope, Cape of, 232
Gormflaith, 248, 349
Grammont, Duc de, 203
Grant, Anne, 126
Grantley, Lord, 240
Grattan, Lady Laura, 52
Grierson, Constantia, 22, 26, 27
Grierson, George, 23
Guarini, 20
Gunning, Elizabeth, 281, 282, 287
Gunning, General, 286, 288
Gunningiad, 287
Gunning, John, 282
Gunning, Maria, 282, 284, 285
Gunning, Mrs., 283, 284
Gunnings, Beautiful, 284, 289
Gushington, Hon. Selina, 238
Gustavus, Vasa (*see* Brooke, Henry)
Gwydir, Lady, 98

HALL, Bishop, 67, 154
Hall, S. C., 222
Hall, Mrs. S. C., 105, 115
Hamilton, C. W., 292
Hamilton, Duke of, 285
Hamilton, Duchess of, 288
Hamilton, Mrs., 48
Hammond, Anthony, 6, 7
Hampton Court, 232, 239
Ham's, 309
Hamwood, 292
Harmonia, Lady, 66
Harris, of Covent Garden, 292
Hayes, John, 275
Hober, Reginald, 124, 125
Hemans, Captain, 114, 115, 116, 117
Hemans, Felicia Dorothea, 108, 142
Hemans, Mrs., 257, 261
Henry VIII., 228
Hennessy, W. H., 348
Hermit of Snowdon, 229
Hibernian Magazine, 339, 348
Hickson, Mr., 307
Highland Society, the, 122
Hill, Dr., 48
Hill, Miss, 156

Hogg, James, 247
Holcroft, Mrs., 269
Hope, Mrs. 98
Horne, R. D., 201
House of Commons, 17, 98, 326
Howitt, Mary, 126

INDUSTRIAL School, 332, 333
Inistiogue, 309
Ireland, 315, 328, 331, 332, 349
Ireland, King's Printer in, 25
Ireland, Lord Lieutenant of, 25, 53, 183
Irish Academy, Royal, 43, 44
Irish Parliament, 53, 55
Irish Rebellion, 310
Irving, Washington, 339
Islington, 223
Italian Opera, 302

JEFFRIES, Miss, 285
Jeffrey (Quarterly Review), 89
Jewsbury, Miss, 126
John Bull, 262
Jones, Mr. 324
Jones, Sir William, 36
Jordan, Camille, 84

KAUFFMANN, Angelica, 148
Katie's Letter, 237
Kavanagh, Mrs., 294
Kean, Charles, 151
Kemble, 202
Kenny, 269
Kentucky, 245
Kildare, Lady, 330, 331
Kilkenny, 292, 293, 300, 301, 307, 313
King's Printer in Ireland, 25
Kosciusko, 84, 149

LADIES of Llangollen, the, 291, 326, 351
Lady of La Garaye, the, 256
La Harpe, 84
Lambart, Miss, 335, 337
Lambart, Mr., 337
Lament of the Irish Emigrant, the, 234, 237
Landon, Letitia Elizabeth, 140

INDEX. 357

Landor, Walter Savage, 221, 222
Lawrence, Sir Thomas, 179, 202
Lefanu, Mrs., 182
Lennox, Lady Louisa, 330, 334
Lennox, Sarah, 331
Leopold, H.R.H. Prince, 146
Lispings from Low Latitudes, 238
Literary Gazette, 190
Llangollen, 291, 300, 309, 310, 316, 322, 323, 324, 327
Llangollen, Cottage of, 291
Llangollen, Vale of, 329
Lockhart, J. G., 248, 251, 256
Londonderry, County of, 330
Londonderry, Lady, 99
Londonderry, Lord, 99
Long, Mr., 307
Longmans, Messrs., 179
Lord Berner's Version, 228, 229
Lord Lieut. of Ireland, 25, 53, 183
Lost and Saved, 265, 266
Lushington, 269
Luttrell, 96
Lyons, Col., 304
Lysaght, Edward, 158

M'KENZIE (Printer), 47
 Macklin, Miss, 14
MacOwen (*see* Owenson)
Madden, Dr., 203, 218
Magazine, Gentleman's, 230
Magazine, New Monthly, 134, 191, 211, 222, 223, 247
Magdalen, 302
Marellet, Abbé, 84
Mathews, Charles, 322, 323
Mathews, Charles, Sen., 202
Mathews, Charles, Jun., 203, 204
Mayo, Viscount, 282, 283
Meares, Miss, 27
"Mediæval Period," 349
Medows, Mrs., 302, 306
Melbourne, Lord, 242, 243, 270
Milford Haven, 309
Milman, 125
Milton, 437
Mitford, Mary, 126
Molesworth, Charlotta Amelia, 18
Molesworth, Mary, 16
Molesworth, Robert, Viscount, 16, 17, 18
Molière, 11
Monk, Henry Stanley, 21

Monk, Hon. Mrs., 16, 21, 27
Monk, George, 16
Monk, Sarah, 21
Montague, Mrs., 291
Montmorenci, 84
Moore, Thomas, 61, 75, 76, 97, 164, 185, 188, 213, 342
More, Mrs. Hannah, 146
More, Sir Thomas, 151
Morgan, Sydney, Lady, 156
Morgan, Dr. Sir Charles, 181, 182, 183, 184, 191, 194
Morning Chronicle, 106
Mornington, Lady, 315
Mornington, Lord, 330
Mountjoy, Lord, 205
Moxon, 269
Murphy, 314
Murray, Captain, 200

NAAS, 303
 Napiers, 334
Napoleon, Louis, 219
National Assembly, Letters to the, 228
New Monthly Magazine, the, 134, 191, 211, 222, 223, 247
Newcomens, 302
Newmarket, 375
Normanby, Lord, 96
Norton, Hon. George Chapple, 240
Norton, Hon. Mrs., 232, 233, 239, 241, 243, 245, 261, 262, 264, 270, 271
Norton, Mr., 242, 243, 246
Norris, Sam, 244, 245, 246

O'BRIENS, 303
 O'Connell, the, 187, 188, 191
Old Sir Douglas, 266
O'Mailly, Grace, 349
O'Menra, J., 188
O'Neil, John, 70
O'Neil, Lady, 70, 72
Ormond, Earl of, 292
Ormsby, Sir Charles, 178
Orrery, Earl of, 70
Orrery, House of Cork and, 70
Oswestry, 322
Owenson, Mrs., 162
Owenson, Olivia, 162, 176, 177, 178, 195

INDEX.

Owenson, Robert, 156, 158, 160, 161, 162, 176
Owenson, Sydney (Lady Morgan), 60, 156, 197

PALMERSTON, Lady, 98
Palmerston, Lord, 201
Paris, 292
Park, Mr., 304, 306
Parliament, Irish, 53, 55
Patton, Mr., 244, 245
Penrose, Mr., 338
Percy, Caroline, 86
Petersham, Lady Caroline, 287
Petrie, George, 343
Phillips, Sir Richard, 171, 172, 173, 178, 180
Pitt, Mr., 173
Pleasures of Hope, the, 325
Pons, Miss, 305
Ponsonby, Chambre, 293
Ponsonby, Miss Sarah, 291, 292, 293, 294, 297, 298, 300, 301, 302, 303, 304, 309, 310, 312, 316, 322, 323, 328, 329
Pope, Maria, 350
Porkington, 323
Porter, Anna Maria, 143, 149
Porter, Dr., 152, 155
Porter, Jane, 350
Porter, Mrs., 143, 144, 146, 147
Porter, Robert Ker, 147, 152
Porter, the Misses, 143, 155
Power, Edmund, 198, 200
Power, Marguerite, 199, 200
Power, Mary Ann, 203
Power, Robert, 201
Priory Gardens, 286
Pritchard, Mrs., 99
Prude, the, 225
Psyche (*see* Tighe, Mrs. Mary)

QUARTERLY REVIEW, 89, 94, 95, 179, 184, 185, 186, 190
Queen, H.M. the, 152, 153
Queen Mary, 226

RADCLIFFE'S, 303
Ranelagh Gardens, 53
Rath Castle, 337

Rathdrum, 313
Recamier, Madam, 84
Recollections of a Faded Beauty, the, 257
Reynolds, Sir Joshua, 100, 148, 285, 287, 288
Rich, 10
Rich, Charles (afterwards Earl of Warwick), 64, 65
Richards, Mrs., 314
Richmond, Duke of, 178, 183, 286, 331
Robinson, Henry Crabb, 268
Rochfort, Mrs., 302, 303
Rockingham, Marquis of, 339
Rogers, 268, 269
Rogers's, 96
Romney, 52
Rosanna, 313
Rousseau, 85
Rowe, 8
Royal Oak, 303
Royal Family, the, 146
Royal Irish Academy, 43, 44
Ruler of the Islands, 247
Russell, Lord, 202
Rutland, Duchess of, 98
Ryves, Miss, 225, 226, 227, 229, 230, 231
Ryves, Jerome, D.D., 225

ST. GEORGE, Lady, 60
St. James, 290
St. Joachim, Order of, 149
St. Leger, Hon. Elizabeth, 275, 276, 277, 278, 279
St. Leger, Right Hon. Arthur, 275
St. Marsault, Countess de, 199
St. Patrick's Hall, 53
St. Patrick's Cathedral, 133, 158, 159
St. Valentine's Day, 285
Saturday Review, 265, 267
School for Scandal, 303
Scott, Sir Walter, 97, 100, 101, 102, 104, 125, 127, 141, 151, 154, 350
Scottish Chiefs, the, 350
Segur, Comte et Comtesse de, 84
Sharpe, 96
Sheeley, Miss, 199
Sheridan, Caroline, 241
Sheridan, Helen Selina, 232, 233
Sheridan, C. E. S., 239, 240
Sheridan, Mrs. Thomas, 237
Sheridan, Thomas, 232

INDEX.

Sheridan, Richard Brinsley, 11, 12, 31, 93, 99, 100
Shuldham, Lord, 306
Sicily, 342
Siddons, Mrs., 75, 99
Siddons, Sarah, 350
Sierra Leone, 263
Smith, Mrs. Charlotte, 70
Sneyd, Elizabeth, 77
Sneyd, Honora, 77
Social Compact, 228
Somerset, Duchess of, 233, 239
Sonnet, 324
Spedding, 269
Spencer, Edmund, 56
Speranza (see Lady Wilde)
Spring, 249
Staël, Madame de, 74, 96
Stanhope, Leycester, 243,
Steele, Sir Richard, 8
Stirling-Maxwell, Lady, 239, 241, 246, 247, 248, 252, 256, 257, 259, 261, 262, 265, 266, 267, 268, 270, 271, 350
Stirling-Maxwell, Sir William, 271
Stockdale and Miller, 180
Stokes, Dr. W. J., 243
Store Street, 230
Stuart of Dunleath, 263, 266
Sturgeon, Captain, 338, 339
Suard, 84
Summer, 249
Sutherland, Duchess of, 252
Swift, Dean, 20, 27, 83

T——, Miss, 41, 46
Tasso, 20
Taylor, Mrs., 306
Teddington, 289
Tennyson, 269
Terence's Farewell, 263
Thaddeus of Warsaw, 350
Thackeray, W. M., 217
Theatre, Smock Alley, 279
Theatre, Aungier Street, 279
The Arab's Farewell to his Horse, 257
The Bay of Dublin, 237
The Blind Man to his Bride, 259
The Child of Earth, 259
The Child of the Islands, 248
The Cow with the Crumpled Horn, 289
The Debt of Honour, 226

The Dream, 252, 254
The Graves of a Household, 257
The Mother's Heart, 257, 258
The Lady of La Garaye, 256
The Lament of the Irish Emigrant, 234, 237
The Pleasures of Hope, 325
The Prude, 225
The Recollections of a Faded Beauty, 257
The Times, 266
The Undying One, 247
The Wandering Jew, 247
The Widow to her Son's Betrothed, 259
Thomas Street, 336
Thomas Town, 294
Tighe, Henry, 55, 56, 310
Tighe, Mrs., 52, 63, 132, 294, 303, 307,, 308, 309, 310, 312, 315
Tighe, Mrs. (of Rosanna), 55
Tighe, R., 313
Tighe, Right Honourable William, 52
Tighe, William, 61, 63
Timolin, 303
Townshend, Viscountess, 287
Tweeddale, Marquis of, 233
Tweeddale, Marchioness of, 286

UNIVERSITY of Cambridge, 6

VAUXHALL, 285
Viceregal Court of Dublin, 53, 284
Virginia, 244
Voice from the Factories, 247

WAGNER, Mrs. (Mrs. Browne), 109
Wales, 322
Wales, Princess of, 179
Wales, Caroline, Princess of, 17
Walker, Dr. Anthony, 68
Walker, Joseph C., 33, 34, 43, 45, 49
Walpole, Horace, 281, 284, 288, 289
Warrens, 303
Waterford, 294, 309, 311
Warwick, Charles, Earl of, 64, 67
Warwick, Countess of, 64, 69
Warwick, Robert, Earl of, 65
Wellington, Duke of, 315
Westminster Abbey, 245

Westminster County Court, 245
Wexford, 314
Whately, Dr., 136
Whitbread, 98
White, Lydia, 60, 99
Wicklow, County of, 335, 337
Wilberforce, William, 219, 319, 322
Wylde, Lady, 108, 212
Wilkes, 9
Wilkie, 202
Winchilsea, 275
Winter, 249

Wiseman, Cardinal, 195
Woffington, Peg, 31, 280, 284
Woodstock, 293, 300, 301, 303, 307
Woodward, 14
Worcester, 288
Wordsworth, William, 130, 131, 137, 324, 325, 351
Wycherly, 29

YORKSHIRE, 288
Young, Dr., 308

THE END.

This book is a preservation photocopy.
It was produced on Hammermill Laser Print natural white,
a 60 # book weight acid-free archival paper
which meets the requirements of
ANSI/NISO Z39.48-1992 (permanence of paper)

Preservation photocopying and binding
by
Acme Bookbinding
Charlestown, Massachusetts
1995

www.ingramcontent.com/pod-product-compliance
Lightning Source LLC
Chambersburg PA
CBHW030744250426
43672CB00028B/394